BATTLE DRESS

BATTLE DRESS

By

FREDERICK WILKINSON

A Gallery of Military Style and Ornament

DOUBLEDAY & COMPANY, INC.
GARDEN CITY,
NEW YORK.

Other Books in the Series

ANTIQUE FIREARMS (1969)
By Frederick Wilkinson

ENGLISH AND IRISH GLASS (1968)
By Geoffrey Wills

ENGLISH POTTERY AND PORCELAIN (1969)
By Geoffrey Wills

EDGED WEAPONS (1970)
By Frederick Wilkinson

Published in Great Britain by
GUINNESS SIGNATURES
24 UPPER BROOK STREET, LONDON, W.1., ENGLAND

Printed in 10pt Century Series 227
by McCorquodale and Company Limited, London, England.
Monotone and 4-colour half-tone blocks by Gilchrist Bros. Ltd., Leeds, England.

CONTENTS

CORRECTIONS

pages 14, 30   The miniatures illustrated in Plates 2 and 4 were attributed to Richard
                Courtenay in error; they are in fact, Russell Gammage figures.

page 46   The correct spelling is *sabaton*.

page 54   Fig. 45; the correct term for the cod piece is *brayette*, not *brazette*.

INTRODUCTION

MILITARY finery has long afforded men an outlet for their natural vanity, although some of their fittings were entirely functional, and designed to serve the serious purpose of self-defence; but style and practical value often combined to produce costume which retained its hold on the imagination long after its practical function had disappeared. Good quality armour has been described, and rightly, as sculpture in steel, and is no less valid artistically for having been conceived for the strictly practical purpose of deflecting the blades of enemies.

With the decline of armour, the soldier's need for display was gratified in ever more extravagant fashion. The gorgeous colours, the loops and plumes, buttons and badges, lace and brocade served several purposes simultaneously. They set the military man apart from the mass of the population, and gave him an air and a sense of his own prowess. The growth of uniform dress fostered *ésprit de corps*, and extended this personal confidence to confidence in the regiment, the corps, and the whole army. So extravagant were some of these uniforms that comfort and practical considerations were sacrificed to the demands of appearance; and despite the efforts of a few clear-sighted men it was not until comparatively recent times that the gaudy inessentials began to disappear, abandoned in the face of a technology which was fast removing even the illusion of romance from the dirty business of war. This simplification of military dress accelerated enormously in the last half of the 19th Century, until by the second decade of this century drab khaki and grey had replaced the crimsons, yellows and blues entirely, and steel helmets had returned to the battlefield, ousting the elaborate shakos, bearskins and tschapkas.

No sane person feels an enthusiasm for war itself; but it is equally un-balanced to ignore the enormous part it has played in the history of mankind, and only the most rigidly puritan can deny the colour and glamour of dead empires and remembered battles. The interest in all things military has become very widespread over recent years, and the collection of militaria has become an important part of the antique market. This volume could not hope to include more than a cursory selection from such a huge and complex field, and many fascinating areas have necessarily been ignored; but as a gallery, a series of brief glimpses of military fashions and fancies over the centuries, it is hoped that it will give interest and pleasure to the collector and general reader alike.

As always the author gladly acknowledges his debt to some very kind friends and collectors who have helped in the preparation of this book, particularly L. Archer, H. Blackmore, S. Durrant, D. H. Gyngell, D. Jeffcoat, G. Mungeam, A. V. Norman, W. Reid, H. R. Robinson, J. F. Winsbury and K. Wynn. All the colour and the majority of the monochrome photographs are again the work of Michael Dyer Associates, and the author wishes to express his very special and sincere thanks to the indomitable Michael Dyer, Paul Forrester and Fred Pryor. The author and publishers also wish to extend their gratitude to the following for permission to reproduce photographs: The Master of the Armouries, H.M. Tower of London (Ministry of Public Building and Works, Crown Copyright, reproduced by permission of the Controller of H.M. Stationery Office); The Trustees of the Wallace Collection; Messrs. Sotheby & Co.; The Director of the National Army Museum; The Director of the Imperial War Museum; The Trustees of the British Museum.

BIBLIOGRAPHY

THE following is a list of the principal sources consulted in writing these *Signatures*:

C. Blair
European Armour, London, 1958.

J. W. Bunkley
Military & Naval Recognition Book, New York, 1943.

W. Y. Carman
British Military Uniforms from Contemporary Pictures, London, 1957.

W. Y. Carman
India Army Uniforms—Cavalry, London, 1961.

W. Y. Carman
India Army Uniforms—Infantry, London, 1969

H. M. Chichester and G. Burges-Short
Records and Badges of the British Army, London, 1900. Reprint, 1970.

G. Cousins
The Defenders, London, 1968.

C. de W. Crookshank
Prints of British Military Operations, London, 1921.

A. Dufty
European Armour in the Tower of London, H.M.S.O., London, 1968.

T. Edwards
Badges of H.M. Services, Manchester, 1943.

T. Edwards
Regimental Badges, London, 1964, 1968.

Lord Egerton of Tatton
Indian and Oriental Armour, London, 1968 (Reprint).

L. Emilio
The Emilio Collection of Military Buttons, Salem, U.S.A., 1911.

D. Erlam
Ranks and Uniforms of the German Army, Navy and Air Force, London, (No date).

C. Firth
Cromwell's Army, London, 1902.

J. Frederick
Lineage Book of the British Army, New York, 1969.

L. and F. Funcken
L'Uniforme et Les Armes des Soldats du Premier Empire, Vols. 1 and 2, Tournai, France, 1968-9.

J. Goggins
Arms and Equipment of the Civil War, New York, 1962.

W. H. Goodenough and J. C. Dalton
The Army Book for the British Empire, London, 1893.

L. L. Gordon
British Battles and Medals, Aldershot, 1962.

Irwin D. Hastings
War Medals and Decoration, London, 1899.

A. Haswell Miller and N. Dawnay
Military Drawings and Paintings in the Royal Collection, Vol. 1, 1966.

G. Hay
History of the Militia, London, 1905.

J. Hewitt
Ancient Armour, 3 Vols., 1860.

T. Holding
Uniforms of the British Army, Navy & Court, London, 1894. (Reprint 1969).

S. Hyatt
Uniforms and Insignia of the Third Reich, U.S.A., 1962.

C. James
The Regimental Companion, London, 1799.

S. C. Johnson
Chats on Military Curios, London, 1915.

S. Johnson
The Medals of our Fighting Men, London, 1917.

S. Johnson
The Flags of our Fighting Army, London, 1918.

R. Kahl
Insignia, Decorations & Badges of the Third Reich and Occupied Countries, Kedichem (Holland), 1970.

P. Kannik
Military Uniforms in Colour, London, 1968.

E. E. Kerrigan
American Badges and Insignia, New York, 1968.

H. Lachouque and A. Brown
The Anatomy of Glory, London, 1962.

C. C. P. Lawson
A History of the Uniforms of the British Army, Vols. 1-5, London, 1940-67.

Lieutenant Colonel in the British Army
The British Army, London, 1899.

D. Littlejohn and C. Dodkins
Orders, Decorations, Medals and Badges of the Third Reich, California, 1968.

G. MacMunn and C. Lovell
The Armies of India, London, 1911.

Sir James Mann
Wallace Collection Catalogue of European Arms and Armour, 2 Vols., London, 1962.

R. Nevill
British Military Prints, London, 1909.

A. V. Norman
Arms and Armour, London, 1964.

C. Oman
A History of the Art of Warfare in the Middle Ages, London, 1924.

H. Parkyn
Shoulder-Belt Plates and Buttons, Aldershot, 1965.

P. Pietsch
Formations-und Uniformierungsgeschichte des Preussischen Heeres, Vol. 1, Hamburg, 1963. Vol. 2, Hamburg, 1966.

R. Rankin
Helmets and Headdress of the Imperial German Army, 1870–1918, Connecticut, 1965.

W. Richards
Her Majesty's Army, 3 Vols., London, (No date), circa 1900.

W. Richards
His Majesty's Territorial Army, 4 Vols., London, (No date), circa 1910.

H. Robinson
Oriental Armour, London, 1967.

Sir Sibbald Scott
The British Army, London, 1868.

A. Snodgrass
Arms and Armour of the Greeks, London, 1967.

P. Stahl
Die Waffen SS, 1969.

G. Tylden
Horses and Saddlery, London, 1965.

L. Vallet
Croquis de Cavalerie, Paris, 1893.

G. Watson
The Roman Soldier, London, 1969.

G. Webster
The Roman Imperial Army, London, 1969.

V. Wheeler-Holohan
Divisional and Other Signs, London, 1920.

A. S. White
A Bibliography of Regimental Histories of the British Army, London, 1965.

F. Wilkinson
Badges of the British Army, London, 1969.

F. Wilkinson
Militaria, London, 1969.

Y. Yadin
The Art of Warfare in Biblical Times, London, 1963.
Badges and Their Meaning, London, (No Date).
General Regulations and Orders 1799.
A Manual for Volunteer Corps of Infantry, London, 1803.
Regulations and Instructions for the Infantry Exercise, 1819.
Rules and Regulations for the Sword Exercises of the Cavalry, 1803.
Standing Orders and Regulations for the Army in Ireland, 1794. Reprint, London, 1969.
The Volunteer Force and the Volunteer Training Corps during The Great War, London, 1920.

The
Ancient World

1

The Ancient World

THE early history of man's defensive equipment must be very much a matter for conjecture, since no reliable evidence has so far been discovered. It is, however, quite permissible to draw from the condition of surviving primitive cultures inferences as to the activities of prehistoric man; this type of speculation is recognised as a valid basis for hypothesis in many fields of study.

In the beginning, man probably used only two forms of offensive weapons—missiles in the form of stones and rocks, and clubs selected from conveniently shaped branches. Against these weapons there are two methods of defence—dodging and parrying—and the second presupposes some form of shield. The idea no doubt germinated slowly, and eventually some unknown

genius produced a shaped shield fashioned from a piece of wood and fitted with a handle. Today the aborigines of Australia still use a shield which is no more than a solid piece of wood with a slot cut into the back to form a simple hand-hold. The protection afforded by this shield depends on the skill of the user in manoeuvring it to meet a blow; and in due course some other prehistoric innovator must have grasped the principle that the larger the shield, the greater was the degree of permanent protection. Thus emerged the more usual style of shield, with a large surface area.

As more sophisticated weapons were evolved, in the form of flint-headed arrows and axes, so the need for protection became greater, and shields of increased size and strength evolved in their turn. This competition between offence and defence was to become the main stimulus to designers throughout the history of warfare; each new advance in weaponry is countered, sooner or later, by the armourer, and his improvement is, in turn, negated by the weaponsmith.

The first positive evidence for the use of shields is to be seen in wall paintings of Pre-Dynastic Egypt, dating from perhaps 4000 B.C. It seems fairly certain that the shields were rectangular and it is highly likely that they were made of animal skin strengthened with wood. Even today in remote regions shields of skin are in use, and

Title page, *Fig. 1: Archer of the army of King Ashurnasipal of Assyria, clad in a long coat of scale armour, draws his bow while protected by a shield-bearer; a wall carving from the palace of Ashurnasipal II, c. 879 B.C. (British Museum.)*

Above right, *Fig. 2: Egyptian infantry of c. 1900 B.C., armed with typical axes and carrying small shields with simple applied decoration.*

Left, *Plate 1: Heavily armoured Greek hoplite, with crested Corinthian helmet, metal cuirass and greaves. (Model by Richard Courtenay, painted by L. Archer.)*

Fig. 3: Egyptian troops, as depicted on a bas-relief at Thebes; the soldier at the rear carries a simple shield with a boss. 13th Century B.C.

there is no reason to suppose that the choice of materials has altered since the earliest times; if this is the case, the hides of elephant, rhinoceros and crocodile were employed.

By 3000 B.C. the warriors of Assyria are depicted as carrying considerably larger shields. By this period the *phalanx* had been developed—the tight-packed formation of foot-soldiers comprising a solid block of spearmen, the rear ranks carrying longer weapons which projected between the men in the front ranks to form a wall of points. This formation is shown on a carving dating from the third millennium B.C. which is known as the "Stele of Vultures". The soldiers are protected by shields which extend from neck to ankle; they are shown using both hands to grip their spears, and this presumably argues that the shields were hung from the neck or shoulders by

straps. A new feature of the shields in this carving is represented by circles drawn on the front faces—it could well be that these are metal discs added for extra strength.

Bitter experience brought home to prehistoric man his extreme vulnerability to potentially fatal head wounds, and thus evolved the helmet—the most basic piece of armour worn on the body. Although it is only conjecture, it is likely that the first models were no more than caps of woven grass or reeds, or leather. On the "Stele of Vultures" the troops are depicted as wearing close-fitting helmets with slightly conical crowns and neck guards reaching to the shoulder; there also appears to be a nasal guard. What material was used in their construction is not known, although if they were produced in quantity it seems unlikely that sufficient bronze would have been available. Certain tombs excavated at Ur were found to contain metal helmets, but since they were royal tombs they may have been atypical. One of the helmets found at Ur is fashioned from gold, in such a way as to resemble hair, but this may confidently be described as ceremonial rather than practical. Accadian sculpture of the same period often shows the king wearing a helmet decorated with curving horns—a fashion occasionally encountered in Europe at a much later date.

One of the most important steps in the evolution of the fighting man's armour apparently took place during the second millennium B.C. There is in the British Museum a decorated panel known as the "Standard of Ur", on which is depicted a column of soldiers each of whom wears a loose cape reaching to the feet; the surface is decorated with a series of rings, and since they carry no shields it is reasonable to assume that these are some kind of protective garment. Such a reinforced leather cape would be quite effective enough to turn away the point of a spear, or an arrow fired from a medium-powered bow. This was almost certainly one of the earliest pieces of personal armour, and it is perhaps ironic that the "buff coat" of the 17th Century was the last form of protective garment to be worn generally. These armoured troops are shown wearing helmets of the type described above, and from their heavy protection may be deduced to represent front line "shock troops".

The important advance in military technology indicated by the reinforced cape was not to become widespread immediately; in Egypt at this period the shield was still the main form of defence. Most were large, fully the height of a man, with a wide base and a gentle taper towards the top, which was roughly conical. Wall paintings of about 1900 B.C. show smaller versions of these shields in use, and the surfaces appear to have been decorated with various patterns. Some display a series of dots, which may represent some form of reinforcement. With the advent of the New Kingdom in Egypt (c.1560 B.C.) there seems to have been a general reduction in shield size, paralleled by the general adoption of a roughly rectangular shape. Those examples found in the tomb of Tutenkhamon (c.1355 B.C.) are of wood covered with antelope skin, and a wall painting of the 13th Century B.C. shows a shield maker at work busily stretching skins to fit over wooden shields. Other features found in wall paintings of this period include pictures of troops wearing horned helmets and carrying round shields, which probably represent mercenaries employed by the Egyptians. During this period soldiers from Palestine and Syria are shown with rectangular shields fitted with bosses or reinforcing discs. A third type of shield was favoured by the Hittites of Asia Minor, the race usually credited with the introduction of iron-working; this was the "violin" or "figure-of-eight" shield. The origin of this shape is obscure, but it may have been introduced in order to reduce the weight by narrowing the "waist" of the shield, without materially affecting the degree of protection it offered.

I T was during the period between roughly 1500 and 1200 B.C. that scale armour became, if not common, then at least more widely distributed. It appears to have originated in the area of Palestine and Syria, for in Egyptian wall paintings Canaanites are usually depicted as wearing this form of protection. Tuthmosis III, king of Egypt in about 1440 B.C., describes in one of his accounts of the battle of Meggido how he took 200 sets of scale armour; and a wall painting of Tuthmosis IV (c. 1415 B.C.) shows a chariot driver wearing just such a coat of scales. In this scene the painter has realistically shown

Fig. 4: A mercenary of the time of Rameses II, with the long, tapering sword, round shield and horned helmet typical of the "Sea People". Circa 1250 B.C.

the driver wounded by an arrow which has pierced a most vulnerable spot—the armpit.

Scale armour is, of course, a logical development of the basic philosophy of the shield and reinforced cape, and was to remain a common type of body defence throughout the history of warfare; indeed, though the materials have changed from bronze and iron to highly sophisticated plastics and alloys, the basic system is still in use in the bullet-proof waistcoats and "flak jackets" which have re-appeared in the equipment of the combat infantryman over the last few years. Small plates of metal, varying in size so as to accommodate themselves to the movement of the body, are stitched or riveted to a fabric or leather garment. It is a technique which was to be adopted by the Assyrians, Egyptians, Canaanites, Hittites—indeed, by most of the races of the Middle East. It is, however, capable of only limited development for two main reasons; firstly, it is a heavy form of defence, and secondly, it is necessarily rather vulnerable, as it is difficult or impossible to adapt the system to cover some parts of the body. It is naturally impossible to shape plates so that they sit comfortably and manageably in position in, for instance,

Below, *Fig. 5: Pharoah Sethos I (c. 1318–1304* B.C.) *charges the Libyans in his chariot, the reins tied around his waist to leave his hands free for sword and bow; a wall painting from Karnak. (British Museum.)*

Opposite, *Fig. 6: Another view of a scale-clad archer, carved on the wall of Ashurnasipal's palace. (British Museum.)*

the armpit. Nevertheless, provided that no very energetic movement was required, scale armour provided a very satisfactory protection for the greater part of the body.

Scaled tunics are featured in many illustrations from Egypt, and actual fragments have been excavated. Individual scales vary in size, ranging from approximately 2½ by 1½ inches, to 4 by 2 inches and 4¾ by 2½ inches, and less than one-tenth of an inch thick. The construction of these scaled coats was both lengthy and complicated; contemporary records list the number of scales used on various armours, and they range from 680 to 1,035. As each scale probably required at least five or six stitches to secure it to the basic garment, the labour and time involved in making one tunic may be imagined. The scales had to be arranged so that, as far as possible, they overlapped to give the maximum coverage with the minimum of gaps. In paintings they are usually shown as having some kind of strengthening or binding at the neck and sleeves, the latter usually extending half way down the arm. The Egyptians do not appear to have adopted scale armour immediately, although a wall painting shows Rameses II fighting against the Hittites at the battle of Kadesh and wearing a close-fitting coat of scale armour extending from neck to shins, with sleeves nearly to the elbow. He is depicted standing in his chariot, and it is interesting to note that the reins from the two-horse team are knotted around his waist, leaving his hands free to manipulate his war-bow. The Hittite enemy are also shown in scale armour.

A point to consider when studying the use of scale armour by the various nations of the area is the fact that such use presupposes a good and regular supply of metal and a community of skilled smiths to work it. The amounts of metal required to equip large bodies of troops with scale armours must have been considerable.

With the rise to predominance of Assyria, the art of warfare became highly organised;

this energetic and skilful race devoted much of their resources to the development of a first-class fighting force. During its comparatively short but spectacularly successful history, this ruthless army was characterised by a high degree of specialisation; troops were allocated to, and probably trained for, various specific rôles in battle. Foot-soldiers formed by far and away the largest part of the Assyrian army, and spearmen were equipped with a circular shield and a crested metal helmet. Shields were comparatively small, allowing a reasonable agility. In the 6th Century B.C. the spearmen of Sennacherib carried either round or large rectangular shields, some of which appear to have been made of plaited reeds or vines, presumably to reduce weight as far as possible.

Assyrian military campaigns sometimes involved the capture of fortified cities, and their military engineers devised large shields to protect the troops during siege

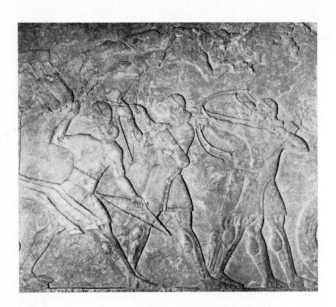

Left, *Fig. 7: This carving shows enemy archers, some fleeing before Ashurnasipal's chariots, others making a stand. (British Museum.)*

Right, *Fig. 8: Protected by his shield-bearer, an Assyrian archer kneels before a siege tower and aims at the walls of an invested city. The conical helmets are typical. (British Museum.)*

operations. These also appear to have been of plaited reeds; some were portable, others were obviously fixed defences. Many had the top section curved back to give protection from archers on the city walls.

Less numerous than the spearmen, but possibly of more decisive importance in battle, were the Assyrian archers, who used a powerful recurved bow of composite construction. These bowmen are almost invariably shown as wearing short-sleeved coats of scale armour reaching to the knee, while their helmets were fairly round, and crested. So important were the archers considered that many of them were accompanied by assistants, whose task it was to carry a shield to defend the archer during the attack. Later, in order to save man-power, Sennacherib introduced larger static shields; this reduced the need for personal protection, and the archers subsequently wore scale tunics of waist length. This principle of pairing archers with shield-bearers was even extended to the cavalry; during the reign of Ashurnasirpal in the 11th Century B.C., these two-man teams are shown operating together—the archer shooting, while the second rider guarded him with a shield and controlled both horses. There is some evidence to suggest that the horses themselves were protected with leather coverings. Cavalry helmets differed from the infantry pattern in that they lacked crests, a very sensible omission for horsemen, though not copied by European armies even in the 19th Century A.D.

Another innovation by the Assyrians was the siege engine. These came to their fruition during the Middle Ages, but the Assyrians had been the true pioneers. Sculptures from the reigns of Ashurnasirpal, Sargon and Sennacherib, covering two centuries, show their armies using wheeled battering rams. Some assessment of their size can be made from the fact that many of them are covered with wicker shields. Assuming these to be the same size as those carried by the infantry, Professor Yadin (in his *The Art of Warfare in Biblical Lands*) makes an inspired guess that the rams were approximately 12 to 18 feet in length and 6 to 9 feet high. Some were actually higher at the front, where the housing rose to form a kind of turret. The actual ram is often shown as having an iron head or point. Obviously the shock troops backing up the battering rams were fitted out for maximum protection, and are shown on sculptures wearing scaled coats reaching to the ground.

which shared certain common features. Through the surviving works of the poets Homer and Hesiod, apparently writing in the 8th Century B.C., much is known of the minor details of life and death, war and peace in the early period of Greek culture. Archaeological evidence has frequently confirmed their accounts of warfare.

Excavations carried out at Mycenae in Southern Greece have unearthed several fragments of metal which are almost certainly pieces of scale armour. These form bronze discs with holes pierced in them in a way which suggests that they were designed to be sewn to a garment in exactly the same manner as those of Assyria. Circular plates are not an ideal shape for scale body armour —they do not overlap so well as rectangular or oval scales—and it may be that they were intended for a helmet; this obviously would not need to be as pliant as body armour, and the shape would therefore be less important. These scales have been dated at approximately 1600 B.C. Another item discovered at Mycenae was a piece of folded linen; the multiplicity of the folds suggests that it was almost certainly some form of "soft" or padded armour.

One very interesting discovery certainly confirmed one of Homer's previously obscure remarks. He made reference in his epics to helmets with boars' tusks arranged on the outside; and during the Mycenae excavations a large number of boars' tusks came to light. A German scholar saw a connection, and it was realised that this particular helmet was made by slicing or shaving tusks to flatten them on one side, the flat faces then being fastened to a leather or linen cap. Alternate rows of tusks faced in opposite directions, and the result was exactly as shown in a Mycenaean carving. Two cheek-pieces were similarly reinforced; and, presumably, the tusks were robust enough to offer reasonable protection—this very striking type of helmet was certainly in use over a considerable period. The style was still employed some 300 years later,

UNDER the leadership of their fierce, war-like kings the Assyrian armies spread their control across the Middle East, and before long their kingdom had become an empire. Despite its apparent vigour and stability, however, it was to be a short-lived empire; a combination of weaker kings and stronger enemies led to its collapse in 610 B.C. As the old powers faded, new ones were rising, and across the Mediterranean new cultures were maturing. There had been several mass migrations in Asia and Europe, and into Greece came one group known as the Dorians, who were to sweep away Mycenae and later to found Classical Greece. A strong national or tribal unity was apparently lacking in these peoples, for in Greece there evolved not one nation but a whole series of city-states. Thebes, Athens, Sparta, Mycenae are names that became landmarks in the development of European civilisation; they represent cultures which differed in many ways, but though other helmets composed entirely of bronze but basically similar in shape were also being used.

In addition to this form of helmet the Mycenaean warrior relied heavily on his shield for protection, and the two common types were both of large size. In surviving representations of these shields they are shown with a speckled surface, not unlike the much later Zulu pattern; this would suggest that they were of oxhide on a wooden frame, and similar to those of Ancient Egypt. The commonest type, which also recalls the design favoured by the Hittites, was of "violin" shape; the other favourite style was of rectangular shape with a curved top. Both types of shield were curved horizontally to enclose the body and give maximum protection, and seem certain to have been fitted with a strap for slinging on the back when not in use.

All forms of armour so far discussed have been of a scale construction, and it is perhaps strange that no evidence of the use of plate armour has so far been discovered in the Middle East. Under these circumstances it is quite remarkable that one of the earliest known forms of this defence should also be one of the most advanced. A warrior's grave excavated at Dendra, not far from Mycenae, and dating from the late 15th Century B.C., revealed an amazingly complete plate armour of bronze. It consisted of a main, tubular body defence with a

Opposite, Fig. 9: Detail from a large clay mixing-bowl of c. 380–370 B.C.; the painting depicts the sack of Troy. Note the Corinthian-style helmet, worn pushed back on the head. Below, Fig. 10: A Greek bronze helmet of the Chalcidian type, found in Salonika and dating from the 5th Century B.C. (Both British Museum.)

series of broad bands hanging down to protect the thighs—less at the front than the back, to enable the wearer to walk with more freedom. A rather crudely fashioned throat guard, or gorget, appears a little wide by more recent standards; but it is flanked by two well-shaped shoulder guards, which again have extra plates attached. Remnants of leg armour—greaves—were also present in the grave; so that with a helmet, either of bronze or boars' tusks, and shield, the Dendra warrior must have been comparatively invulnerable if rather restricted in his movements. There is evidence to suggest that this armour was not unique, but it seems to have enjoyed only a very limited use, disappearing in the 14th Century B.C. and not reappearing until the 15th Century A.D. It may be that the armourers had over-reached themselves; in offering such complete protection, they may well have so increased the weight of the armour that the wearer's mobility was reduced to an unacceptable level—although it has been suggested that these plate armours were intended for use by warriors riding in chariots.

Paintings from about the 14th Century B.C. suggest that the main form of defence was then some type of body armour fashioned of material—perhaps leather—and probably reinforced with an occasional group of scales. During this late period of Mycenaean history a variety of shield shapes were in use, ranging from quite small circular models to the large "violin", which was still very popular. Nearly all types were reinforced with scales and strips of bronze.

Despite its comparatively advanced culture, Mycenae was overwhelmed and eventually disappeared from the main paths of history in about 1200 B.C.; and for the next four centuries there is a dearth of information about the armour of the Greeks. It was a period not dissimilar to that following the withdrawal of the legions from Britain—an Age, if not exactly Dark, then certainly obscure. Little evidence of metal body armour has been found, and there are grounds for thinking that soft, fabric protection was once again predominant.

From about 800 B.C. conical helmets began to appear in paintings, rather similar to those of Assyria, even to the crest on top. Shields are usually shown as being round and fitted with a central bronze boss. The "violin" type is shown in a very exaggerated form, with two great segments cut out from the sides; but A. Snodgrass (*Arms and Armour of the Greeks*) suggests that these shields were not in fact representative of those in contemporary use, but conventionalised forms traditionally used when depicting the deeds of historical heroes, by then, presumably, established in folk-lore.

From about 700 B.C. there are increasingly frequent representations of a style of helmet known by the Greeks as the Corinthian. This wonderfully attractive design represents a superb technical mastery of bronze-working, for it is fashioned from one piece of metal without joints of any type. It completely covers the head, the base line following the line of the shoulders and projecting slightly downwards over the chest. At the front a T-shaped opening accommodates eyes and nose, and the latter is protected by a bar projecting down from the middle of the brow. This style of helmet remained in use for many centuries, although in Greece it had largely been abandoned by the 5th Century B.C. It was padded on the inside, and no doubt offered excellent protection, but the wearer must have been handicapped by restricted vision, and, particularly, hearing. Later versions appear to have been so shaped that they could be worn pushed back from the face. Another style, known as the Chalcidian, is a smaller version of the Corinthian with a smoother outline and, significantly, cutaways leaving the ears uncovered.

Naturally these were not the only types of helmets in use; most were simpler in design, and these are generally known by the areas in which they appear to have originated or enjoyed widespread use—although

these were not the contemporary terms. Illyrian helmets dating from the 7th Century B.C. were much simpler than those described above, being essentially a bowl-shaped skull-piece with triangular face guards projecting well down over the chest. The technical problem of beating out a helmet from a single piece of metal was overcome in this style by fashioning it in two pieces and joining them along a lateral ridge running across the skull, although some later models were made in one piece. Boetian helmets were possibly the simplest of all, resembling metal hats with wide, forward-sloping brims.

For centuries the main fighting unit of nearly all Greek armies was the solid block of spearmen—the phalanx. It was not a new formation, and as we have seen it had appeared at a very early date in the Middle East. A great mass of heavily armoured soldiers, known in Greece as *hoplites*, pressed forward in close-packed ranks with shields forming a solid wall and spears at the ready; when the opposing phalanxes met, each hoplite strove to stand his ground, thrusting and stabbing at the enemy's unprotected throat and groin. The essence of victory was to maintain the ranks; the phalanx that failed to keep in solid formation was broken, and the battle was lost. In these conditions it was essential that the hoplites be well protected;

each wore a breast- and backplate of beaten bronze, a cuirass simply shaped to the body with a shallow, upstanding collar and a slightly flared waist. His shins were protected by shaped bronze plates—greaves—sometimes secured by lacing but often held in place by the springiness of the metal itself. Completing his defence was a circular shield some 3 feet in diameter, fashioned of wood and reinforced with strips or plates of bronze. On the back was a bronze strip through which the hoplite passed his left arm to grasp a leather thong secured to the edge of the shield.

For many centuries this type of equipment was standard; but changes began to appear around the 6th Century B.C. The heavy, solid metal cuirass was largely replaced by a lighter quilted model fashioned of leather or folded linen and possibly reinforced with bronze discs. In some ways this resembled the later Roman legionary's *lorica segmentata*; it was opened down the front and secured by laces, and the shoulder guards, secured at the back, were passed over the shoulders and similarly laced at the front. Full cuirasses were still used, but from the 5th Century B.C. there was a fashion for plates moulded to represent the muscles of the torso. Occasionally metal guards were worn on wrist, upper arm, ankle and thigh.

In addition to the heavily armoured hoplites, Greek armies included numbers of lightly armed skirmishes whose task it was

to harry and pursue an enemy. This group included archers, slingers and spear-throwers, and since mobility was the core of their function they required less personal protection. Their shields were lighter, commonly made from plaited or woven wicker and covered with animal hides—goat and sheep were both popular. Some of these shields were circular, while others were curved rather like a new moon. It is of interest to note that the javelins thrown by these skirmishers were fitted with loops part way along the shaft; the fingers were inserted in these, so that they acted as a "spear thrower" and lengthened the arm to give added power to the cast.

Horsemen had not figured prominently in Greek armies, the emphasis always being on massed infantry. There had been some considerable use of chariots in the early days but by the 5th Century B.C. these seem to have been abandoned to a great extent. During the wars between Greece and Persia cavalry had been deployed against the Greek hoplites with little success, but the Greeks were sufficiently impressed by the potential of this arm to begin building up their mounted troops. Xenophon (c. 430–

335 B.C.), a Greek writer with military experience, described what the well-equipped cavalryman should wear. He advised an open-faced helmet such as the Boetian type, since this style assured the rider of wide, clear vision. The cuirass, said Xenophon, should be light and non-restrictive, with thigh defences, and in addition the rider should wear a guard for the left arm which was occupied with holding the reins. This idea of a "bridle gauntlet" was to be revived in the 17th Century, although Xenophon's was apparently larger and made of leather. He also recommended that the horse should be armoured, although this form of defence did not really flourish until the 15th Century.

Greek armour was often technically far in advance of its period, and was certainly superior to that produced in the Middle East. The contrast was always between plate and scale, and it is interesting that this difference in emphasis was to continue for centuries. Oriental armour was almost invariably constructed of mail, scales or a mixture of the two, while Europe developed an elaborate system of armour based on the increasing use of solid plates.

The Age
of the Legions

2

The Age of the Legions

HAVING proved his worth, the hoplite spearman fighting in the massed phalanx retained his mastery of the battlefield for many centuries; but when war broke out between the two dominant city-states of Athens and Sparta in 431 B.C. a chain of events was set in motion which was to lead to sweeping changes in military thinking, and the abandonment of the phalanx until its revival in a modified form in the Middle Ages. Athens, weakened by an appalling epidemic of the plague, was finally overcome. Sparta's triumph was, however, to be relatively short-lived; despite their reputation of hardiness and military skill second to none, the Spartans were in turn defeated by the army of Thebes. A period of bickering and intermittent warfare among the Greek city-states left them virtually defenceless against a new power which had risen in the North.

Title page, Fig. 15: Roman cavalry parade helmet of thin bronze embossed with scenes of combat, and probably gilded originally. (British Museum.)

Left, Plate 3: Superb full-sized facsimile of a Roman legionary's helmet and lorica segmentata, *fashioned by H. Russell Robinson Esq. The* lorica, *made in four separate sections, is based upon examples found at Corbridge-upon-Tyne, a Roman military site three miles south of Hadrian's Wall; it weighs approximately 12 lbs.*

From Macedon came King Philip and his brilliant son Alexander, and under these two great leaders changes in the structure and uses of armies were introduced. From its previous position of relative unimportance in Greek warfare, Alexander raised the cavalry to a central place in military tactics; led by their young king in person, the Macedonian "Companion" horsemen made an enormous contribution to the many victories which distinguished the career of the legendary conqueror.

The phalanx was increased in size and the pike carried by the foot-soldiers was lengthened until it was some 18 or 20 feet long. The troops continued to carry the *hoplon*, or great circular shield, but although it is difficult to be precise, the evidence certainly suggests that the men of the phalanx no longer wore the heavy metal cuirass. Metal helmets and greaves seem to have been retained by the majority of the infantry. This reduction in the protection worn by the foot-soldier was paralleled by an increase in cavalry armour; the horsemen were equipped with high-domed Thracian helmets and one of the modelled styles of cuirass.

Under the leadership of Alexander the Macedonian and Greek armies travelled thousands of miles, tearing down the Persian empire and eventually reaching India. Here it was that they met, for the first time, the war elephant. These great beasts were to be pressed into service for many centuries, crossing the Alps with

Hannibal and suffering throughout the Punic Wars between Rome and Carthage.

Alexander the Great, the young conqueror with a vision of supra-national unity and brotherhood, died on a sick-bed before his dazzling victories could be consolidated, and the vast empire which he had carved out fragmented. From this point onward Greek ascendancy disappeared, and the pivot of European history moved westward to Italy.

The Greeks had strong contacts with Sicily and Southern Italy, and excavations in this area have revealed many common features with the arms and armour of Greece. In the 4th Century B.C. the warriors of Southern Italy were still equipped in the style of the old Greek hoplite. Traditionally it was in 753 B.C. that the town of Rome was founded on the seven hills above the Tiber; as befits such a significant historic event,

the facts are obscured by abundant myths. At first Rome was a small community, which struggled to survive. The Etruscans, whose culture was based to the north of the young city, were only fought off with difficulty; but Rome prevailed, and flourished, surviving even such disasters as the sack of the city by the Gauls in 390 B.C.

External pressures forced the Romans to create an army in self defence. At one time

Below, Fig. 16: A legionary's bronze helmet, dating from the 1st Century A.D., found in a canal between Tring and Berkhamsted. The rear peak guarded the neck, and the holes indicate where the missing brow peak was originally mounted. Right, Fig. 17: A bronze shield, 44 inches long, found in the River Witham in Lancashire. Dating from between 250 and 150 B.C., it was originally decorated with the figure of a wild boar; it probably differs but little from the shields carried by the Britons who opposed Caesar's landing. (British Museum.)

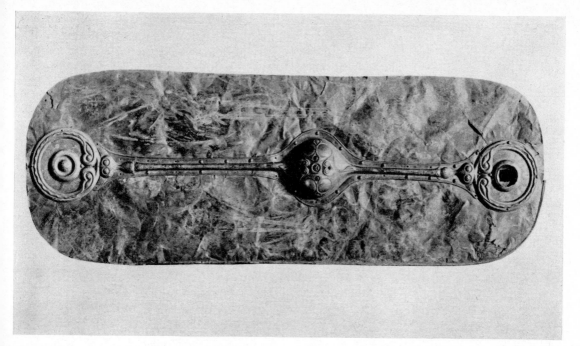

this army met the great Macedonian phalanx in battle, and was defeated; but at the battle of Pydna in 168 B.C. they found the secret of dealing with this formation. By superior mobility they turned the flank of the phalanx, and attacked the more vulnerable face of the formation with devastating results.

Gradually Rome extended her influence, until the greater part of the Italian peninsula was under her control. This expansion was a self-sustaining process, and the leaders of the city looked further afield until their eyes fell upon Sicily. It was here that they came into violent contact with the borders of another vigorous Mediterranean culture—Carthage, the powerful North African city-state. Although Rome was victorious in this First Punic War, Carthage was resilient; despite enormous geographical and military obstacles her greatest general, Hannibal, defeated the Romans on their own ground, and it was only his recall to Carthage to fight a Roman expeditionary force which saved the whole of Italy from Carthaginian domination. A series of clashes followed until, in 146 B.C., the city

was captured and brutally destroyed, leaving Rome the dominant power in the Mediterranean. From this first step on the road to empire, Rome developed into one of the greatest power structures the world has ever known. The success of Rome may be attributed to two basic factors; and the first was the Roman genius for adaption. They were not great innovators, but were enormously successful at developing and shaping ideas and institutions in their own best interests. The second factor was the Roman legion.

The legions were not a constant and unchanging force over the whole period of Roman history, and conditions of service varied. It seems that in the early days of the Roman Republic liability for service depended on a property-owning qualification. According to the writer Polybius, the legion was divided into thirty *maniples*, of which ten were allocated to each of three lines of battle—the *hastati*, *principes* and *triarii*. Reforms took place around the end of the 2nd Century B.C., including the removal of the property limitation; all Roman citizens now became liable for service. It

Above, *Fig. 18: Horned bronze helmet found in the Thames near Waterloo Bridge, and dating from the 1st Century* B.C. *The studs were at one time decorated with red enamel.* **Opposite,** *Fig. 19: This bronze helmet of the 1st Century* A.D. *is probably of North British origin; its shape is strongly reminiscent of the Roman legionary style.* (*British Museum.*)

was at this time that each legion was presented with a standard in the form of the Roman eagle, which came to represent the spirit of the legion. It occupied a place in the minds of the soldiers mid-way between a religious relic and a battle flag. Where the eagle was raised, there was the heart of the legion. In defeat, it was the rallying point, and the site of the last stand. In victory and attack, the eagle led the legion; when the advance faltered, the eagle-bearer might stimulate the flagging legionaries into renewed effort by pressing forward and exposing himself to danger, knowing his comrades would follow—for to lose the edge in battle was unimaginable disgrace.

A third reform carried out at this time was the decline in the use of Roman citizens in the cavalry and lightly armed skirmishers. Such groups were still widely employed in a variety of rôles—reconnaissance, flank protection, forward garrison duty, battlefield support—but they were recruited almost entirely among foreign populations who did not qualify for Roman citizenship (although they were frequently officered by Romans). These auxiliary units raised among conquered races became a feature of the Roman

army for many centuries; but the core on which the power of Rome was built was the disciplined, trained, uniformly equipped Roman heavy infantry—the legion.

At this period the legion comprised ten cohorts each of six centuries, totalling approximately 4,000 men. Generally speaking the number of legions in service never exceeded thirty-three. Most were known by a number and a name or honour-title, this latter being based on any one of a variety of factors—the Emperor who first raised the unit, the area in which the legion was first recruited, some figure from the Roman pantheon of gods, or occasionally, some great victory. Some legions also adopted particular unit symbols, in addition to the eagle which was common to all. The ill-fated Ninth Legion, originally raised in Spain (for it must be remembered that Roman citizenship did not depend on birth) was known as "IX Hispana". The renowned Twentieth Legion, which played a great part in the campaigns in Britain, was "XX Valeria Victrix", and bore the sign of the charging boar; while the Fourteenth Legion, formed from two earlier formations, took as its title "XIV Geminae"—"The Twins".

One special unit which should perhaps be mentioned was the Praetorian Guard; essentially the body guard of the ruler, they were given permanent establishment by the Emperor Augustus in 27 B.C. In 23 A.D. Tiberius moved them all into the city of Rome, and their rôle became rather more sinister; they became the personal police of the Emperor, a threat hanging over the city, and a vital factor at all stages of the violent and bloody power struggles which bedevilled Rome throughout her history. Their strength probably never exceeded 16,000, but until their disbandment by Constantine in 312 A.D. they exercised an influence out of all proportion to their strength. "Who had the Praetorian Guard, had Rome"— and it is hardly surprising that they were a privileged force; it is believed that under

Augustus the praetorian received twice the wages of the ordinary legionary.

Although the liability to serve in the army was incumbent on every Roman citizen, the majority of recruits were in fact volunteers. Augustus decreed in 13 B.C. that the term of service in the legions was to be twenty years. For the last four years of his service, the legionary was in theory relieved of routine duties and lived in special quarters when not actually in the field. In A.D. 6 the conditions of service were changed, the final five of a legionary's twenty years being fixed as the "privileged" period. These provisions could be set aside in time of emergency; indeed, one of the main grievances quoted in surviving accounts of potential or actual mutiny among the legions was the retention of men in the ranks after their term had expired. When the legionary was finally released from service he received a grant of land; various areas of the empire were set aside for these land grants, a useful secondary result being that behind the military defences of the various provinces, hardy communities of veterans sprang up, who could be counted upon to help defend their lands against barbarian incursions in times of emergency, and who provided a stabilising influence on society.

To "join the eagles" was by no means a matter of simply enlisting. Unless the applicant could produce a letter of reference from some person of respectable standing, it was difficult to gain acceptance. He also had to be a full Roman citizen, although there is evidence to suggest that this barrier could be overcome, the sons of serving soldiers enjoying preference in this respect. A new recruit was subjected to a medical examination and, according to Vegetius, there was a minimum height requirement of 5 feet 8 inches—although this was lowered to 5 feet 5 inches in the 4th Century A.D., when manpower shortages were becoming a matter for concern. Once accepted for service, the recruit was given a small payment—rather like the "Queen's Shilling" in Victorian England—and was then sent to join his unit, travelling in a group and under the control of a "recruiting officer" or some other military functionary. He took an oath binding him to give unquestioning obedience, and certain documentary evidence suggests that he was marked in some way—in the 4th Century, apparently by being branded on the arm. Once the recruit had arrived at his unit's official depot his name was entered on the nominal roll, and he became a trainee legionary.

The initial stage of his training consisted of a great deal of hard physical exercise, to prepare him for what would undoubtedly be an extremely harsh and arduous life. In summer the legion was expected to march twenty miles in five hours, and in times of urgency, at the full military pace, twenty-four miles in five hours.

Even more important than physical training was, of course, the use of weapons. Basically the legionary relied on two weapons. The first attack on the enemy

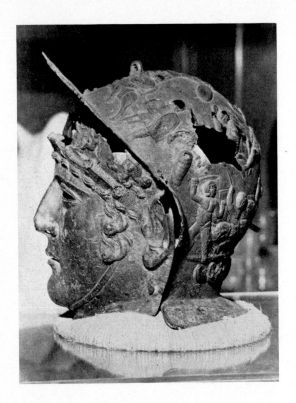

would be a barrage of spears, and the legionary's throwing spear, or *pilum*, was generally made according to standard pattern. About 6 feet long, it consisted of a wooden shaft making up about half the total length, to which was fixed a long shank of soft iron with a fairly small head. The pilum remained the prime assault weapon of the legions until at least the 2nd Century A.D., although it underwent small modifications. The main one was designed to ensure that expended spears could not be thrown back at the legionaries; either the shank was made of iron so soft that on striking a shield or the ground the weight of the wooden shaft caused it to bend and become useless until it could be hammered straight; or the shank was fitted to the shaft with a wooden pin, which broke on impact.

When the spears had been thrown, the legion closed in for the style of combat which was its great strength, and which won for Rome mastery of most of the known world. In close but flexible ranks, manoeuvring into various formations on the word of command, the iron-clad legionaries closed with the enemy shoulder to shoulder, protecting themselves and each other with a shield-wall, and stabbing around it with the wicked Roman short-sword—the *gladius*, or Spanish sword—a wide, double-edged weapon with a blade about 20 inches long. Fitted with a simple bone or wooden handle, the gladius was carried in a brass-mounted leather sheath slung from a cross-belt or baldric, hanging high on the right side of the body, the hilt against the ribs. Because of its short length and lack of rigidity in the scabbard fitting on the belt the sword could be drawn with the right hand without difficulty.

In order to toughen their recruits, the Romans issued them with shields and swords of much greater weight than the standard issue models. After practising until they were competent to handle these overweight weapons, the recruits would have found the issue swords and shields light and easy to manipulate. While most of the Greek swords had been intended primarily for slashing, the Roman legionary was taught the paramount importance of the point; for hours and days he stood in front of a 6-foot wooden stake driven into the ground, sweating under the weight of his practice shield, thrusting and stabbing until he was completely proficient in the art of handling his sword. After he had reached a certain level of skill, the recruit was permitted to indulge in mock combat with another soldier; and if he failed to show sufficient promise during the early days of his training, then, according to the 4th-Century writer Vegetius, his rations were cut until he showed some improvement! The wooden stake was also used as the target for pilum practice.

In addition to weapon training the recruits had to do a certain amount of route marching, and Vegetius states that they had to carry up to 60 pounds weight in addition to their weapons and personal equipment. It was no doubt in the course of these route marches that the recruit was instructed in the art of making camp—for every overnight halt by the legion was protected by the construction of a fortified camp to a fixed design. Under normal circumstances a ditch was dug and a wall built up to a height of about 3 feet; if attack was thought to be imminent the ditch was made deeper. Vegetius states that it should be 9 feet wide and 7 feet deep, or 12 feet wide and 9 deep if a really major attack was expected. The earth dug out was used to build up a wall 3 or 4 feet high, into which were thrust pointed stakes, which were part of the marching kit of every legionary. The soldiers practised making camp under imminent danger of attack, with half the infantry and the cavalry units drawn up in line of battle while the rest were digging the ditch.

On reaching the end of his training the recruit joined the ranks of the legion, and faced a variety of occupations. He might be allocated to a specialist job such as tilemaker, sword cutler, or blacksmith; if he received such a posting he would be exempted from general duties—standing guards, road-making and so on. During the 2nd Century A.D. the legionary might be appointed as a *principalis*, usually meaning an exemption from general duties and service in a more scholastic capacity—in effect, an "orderly room clerk". Over the generations other specialist posts were created; but throughout the history of the legions, the backbone of the whole structure was provided by the centurions. A man of proven professional skill, the centurion may be described as an N.C.O. in social terms, but an officer in all else. He could be transferred from legion to legion, and his appointment and postings were all subject, theoretically, to the Emperor's approval. There were about sixty centurions in each legion, graded in seniority; the senior centurion, or *primus pilus*, was a man of enormous importance, whose professional-

Opposite, *Fig. 20: Another view of the cavalry officer's parade helmet; note the separate visor. This fine piece was found on the site of a garrison in the north of England.* **Above**, *Fig. 21: A bronze Roman shield boss, engraved with a series of trophies and figures around the edge and with a single figure on the dome. 2nd Century* A.D. *(British Museum.)*

ism underpinned the efficiency and morale of the legion, especially as the *tribunes*, or officers, were often aristocratic sprigs with little military experience.

In the early days of the Republic service in the army had been an obligatory duty of the citizen, and there had been no question of payment. However, the idea of wages was certainly well established by the middle of the 2nd Century B.C. From the legionary's pay certain deductions were made for food, clothing, replacement of weapons and so forth; what proportion of the wages these deductions represented is not clear, but they are thought to have been fairly high. Payment was normally made in three instalments, in January, May and September; naturally, the higher grades received higher pay.

Service in the legion was unquestionably a hard life; and a particularly disgraceful defeat, or a mutiny in an army where discipline was so vital, could lead to the terrible punishment of decimation. Each tenth man, drawn by lot, was clubbed or stoned

officer with an administrative background, particularly if the legion was quartered at its permanent depot, the senior centurion wielded great influence.

THESE, then, were the men who won, and for centuries on end held secure, the greatest empire in the history of the world. What of their equipment? The available evidence suggests that the early legionaries wore a mail shirt known as the *lorica hamata*. The origin of mail, a form of defence using interlocking rings, is obscure; this question will be discussed in detail in a later Signature, but the earliest known fragments were found in Denmark and date from the 3rd Century B.C. Some authorities suggest that the Romans received their idea of mail via the Greeks from the Persians; but others argue that Western European mail was of Celtic origin, and there seems to be more evidence of this—especially as the Romans referred to it as "Gallic mail". Mr. H. Russell Robinson, undoubtedly the foremost British expert on Roman armour, has traced its first appearance on sculptures relative to the Roman army to about 168 B.C., and its use continued until the middle of the 1st Century A.D. The legionary's head was protected by a bronze helmet, the *galea*, which had a hemispherical dome with a rounded peak at the rear—giving it something of the appearance of a jockey's cap turned backwards. A flat bar followed the contour of the brow and afforded extra protection, and the sides of the face were covered by wide cheek-pieces tied by a thong under the chin. In the early days of the Republic the shield carried by the legionary was large and oval in shape, but by the 1st Century B.C. the *scutum* was in general service. This was a tall, rectangular shield, curved horizontally and fitted with reinforcing strips and a central boss. This covered the hole cut to accommodate the hand which gripped a bar running across the inside. The shield weighed something in the region of 12 pounds, and one passage in

to death, while the nine shaken survivors suffered some minor punishment such as a reduction in rations. This ghastly penalty does not appear to have been invoked very often from the time of the Empire onwards. In cases of individual cowardice or disobedience a range of punishments were available, ranging from a few casual welts with the centurion's staff, through dishonourable discharge, to the death penalty.

The composition of the legion varied during the long history of Rome, but essentially it consisted of eight-man squads, known as *contubernia*, ten of which made up a century. Two centuries were counted together to form a maniple, or company; and three maniples formed one cohort, or battalion, of about 480 men. Ten cohorts made up one legion, which may thus be compared loosely to a modern brigade group. In command of the legion was the Legate—*legatus legionis*; below him came the senior tribune, and third in line was the camp prefect. As this latter might be an

Caesar's commentaries suggests that it was carried with some sort of cover over it when not in use. Greaves were not normally worn. The gladius, as already described, hung in its sheath on a belt crossing the left shoulder, and an iron dagger, or *pugio*, was also slung on the right hip, on the waist belt or *cingulum militare*. This was decorated with a number of fancy metal plates, often embossed or silvered and occasionally even gilded. From the centre of the belt in front hung an apron comprising a number of leather straps reinforced with metal plates, which afforded some protection to the lower abdomen and genitals. On the column erected by the Emperor Trajan (53–117 A.D.) to celebrate his victories, this apron is shown as being worn tucked up into the belt when the legionaries were on the march; it was some 15 inches long, and would presumably tend to bang on the legs.

Beneath his mail shirt the legionary wore a linen undergarment and a woollen tunic, the latter short-sleeved and reaching to the knee. The practice of wearing tight-fitting leather breeches (*braccae*) became general; these reached to the calf. Since so much of their time was spent in marching, the footwear of the legionaries was obviously of extreme importance. They wore *calligae*, thick, heavy leather sandals studded with iron nails and secured by a length of thonging or narrow strap which extended well up the shin.

The standard-bearer occupied a post of great importance, and over his uniform this soldier wore an animal skin. This is traditionally represented as being the hide of a leopard, but in fact the skins of lion, boar and bear were also used; it was normal for the upper portion of the animal's head to be left attached to the skin in such a way that it could be draped over the standard-bearer's helmet, with the front paws hanging down over the shoulders and fastened on the chest. As described above, the eagle standard had a unique significance for the legionaries; among other customs,

Opposite, Fig. 22: Protective cage for the eye of a horse, discovered on the site of a Roman fort at Ribchester; late 2nd or early 3rd Century A.D. Auxiliary formations such as cavalry squadrons usually formed the garrisons of frontier forts, the main legionary strength being held in reserve in the major depot cities. Above, Fig. 23: The magnificent helmet found in the 7th Century Sutton Hoo ship burial; eyebrows and moustache are embossed and gilded. (British Museum.)

it was the signal for the end of the march and the siting of the camp when the standard was planted in the ground, and when it was uprooted again, the camp was struck.

During the 1st Century A.D. the legions began to adopt new forms of equipment, the most important of all being in the style of body armour. In place of the mail shirt there was a fairly rapid adoption of the *lorica segmentata*. Understanding of this form of defence has been rather sketchy until quite recently when, thanks to extensive research and a deep understanding of the technical problems, H. R. Robinson constructed facsimiles which clearly show the methods of manufacture and use.

Fig. 24: Reconstruction of the shield from the Sutton Hoo ship; it is of higher quality than was usual, but is otherwise typical of the period. (British Museum.)

The lorica segmentata is composed of a number of metal strips which are united to form four separate units. The main body armour comprises two sections, with seven or eight strips curved to fit the body, the lower one being rolled over along the bottom edge. Each strip is riveted on the inside on to a long leather strap which holds the pieces firmly but flexibly together. These two sections are joined together by a series of hooks and thongs. To protect the upper part of the body and the shoulders two other sections are attached, also made up of curved strips hinged and leathered together. The extremities of these two shoulder-pieces are secured to the lower section of the body armour. The whole armour was extremely pliable, allowing easy movement of the body and arms; and when not in use the lorica folded up until it

could be carried with comfort in a small cloth bag. The weight was, again, in the region of 12 pounds. This type of armour was introduced during the first half of the 1st Century A.D. and continued in use until at least the beginning of the 3rd Century, when there was a gradual reversion to the use of mail. Officers wore a slightly different form of protection, often depicted as a moulded cuirass, with metal greaves and the sword slung on the left side.

The helmet of the legionary also became more complex. Not only was iron substituted for bronze, but the construction was redesigned to give greater protection. A dome, again reinforced with a brow peak, projected lower at the back to cover part of the neck; and from the base of the skull a wide, sweeping neck guard stood out to protect the neck and the upper part of the shoulders. Wide cheek-pieces, shaped to offer the greatest protection, were fitted at the temples and laced under the chin. On top of the helmet was a detachable crest fitting; this was a small support into which could be clipped a curved crest holder which was laced to hooks mounted on the brow and rear of the helmet. The crest would have been made up either of feathers or, more likely, horsehair; and although there are references to coloured crests Mr. Robinson suggests that the two predominant colours were in fact black and white. These plumes and crests were normally worn only for parades and ceremonial occasions; the legionaries' crests ran from front to back, and those of centurions transversely, from side to side. From the centre of the neck guard projected a hinged handle, to facilitate the slinging or carrying of the helmet when it was not required; on the march it was carried slung from the neck and there was a small loop inside the neck guard through which a thong could be passed. Strength alone would not afford the maximum of protection, and to reduce the force of a blow the inside of the helmet was lined with padding; since there are no holes for lacing in this lining, it was presumably glued in place. It is known that certain helmets were specifically designed for parade use. One example in the British Museum is of very thin metal, elaborately embossed, and has a full visor fashioned as a face mask.

Cavalry was never very popular with the true Roman, and during the early part of the Empire's history the majority of the mounted troops were Spanish or Gallic auxiliaries. These troopers appear to have worn helmets which are not dissimilar to some worn in the 16th Century. They are basically the same as the legionary pattern, but extra fittings cover the face except for an opening which leaves eyes and mouth clear. For body protection the cavalry tended to favour either a mail shirt or scale armour. Another important difference in cavalry equipment was the sword; in place of the legionary's short, wide gladius, the trooper carried a longer, narrower style of weapon known as a *spatha*. In addition he carried a lance, which could either be braced under the arm, or used over-arm to stab and thrust. On horseback the heavy scutum would have been unwieldy, and the cavalry carried a round shield of lighter construction. Contemporary references suggest that, in some cases at least, the horses were fitted with armour for the head, breast and flanks. Several bulbous cages have been excavated which are presumed to have been horses' eye-guards. Some units of cavalry in the armies of the late Empire, known as cataphracts, were apparently very heavily armoured; fragmentary evidence suggests that some cavalrymen and their mounts were completely covered from head to foot with armour, probably of scale construction. This innovation is generally associated with the Eastern Empire, and was characteristic of the way the life style of the Roman administration and armies in that area was influenced by Eastern rather than Western European ideas in the later years.

Fig. 25: A detail of the Sutton Hoo shield, showing the large central boss with its decorative work. (British Museum.)

For centuries the great Roman armies were steadily diluted by the admission of auxiliaries and barbarians into the service, and the great legionary ideal steadily declined. Under the crushing pressure of mass barbarian migrations on her frontiers, Rome resolved the manpower problem by the dangerous course of filling her ranks with a greater and greater proportion of mercenaries. In this climate the essential discipline and professionalism of the legions became weaker and weaker; generations of treachery and civil war, as rival leaders and factions wrangled over the seat of Imperial power, allowed the rot to spread, and influence passed from Rome to Constantinople, capital of the Eastern Empire. By the beginning of the 5th Century the entire structure was crumbling. Migrations of Goths, Saxons, Angles and

Jutes were shaping a new Europe; and in Britain the effect had been noticeable long before the traditional date of 410 A.D., when the legions were finally withdrawn. Raids by the marauding tribesmen of Northern Germany and Denmark had forced the Romano-British Government to appoint a Count of the Saxon Shore, whose responsibility it was to guard against these incursions. Forts were built on strategic sites, and a watch system was instituted to enable a quick response to hostile landings. With the withdrawal of the legions and the collapse of firm central government, the country lay, not completely, but largely at the mercy of these and other invaders.

From the North came the Picts, the painted men of Scotland, who for centuries had made sporadic raids against and over Hadrian's Wall; from the East came the Saxons and Angles; and all of Britain lay in the shadow of attack. Tradition has it that in order to fight fire with fire one of the British kings in South-East England hired a force of Saxon mercenaries led by Hengist and Horsa to protect his lands from other invaders. Realising their own strength and the weakness of the local population, the Saxons gradually assumed greater and greater power. Soon the so-called Dark Ages descended upon Britain; what had been a prosperous, unified province of Rome fragmented into warring petty kingdoms, and for 500 years the forces of ignorance and barbarism held sway. The wattle and daub of the Saxon *tun* replaced the marble and statuary of the Romano–British villa, and the bright flame of civilisation was dimmed. Records of this period are sparse and knowledge of it is limited, but archaeological evidence suggests that beauty and craftsmanship were still appreciated and enjoyed.

This was the period of King Arthur, about whom little is known but much is assumed. Like all folk heroes he became a peg on which to hang a host of stories; but he is of little interest in the fields of arms and armour, beyond the emphasis the stories

Plate 4: *Types of the Roman army— legionary, standard bearer, and centurion. The legionary* (left) *carries a* pilum *and a large shield—*scutum*—and the standard bearer wears the traditional animal skin. Unlike most troops, centurions did occasionally wear greaves. (Models by Richard Courtenay, painted by L. Archer.)*

place on the importance of the war-horse.

During this shadowy period the style of armament is known to have changed. Shields regained their importance in the absence of formalised body armour, and most appear to have been circular and fitted with large central bosses. These covered the hole which accommodated the hand grip on the central bar, in the Roman fashion. Some shields belonging to nobles and royal figures were decorated with enamelling and precious and semi-precious stones, and literary evidence supports the idea of painted shields. The best-known survival is, of course, the superb example found in the 7th-Century Sutton Hoo ship burial.

This same hoard provides the best example of a contemporary helmet, though there is little detailed knowledge of helmets of the post-Roman period. The Sutton Hoo specimen bears some decoration which shows a helmet fitted with horns. Whether this is an accurate representation is not certain, but helmets have been found in Gaul dating from about the 1st Century

with very large, horn-like cone projections on each side, so the style seems to have been fairly well established. The Sutton Hoo helmet is of iron covered with bronze foil, and the face is covered by a visor with a gilt nose, mouth, moustache and eyebrows. The piece rather resembles a modern "crash-helmet" and would indeed have been padded on the inside. There is no doubt that this was only one of many styles of helmet in use, for the grave of a Frankish chief of the 6th Century has furnished us with one that is very much plainer, being merely a conical crown with two cheek-pieces and indications that a curtain of mail hung down to cover the back of the neck.

The body protection of this period seems to have been almost entirely of mail, although there is evidence to suggest that a combination of mail and scale armour was worn on occasion. The scales in this case are long strips of metal, and it is believed that they were worn on shins and forearms.

Figs. 26 & 27: Two ivory chessmen from the famous set found at Lewis in Scotland. They date from the 12th Century at least, and possibly earlier, and are thought to be of Scandinavian origin. Fascinating for their significance to the history of the game—they display several characteristics which differ from modern convention, notably in the design of the rooks—the chessmen are also faithful reproductions of the military styles of their period; note the kite-shaped shields and the typical conical helmets with nasal guards. (British Museum.)

Mail
and
Plate

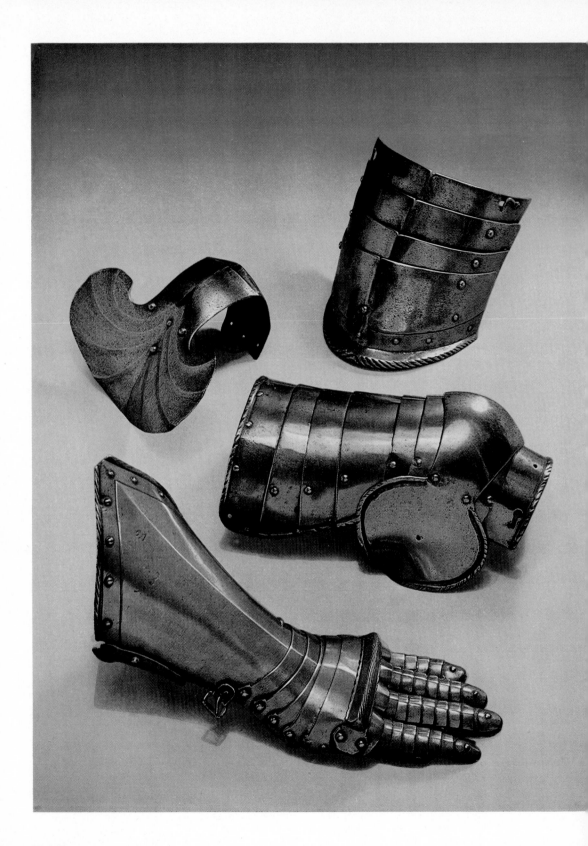

3

Mail and Plate

Title page, *Fig. 28: Sir John D'Aubernon, died 1277; this brass shows the adoption of plate defences at the knee. Sir John wears a hauberk, coif, mufflers and chausses of mail.*

Right, *Fig. 29: Detail of a section of European mail, showing how each link engages with four others. The flattened and rivetted ends of each link can be seen clearly. Actual diameter of each link is approximately ⅜ inch.*

Left, *Plate 5: Armour of the 16th and 17th Centuries.* **Top right,** *the detachable part of a tasset;* **top left,** *knee piece with wing;* **centre,** *right thigh piece with knee piece attached;* **bottom,** *gauntlet with small digital plates rivetted to a leather glove.* *(Gyngell Collection.)*

As we have seen both Greeks and Romans made extensive use of a form of plate armour, but each culture abandoned it and reverted to simpler means of defence. From the 2nd until the 14th Century A.D. the main, although not the only defence was to be mail. The word "mail" derives from the Latin word meaning a net, *macula,* or in Italian, *maglia;* it is often erroneously called chainmail, but mail is the technically correct term.

As already pointed out, the earliest surviving pieces of mail were found in Denmark and date from the 3rd Century B.C. It is of some interest to conjecture on its development for there is no obvious connecting sequence between mail and scale armour—was there a form of scale armour which used rings rather than plates?

It is often difficult, if not impossible, to be sure of our facts concerning early armour; few items dating from before the 15th Century have survived. Much of our knowledge is derived from sculptures, paintings and manuscripts and it is not always easy to know exactly what the artists intended to depict since they often used systems and symbols which may now be misinterpreted. This was especially so in the case of mail, where a variety of shading styles are encountered, and this has led to great discussion as to whether they represented special types or common mail. The general consensus of opinion today is that all styles represent conventional mail.

Obviously the number of links in any mail garment was affected by the size of the link used, but in any piece the number was considerable. When the wire was ready it was probably wound round an appropriately sized former and then cut to produce split rings. The ends of each ring were flattened, overlapped and then riveted together, and each link normally engaged with four others. Shaping was achieved in much the same way as with knitting, by adding or omitting links in specific patterns. The amount of physical labour and time involved

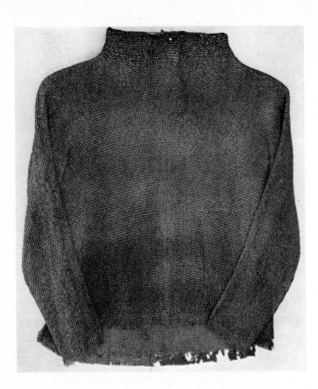

Left, *Fig. 30: A shirt of mail made in Germany during the first half of the 15th Century; it measures 27 inches long, and weighs 19 lbs. 14 oz. (Wallace Collection.)*

Right, *Fig. 31: Mail shirt of very high quality, the neck and sleeves originally edged with a row of brass rivets. In the neck is a brass ring bearing the name of the maker—+ERNART COUWEIN. A German piece dating from the second quarter of the 15th Century, this shirt weighs 19 lbs. 8 oz. (Wallace Collection.)*

was obviously very considerable. It is not, therefore, surprising that the cost of mail was high and in the early days its ownership was restricted to the wealthy and powerful.

Mail was a useful defence, although it was certainly less efficient than plate, since the point of an arrow or lance could pierce the links. Indeed, to receive a wound from this type of weapon while wearing mail could be more serious than in the case of plate, for the rings tended to split and fragment and could be carried into the wound, greatly increasing the risks of infection. However, mail provided efficient protection from sword cuts and arrows striking with less than maximum power. In order to further reduce the shock of a blow, it was common practice to wear a padded garment beneath the mail.

A clever mail maker could shape it to any part of the body, and at one time or another it was used in the construction of hoods, capes, shirts, leggings, mittens and even horse armour. Despite its flexibility it was in some ways less comfortable to wear than

plate; the whole weight of a mail shirt rested on the shoulders, while in a well-designed armour the weight was distributed over the entire body.

This costly form of defence was certainly beyond the means of most of the Saxon raiders of the Dark Ages, and was probably the prerogative of the leaders of the war bands. Very few Saxon helmets have survived, and their structure must be largely a matter for conjecture. Some are known to have been fashioned from a band which encircled the forehead and from which metal strips passed over the head, the spaces between these strips being filled by pieces of horn or metal. There is good reason to believe that many of these helmets were fitted with some form of crest, and it is suggested that this often took the shape of a boar.

During the 9th Century there burst on the scene a new force. In far away Scandinavia there lived a hardy race of people who were farmers, merchants and warriors. They are usually called Vikings although, strictly

Fig. 32: A painting by Matthew Paris, c.1250, shows the aventail tied at the side of the head, quilted cuisses and some form of shin defence laced on.

speaking, this word should apply only to those who actually went raiding. Viking raids were not a new phenomenon in the 9th Century, for there had been intermittent raiding and plundering in the North for some time; but from around 790 A.D. onwards their name begins to occur in the written records of Western Europe. The first raid on English soil is reported in the Anglo-Saxon Chronicle, which tells how the men landed from three ships, and killed the king's officer when he went to the shore to find out what they wanted.

In 793 there was an attack on the island of Lindisfarne when the monastery was destroyed and the monks killed. The Vikings of this particular group, probably from Norway, had travelled from Scandina-

via to Britain in their longships, and fortunately a number of these fascinating craft have survived. One example found at Gokstad in Norway measured some 76 feet in length, 17 feet across and 6 feet deep amidships. Such ships were designed so that they could either be rowed or sailed and they carried at least thirty-two oars, if the Gokstad ship is to be taken as typical. To protect the rowers in action a light rail ran round the sides of the ship, and from this were hung shields. In the case of the Gokstad ship there were thirty-two on either side; they were painted alternatively black and yellow and were so positioned that they overlapped each other to form a defensive wall for the rowers.

As with the Saxons, probably only the Viking leaders owned shirts of mail, or *byrnies*, and these were fairly short, covering only the shoulders and the chest. The less wealthy Vikings relied on leather jackets, padded or reinforced with strips of bone, a style recalling the Mycenaean boar's tooth helmets. Viking helmets were probably fairly small and later acquired a nose-piece, or nasal, which projected straight down over the face to afford some protection against a lateral sword cut. These nasals were a feature of the later Norman helmets. Some of the carvings from Scandinavia show dome-shaped helmets fitted with a spike at the top. Most Viking helmets seem to have been quite plain but there is some slight evidence for the fitting of horns; apart from the decoration on the Sutton Hoo helmet, there are one or two small plaques and figures of the 7th Century which depict warriors wearing horned helmets.

Most Vikings completed their equipment with a large, round, wooden shield; surviving examples are fashioned from a number of boards which are held together by iron bars fitted to the back. Most have a shield boss to guard the hole where the hand gripped a crossbar. Some shields were covered with leather as well as with strips of reinforcing metal, and most appear to have been painted in a variety of styles.

Essentially the Viking was a foot-soldier, but it was common practice for them to round up a number of horses as soon as they landed so as to give them greater mobility during the raid; and many Viking graves contain stirrups and other pieces of horse furniture, although there is no evidence of horse armour. At first the raids were only sporadic, but as the Vikings (or the Danes as the Saxons called them) found that the country lay at their mercy the number of raids increased, until in 860–870 A.D. great armies of Danes roamed the countryside, taking what they wanted and moving on when the pickings were finished.

France was a popular target for the Viking raiders; some found it, in comparison to their rather inhospitable northern lands, a pleasant and comfortable country, and many settled there. In 911 A.D. the French rulers made a treaty with the Vikings and confirmed their lands in return for their allegiance. These Northmen became the Normans, who were to play such an important part in the history of Britain.

Fig. 33: This brass of a member of the Dalson family of Lincolnshire shows all the features of late 14th Century armour. A bascinet with its aventail, and the tight-fitting tunic, or jupon, obscure many of the details of the body defences.

THE story of William the Conqueror, Harold Godwinsson and the Battle of Hastings is so well known as to require no retelling here. For much of the detailed information on these events reference is often made to the famous Bayeux tapestry, but this unique source should be treated with a certain reserve. It is likely that it was not prepared until some time after the events depicted, and it must also be borne in mind that during its long history parts of this tapestry (which incidentally is not a tapestry at all but an embroidered panel) have been repaired and renewed on several occasions; thus there must be a degree of uncertainty about some details. However, the evidence that the tapestry offers as regards the arms and armour of the Normans and the Saxons may be accepted as being broadly correct. In battle the

majority of the combatants are shown clad in mail shirts which vary in detail but generally extend from the shoulder to the knee, while the sleeve reaches to the elbow or just a little below. Knights on horseback and archers on foot are shown apparently wearing mail trousers, but this was almost certainly not the case. Considered from a practical point of view such mail garments would have been, to say the least, uncomfortable, being impossible to ride in, and it is most likely that the trouser appearance is merely a convention showing that the *hauberk* or mail coat was split back and front to enable the man to sit upon his horse. In one or two instances mail is depicted on the inside of the leg, but again this is more likely to be a conventional representation.

In a large number of instances the hauberk has a section outlined on the chest, and it is not at all certain what this represents. This area is rectangular and extends roughly from the shoulders down to the armpit. It may have been intended to show that this part of the hauberk was strengthened, or it may represent a flap of mail covering the slit which enabled the wearer to pull the hauberk on. It may also have indicated some kind of reinforcing plate beneath the mail. Conjecture is hardly fruitful as there is simply no concrete evidence to settle the matter. Many of the hauberks are shown with some form of edging at sleeves and legs. These strips are in various colours but whether they represented a true finishing strip or were purely decorative is not at all clear.

Another minor mystery left unsolved by the tapestry concerns clothing worn under the mail. Commonsense and practical considerations suggest that some form of under-tunic must have been worn. The chafing and pinchings of the metal rings would have been at best uncomfortable and at worst positively dangerous! However, in the narrow bands of decoration which flank the main tapestry, a number of dead warriors are shown being stripped of their mail and as the mail is removed bodies are shown to be naked. It seems logical that the warrior must have worn some form of linen or woollen shirt or even some form of thinly padded garment.

Most knights are shown with their legs encased in apparently conventional stockings, plain or crossgartered, but there are one or two with mail defences known as *chausses* covering the legs. The head was protected by a hood of mail, known as a *coif*, and the tapestry would seem to indicate that some were part of the hauberk while others were separate. The decorations could even be interpreted as showing that some coifs may have been of leather or some form of padded material. Over the coif went the helmet, and these conical pieces

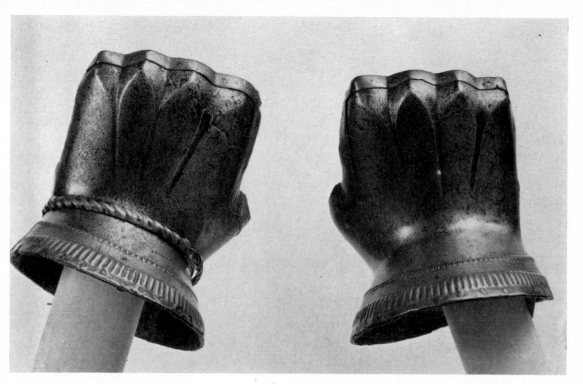

Opposite, *Fig. 34: Based on the brass of Sir John Drayton of Oxfordshire, c. 1425, this shows full plate armour, with full cuirass and fauld and complete limb defences.* **Above,** *Fig. 35: A pair of late 14th Century gauntlets of typical hourglass shape, decorated with brass bands. The finger plates are missing. Milanese, c. 1380–1400. (Wallace Collection.)*

are essentially the same as those of the Saxons and Vikings, some apparently fashioned from metal bands and plates of bone while others were beaten from a single piece of metal. Most have a nasal, and some appear to have had cheek-pieces as well.

Very prominent in all the illustrations is the great shield, which is large and shaped very much like a kite, curving round the body and large enough to extend from shoulder to ankle when seated on a horse. The tapestry indicates that inside the shield were straps known as *enarmes*, and there was probably some padding on the inside of the shield to cushion any shock when deflecting a blow. When not required for immediate use the shield was slung over the

back and held in this position by a longer strap known as the *guige*.

For the remainder of the 11th Century this was the basic defensive style for the knight, but towards the end of the century the hauberk was developed and the sleeves lengthened to the wrist. Coifs were normally fashioned as part of the hauberk, and from the end of the century a flap of mail, known as the *aventail*, was added to the coif; this crossed over the chin and was then secured at the side of the face by a buckle or lace, leaving only a minimum of the face exposed. Padding, either attached to the mail or worn as a separate cap, was worn under the coif. Records dating from around 1150 indicate a greater use of mail leg defences; the simpler form comprised a strip of mail laced in place over the shin and foot, but single-piece stockings of mail were also worn.

Manuscripts dating from the 11th Century and on through the whole of the 12th Century often show the edge of a garment hanging beneath the hauberk and extending

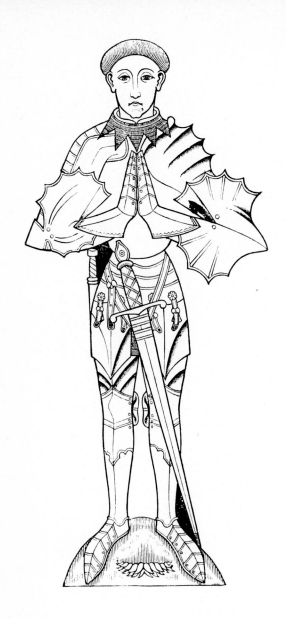

to the knee, and covering the mail was a long fabric tunic known as the surcoat. The origin of this garment, like so many early items of armour, is uncertain, but it seems to have appeared about the time of the Crusades and it is conceivable that it was intended to give the wearer some degree of protection against the hot sun.

During the last quarter of the 12th Century further improvements were taking place; the hauberk sleeves were extended to form bag-like mittens known as mufflers. These were laced along the centre of the palm and when not required could be undone and slipped off. After the middle of of the 13th Century some of the mufflers are shown as having separate fingers, but mittens were the most usual type of hand protection, being mailed on the back only.

Cost must have had a limiting effect on the number of people who could hope to acquire mail and undoubtedly the less wealthy warrior counted himself lucky if he had some form of padded defence; and by the latter part of the 12th Century quilted forms of armour were fairly common. Two names are frequently mentioned—the *aketon* and the *gambeson*; these were often of silk and decorated with embroidery and it seems that this rather richer form of soft armour was occasionally worn over the mail rather than underneath it. During the second quarter of the 13th Century padded thigh defences, the *cuisses*, were often worn either over or under the mail chausses.

M AIL maintained its basic efficiency, but advances in the design and production of swords and axes together with a greater use of powerful bows meant that it could be pierced more easily. Armourers were pressed for better protection, but they were faced with a problem. To strengthen mail meant using bigger links, which made mail stiffer, heavier and less comfortable; and the only alternative was to add reinforcing plates to the mail. There are vague references to some form of extra protection

Above, *Fig. 36: Here the elbow pieces, or couters, have been exaggerated almost to the point of absurdity, and serve as shields; tassets are suspended from the fauld. Brass of Sir Richard Quatremayne, Oxfordshire, c. 1460.* **Opposite,** *Fig. 37: Gothic armour for horse and man, c. 1475–85, with typical German outline and fluting. Mail is still used to protect vulnerable points such as the armpits. This armour was made for a member of the von Freyberg family, who lived in a castle in the Bavarian Alps. (Wallace Collection.)*

in Viking times when there is reason to believe that they may have worn a small breastplate beneath the byrnie. Certainly in the 12th Century there are references which could be interpreted as applying to some form of plate reinforcement. However, it is only from the middle of the 13th Century that positive evidence for the use of plate armour begins to increase. The first illustrative evidence of this development occurs in brasses and illuminated manuscripts which show the addition of small plates, known as *poleyns*, to the leg defences at the knee. At first these devices are fairly small but by the last quarter of the century they were quite large and covered the entire knee. Similarly, about the same time small round plates (*couters*) are shown fitted to the elbows of the hauberk. Naturally the process was extended, and there is every indication that around the middle of the 13th Century crude plate defences, little more than half-cylinders, were being fitted to the shins. Protection for the body was increased by the rivetting of metal plates, too large to be classed as scale armour, to the inside of the surcoat. A shirt-like garment of leather or stout fabric lined with metal plates, known as a "coat of plates", was also very popular during the 14th Century.

Early in the 14th Century neck guards of plate, termed *gorget* or *bevor*, were being

used, although at first they were no more than a high-standing collar of metal. Defences for the arm, *vambraces*, were developed and by the second quarter of the 14th Century they appear to have been fairly complex, comprising a shoulder guard known either as the *pauldron* or *spaulder*, an upper arm defence, a couter at the elbow, and a forearm defence. Despite the steadily "creeping" spread of plate defences over the mail, the latter was still considered to be the main defensive equipment, the plate additions being merely a desirable "extra".

The whole assembly was still worn over padded undergarments of various kinds, and partially covered by the simple surcoat. This remained largely unchanged until the mid-13th Century, when it is often depicted as having long sleeves. During the second quarter of the 14th Century the front was shortened, presumably to prevent entanglement with the feet and stumbles. The long surcoat is no friend to the historian; its folds hide the details of the defences worn under it on most of the monuments, brasses and illustrations of the period, so that little can be known for certain of the development of body armour during the latter part of the 14th Century. However, it seems probable that the coat of plates was developed somewhat and the size of the plates increased so to form a simple form of the Roman lorica segmentata. Solid plates which covered the greater part of the chest were probably in use around the middle of the 14th Century. The size of these plates was gradually increased and by the last quarter of the 14th Century the breastplate reached to the waist and was projected downwards in a series of joined hoops known as the *fauld*—in effect a metal skirt.

B Y the middle of the 14th Century plate armour for the legs and arms was fairly general and the knee guard, the poleyn, had been fitted with a small winged section on the outside to provide protection at the back of the knee, which was also protected by the mail chausses. The arm defences were similarly expanded and the top of the shoulder was then protected by a number of small overlapping plates; the elbow-piece, or couter, was fitted with wings like the poleyn. Gauntlets of plate were fairly common with a slightly widening wrist plate and fingers made up of a number of small separate plates riveted to a strong leather glove. The plates were often thickened at the knuckle with small pyramid-shaped projections and these were known as the *gadlings*—a kind of medieval knuckle duster. Over all went a short, sleeveless surcoat called a *jupon* which usually bore some form of heraldic device.

The many layers of defence now comprised a padded garment, the aketon; mail leggings and hauberk; a coat of plates; and strapped on to the mail, or possibly secured permanently, the various odd pieces of plate. All these garments gave the knight extra weight. The momentum of a charging horse with a weighty man on his back was considerable, and the lance tucked under the arm had an equal momentum. On striking

the target it must have been extremely difficult to retain a grip and prevent the lance sliding through and under the arm. To overcome this a ring was fitted just behind the grip and from about 1380 a small metal arm was secured to the breastplate, so positioned that when the lance was couched under the arm the ring, or *graper*, engaged with this metal arm, or *arrest*. Some of these lance arrests, or as they became known, lance rests, were hinged or made detachable so that when the knight was not on horseback they could be removed. By this means the shock of impact was taken not only by the hand and arm but, through the rest, by the armour and body of the man.

By the first decade of the 15th Century full plate armour had been developed. By now the skill of the armourer had increased considerably and he was competent to produce carefully moulded plates which were graded in thickness, so that at points of maximum danger there was maximum

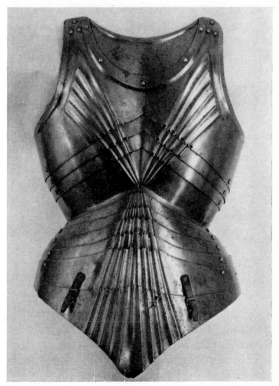

protection. The increased protective efficiency of such armour reduced the necessity
of wearing supplementary defences and from
the early part of the 15th Century the
hauberk, or the smaller mail shirt known
as a *haubergeon*, were far less common; in
place of the full coat of mail an arming
doublet became usual. This was, in
effect, a smaller sized padded aketon with
patches of mail sewn to particularly vulnerable points such as the armpit and inside
of the elbow. The arming doublet was
either fitted with a mail skirt or a carefully
shaped and presumably padded pair of mail
''briefs''. A number of points—leather
laces—were attached to the arming doublet;
these were passed through holes in the
pieces of armour and were then tied to hold
them in position. Many arming doublets
were fitted with an upstanding collar of
mail. In addition the knight of this period
would probably have worn some form of
padded cap and one mid-15th Century
document which details the method of
arming a knight suggests that pieces of
blanket should be fitted at the knees and
around the legs to prevent the edges of the
armour rubbing. After having put on the
arming doublet the knight donned the leg
harness; the greaves and *sabotons* fitted
over the top of the leather shoes and were
secured in position by the various points.
Next he put on the breast- and backplates
with skirt attached; then the arms, which
again were buckled and tied into position;
and the gauntlets and helmet were left until
last.

WITH the appearance of full plate
armour during the 15th Century two
easily distinguishable national styles
emerged, those of Italy and Germany.
German body armours were usually rather
large and were made with a distinctly
angular breastplate fitted with a series of
hoops forming a fauld or skirt which usually
reached almost to the knee. As the century
progressed they became a little less angular,

Plate 6: *Italian anime breastplate of the mid-16th Century; the separate plates are rivetted to leather straps so as to give some slight freedom of movement. Weight, 9 lbs. (Gyngell Collection.)*

and around the middle of the 15th Century
there evolved the Gothic style of German
armour. For the next thirty or forty years
this style remained popular with German
and Austrian manufacturers; although there
were variations on the main theme there
were a number of features common to most
of these armours. The breastplate was in
two overlapping sections and had a rather
narrow waist from which spread a fairly
short skirt of *lames*—a style repeated on
the backplate. Surfaces were decorated
with a series of curved ridges, and where one
of these ridges reached the edge of the plate
the armourers often drew out the metal into
a *cusp*. To increase the decoration the
edges of the main plates were sheathed with
a thin brass strip or pierced with a trefoil
pattern. A mail skirt below the fauld completed the body defence. The legs were protected by a similarly decorated series of
plates which extended well up the thigh,
whilst the plates protecting the feet, the
sabatons, had very pointed toes matching
the then-popular style of footwear. The
arm defences bore the same style of decoration, with fluting and pointed edges.
Gauntlet cuffs swept up to a sharp point,
and the couters tended to be rather large.
The shoulders were protected by a series of
plates forming the pauldrons, which also
had an upturned section which was designed
to prevent a weapon slipping over the
shoulder and on to the throat. A shaped
chin piece, the gorget or bevor, was secured
to the upper part of the breastplate. Gothic
armour was unquestionably one of the most
graceful and aesthetically pleasing styles

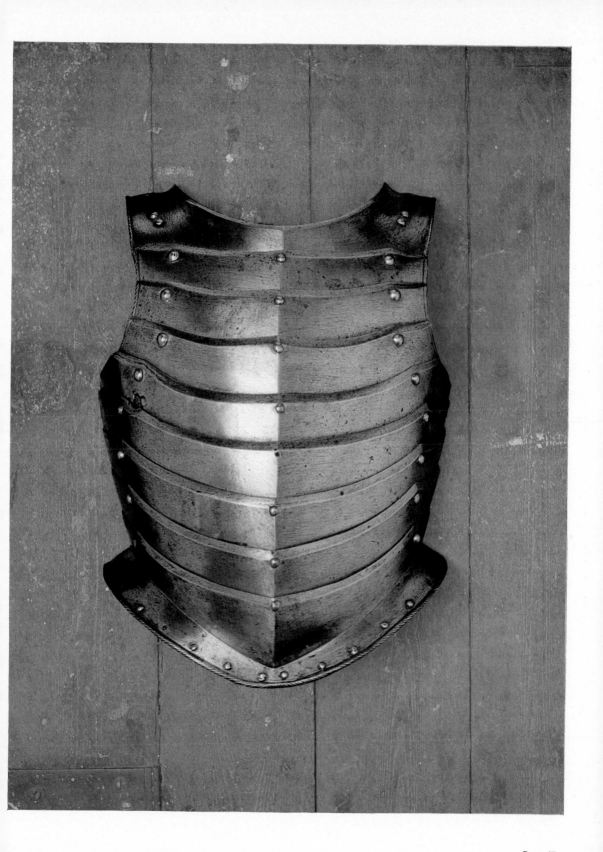

Fig. 40: Italian war armour of Milanese construction; note the hauberk worn beneath the armour, and the mitten gauntlets. This harness is not homogeneous, but is made up from a number of pieces of c. 1480. (Tower of London.)

ever evolved and it was, in addition, an essentially practical design.

Further south in Italy a far more rounded, smoother outline was preferred, and this is one of the distinguishing features of Italian armour of this period. During the second quarter of the 15th Century the lower section of the fauld was often formed into two separate sections to protect the thigh, and for simplicity they were often constructed from a single plate and then strapped to the lower edge of the fauld. These plates, *tassets*, continued to be developed and by about 1450 had the lower end cut and shaped into a triangular form.

From about 1425 the Italian armours were frequently fashioned so that breast- and backplates were hinged on the left hand side and secured by straps and buckles on the right. Shoulders were protected by large curving pauldrons which passed over the shoulders and their size was increased to such an extent that they overlapped at the back; but by about 1490 the size was once more reduced to manageable limits. Like those of the German Gothic style, many pauldrons were fitted with a vertical plate to protect the sides of the neck—the *hautepiece*. Since in most cases the knight used his right hand to wield sword or lance, the right pauldron was usually made smaller than the left to ensure ease of movement.

The Italian and German Gothic styles described above were predominant in Europe during the second half of the 15th Century, but naturally each style influenced the other and by the end of the century many features had been combined to produce a less spiky, more rounded outline on much of the Austrian and German armour.

During this period most armour produced in Europe was of either Italian or German origin. There were a few armourers at work in other countries, but it was centres such as Milan in Italy, Innsbruck in Austria and Nuremburg in Germany which held a virtual monopoly on equipping the nobles and armies of Europe.

4

The
Latter
Days
of Plate

The Latter Days of Plate

Title page, *Fig. 41: Armour for war and the tilt, decorated with etching and gilt bands; French or Italian, c. 1570. (Tower of London).* Right, *Fig. 42: Strictly functional—a black and white half armour with a red cross painted on the breastplate. The lance rest is clearly visible, as are the stop ribs at throat and armpits. Nuremberg, c. 1510.) Tower of London.)*

Left, *Plate 7: Fine quality close helmet, which retains to some degree its original black colouring, and the brass-headed rivets for the attachment of the inside lining. The side bar supports the visor in the raised position. This helmet is probably from the Electoral Armoury in Dresden, circa 1580. (Gyngell Collection.)*

WITH the emergence of the Italian and German styles the art of the armourer had reached a peak of perfection, showing superb technique and mastery of materials. During the 16th Century these skills were developed even further, but during the 17th Century demand declined and the standards tended to fall off.

Not a great deal is known about the manufacture of armour, for it was a closely guarded craft or "mystery", and few details were ever committed to print. However, there are a few contemporary references and illustrations, and these suggest that most of the actual shaping was done while the metal was cold. Plates were shaped by beating them over a series of anvils or stakes using a number of hammers of different weights and sizes. Hammering affected the temper of the metal and it was therefore heated periodically during the shaping process and then allowed to cool before being hammered again. It was necessary to heat the metal to increase its malleability for certain processes such as turning over the edges of the plates. The great majority of the work was done by hand, but there is no doubt that some water-driven power hammers were used to carry out the initial simple shaping. Mechanically operated shears were used for rough cutting, and files and hacksaws obviously played an important part in the process. When the shaping had been completed both inside and outside surfaces bore hammer marks, and it was customary to polish the outside surfaces to a bright, mirror-like finish. Much of the preliminary polishing was also done by water-powered grinding wheels. In expensive armours the surfaces were often decorated by any one of a number of techniques—painting, blueing, gilding, engraving and chiselling which involved the actual sculpting of the metal; there are early references to the covering of armour with expensive materials bedecked with jewels, but this style did not long survive.

Armour manufacturing centres such as Milan and Nuremberg produced large quantities of cheap "munition" armours, but for an expensive, quality armour the process was a long, painstaking job.

Clients ordering armours from a master craftsman sent, if they were unable to attend personally, items of clothing as well as full measurements and relevant personal details. Such information was vital if the armourer was to be sure that the overlapping plates moved freely without chafing or pinching and still left no chinks or dangerous gaps. When he shaped and fashioned the plates it was essential to allow sufficient space for the clothing and padding worn beneath the armour. Many plates were fitted with individual padding and rubbing was reduced by scalloped leather fittings; in addition, arming doublets were still worn beneath the armour. The construction of armour was a skill and craft which involved far more than simply fitting a metal sheath around the body, for it was of vital importance that the armour should not restrict the wearer's movement —it was essentially practical wear. One of the most persistent misconceptions about armour is that its weight was so great that it prevented a knight from rising from a prone position. In fact the comparisons show that a fully equipped cavalryman of the 19th Century was heavier than an armoured knight. Sir David Scott, writing in 1868, stated that the weight of equipment carried by cavalrymen of his period ranged from 98 pounds for the Austrians to 106 pounds for the British. These figures compare with 57 pounds for an Italian field armour, c. 1450, and 71 pounds for an English armour of c. 1590. The specially thickened armour for jousting weighed only just over 90 pounds. This weight was distributed over the body and, for men trained to the wearing of armour, must have represented only a minor inconvenience. Quite apart from contemporary references to feats of arms whilst fully armoured— Shakespeare has King Henry V say "If I could win a lady at leap frog or by vaulting into my saddle with my armour on my back" (Act V, Scene II)—tests carried out with genuine armour have shown that an untrained man can perform all normal actions with ease when wearing armour. It is equally certain that no knight would have been so foolish as to risk his life by wearing equipment which would render him helpless should he stumble and fall.

Each piece of plate armour was shaped and planned with the object of deflecting as

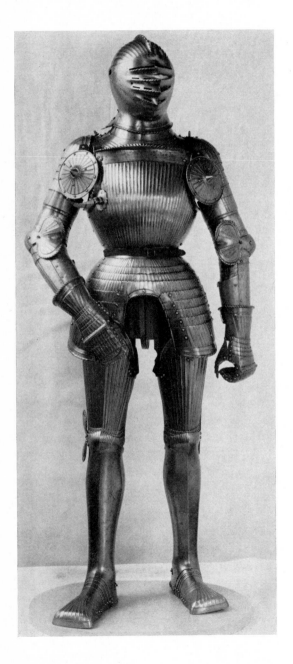

well as simply stopping blows. In general, surfaces were smooth and free of superfluous projections. Fluting on German Gothic armour served a triple function, for not only was it decorative but it gave a little extra strength to the plates as well as reducing the chance of a point sliding over the plate to vulnerable areas. Along the top of breastplates, shoulder pieces and cuisses were secured stop ribs, raised edges which prevented a point riding up and over the edge of the plate. It was a fairly simple matter to protect large areas such as the chest but joints and limbs were far less easy to cover, and the normal method was to fit a series of overlapping articulated strips, or lames. In order to ensure free movement these lames were riveted to leather straps or secured by sliding rivets which held the plates together but also allowed a limited movement. Mail was still used as a defence for these awkward places.

Basically the construction of armour altered but little, although fashions evolved and interacted one with another to producing new styles. Such a combination of German and Italian Gothic led, in the early 16th Century, to a style known as Maximilian, after its supposed association with the Austrian Emperor. The common feature on all Maximilian armours was a pattern of parallel fluted lines on every piece, with the single exception of the greaves which were always left smooth. There was a variation on some Maximilian armours from South Germany for these had the fluting extended into a rather zig-zag pattern, but in general the flutes were fairly close together. Another feature was the adoption of a "roped edge" on the plates, achieved by folding the metal over to give a roll-like border which was then indented with a series of angled lines suggesting the plaiting of a rope.

In areas strongly influenced by Italian armourers the Maximilian fluted armour seems to have become rather old fashioned

*Opposite, Fig. 43: Armour with fluting in the Maximilian style; note that the greaves, as always, are plain. The gauntlets are of the mitten type. German, c. 1515–25, total weight 41 lbs. 13½ oz. **Above**, Fig. 44: Black and white horse armour of Otto Heinrich, Count Palatine of the Rhine, made by Hans Ringler of Nuremberg and dated 1532 and 1536. The rider's armour weighs 57 lbs. 15 oz., and that of the horse 61 lbs. 7½ oz. (Wallace Collection.)*

by the 1520s, although in German-dominated areas it remained popular for another fifteen to twenty years. Even in the German armours the rounded Italianate look was popular and breastplates were rather globose, but from the 1530s they became flatter and more angular with a marked central ridge. Around the middle of the century this medial ridge became quite pronounced, with a central point. During the last twenty years of the century the central projection was placed lower on the breastplate and became the "peascod", with a distinct down-pointing beak at the waist, simulating the civilian style of doublet.

One unusual pattern of breastplate which first appeared in Italy c. 1530 was the *anine* (see Plate 6). These were fashioned of a series of substantial lames, shaped and

united to form a heavy, slightly articulated breastplate. Backplates of the 16th Century were fairly simple and fashioned from one piece of metal, thinner than that used for breastplates, since less protection was necessary. Breast and back were secured by straps which passed over the shoulders and encircled the waist. It was not uncommon for troops to discard their backplates in which case the breastplate was held in position by long straps which crossed over the back.

Gauntlets underwent changes during the first thirty years or so of the 16th Century. Whereas most Gothic gauntlets were fitted with separate fingers, composed of many small plates, most Maximilian examples dispensed with fingers. In their place strips of metal crossed the back of the hand and fingers to form a mitten gauntlet. There was a re-adoption of fingers after about 1530 although mitten gauntlets were made until the end of the century. Cuffs were generally smaller than on Gothic gauntlets and many were made so that they could be opened at the wrist and secured by a spring clip.

Despite the tremendous technical skill of the armourers, the craft was already becoming obsolete during the 16th Century and certain features indicative of its forthcoming downfall were apparent. During the early part of the 16th Century some superbly decorated armours were produced, including some which copied in steel the elaborate puffed and slashed style of civilian costume. Italian armourers excelled in the quality of their embossing, covering helmets and armour with high relief classical scenes and figures. No doubt the superb decoration impressed the customer and made a strong selling point, and provided they were worn only for parades or ceremonies such armours were acceptable—but they were not functional. To perform its task of defending the body effectively armour had to present a strong, smooth deflecting surface and all the folds and embossing destroyed these vital qualities. Blades could become entangled with these projections instead of slipping clear, and this could negate the whole purpose of armour.

Combined with this decorative decadence was the growing effect of firearms. Gunpowder had been known in Europe since the 14th Century and cannon were in use early in this century, but their effect was limited and probably many contemporary militarists viewed them as gadgets which had no future. Handguns were developed, and these led in turn to the muskets and pistols which were to upset the balance of Europe's battlefields. From the 11th Century until the early 16th Century, supported by archers using either the crossbow or the longbow, the mounted armoured knight was supreme on the medieval battlefield. Agincourt, Crécy and Poitiers showed that they could be dealt with by enemy archers, but these marksmen had to train for many months before their aim and expertise were sufficient to pose a serious threat to an armoured knight. Handguns and muskets made it possible to equip a large number of marksmen, who might be individually inferior compared with an archer, but whose massed firepower more than compensated for their poorer aim. A factor of even greater importance was the minimal amount of training that a musketeer required. Although the sequence of loading and firing was complicated the basic movements were simple and could be taught in a comparatively short time. No longer was it necessary to train an archer from youth, increasing the strength of his bow and hardening up muscles for the effort of an 80 pound pull—musketeers could be turned out in a few weeks.

Defence against firearms was perfectly possible and armour strong enough to withstand both musket and pistol balls was produced from an early date. Tests were carried out by armourers to demonstrate the strength of their plates, by discharging a pistol or musket at the armour from a fairly short range. Generally speaking only breastplates and helmets were so tested. This proving of plates is responsible for the great majority of bullet marks seen on pieces of armour in museums. The greater strength required to withstand a bullet was achieved by thickening the plate and this obviously increased the weight of the armour.

INCREASING use of firearms during the 16th and 17th Centuries produced two mutually opposed responses from the military thinkers of the period. On one hand the destructive effects of firearms could be

countered by thickening armour, or alternatively they could be offset by manoeuvering troops quickly and replacing the old massed charge by quick surprise marches and attacks. Pistols, and muskets in particular, were not very suitable for snap shooting and rapid aiming; and once the weapon had been fired it was largely useless until it had been reloaded, and during this period the musketeer was defenceless. Light, quick moving cavalry were obviously difficult targets to hit, but if cavalry were to be free to move at top speed then there was no place for heavy bullet-proof armour. Thus there was a motivation for the abandonment of armour on at least two counts, discomfort and tactics. This movement was not limited to the cavalry; infantry, too, began to reduce body defences and there are accounts of armour being transported in wagons and donned only when action became inevitable. The first to be abandoned by both infantry and cavalry were defences for the lower legs, and half-armours became increasingly common. Known as corslets, these comprised a breast- and backplate, tassets, arm defences, simple gauntlets—often no more than two or three overlapping plates covering the back of the hand—and a light helmet. A cheap version of this corslet, mass produced for armies, was known as the "Almain rivets", and Milan was certainly one of the main centres for such armours.

German mercenaries known as Landsknechts favoured these corslets worn with a collar which protected the neck and shoulders—others preferred a cape of mail, a "Bishop's mantle," which covered the shoulders and reached nearly to the elbows. Many armours of the period were covered with thick black paint except for a border about an inch or so wide, which was left polished bright. The painting was primarily for protective purposes, to guard against rust—a constant problem for campaigning troops.

There was also a return to the use of

Fig. 48: Superb half armour made by Michel Witz the Younger of Innsbruck and dated 1555. It is decorated with etched patterns and a crucifixion scene. The total weight is 43½ lbs. (Wallace Collection.)

lighter, less bulky forms of defence; mail was still used and many officers wore a mail shirt beneath their doublets. Possibly even more popular during the 16th Century were two types of scale armours, or coats of plates —the brigandine and the jack. Brigandines appeared in the 14th Century and remained in use until the 17th Century, and generally had some claim to style, the heads of the rivets which secured the plates in position being gilded or arranged in patterns. A simpler, cheaper version of the brigandine was the jack, which consisted of a number of plates of horn or metal which were held in position between two layers of material, usually by various cross-stitchings—obviously a simple and cheap form of defence.

There was a tendency during the 16th Century, which was emphasised during the 17th, to use at least two main types of cavalry; a heavy cavalry intended to charge —which was the last survival of the old armoured horsemen—and the light cavalry intended for scouting, flank attacks and chasing a defeated enemy. Medium to heavy cavalry usually wore what was known as a three-quarter armour, which had a breast and back, arm defences, gorget, helmet (probably a close one), and leg armour which reached only to the knee. For the lighter cavalry the armour consisted of a cuirass, tassets, gorget, arm defences and an open helmet.

Processes begun in the 16th Century were accelerated by events in the 17th, and the discarding of armour became far more prevalent. Heavy cavalry were still used,

Fig. 49: Half armour or corselet, with morion. The tassets are attached by straps. North Italian, c. 1570. (Tower of London.)

discarded until many retained little more than a breast- and backplate. Arm defences were retained by some, although many discarded pauldrons and vambraces and in their place wore, on the left hand, an elbow or bridle gauntlet. These were designed to protect the hand and forearm which were particularly vulnerable since the left hand held the reins and therefore could not be moved out of danger easily. Most comprised a fairly conventional gauntlet with digital plates and with a cuff big enough to guard the whole of the forearm, reaching to the elbow.

In the case of the infantry the musketeer, from the beginning of the 17th Century, discarded almost all his armour and took to wearing ordinary civilian clothing, usually with a wide-brimmed hat complete with large, colourful feathers. However, to protect the musketeer whilst he was reloading, groups of infantry armed with long pikes were interspaced with the musketeers. Pikemen usually wore a fairly substantial breastplate with a comparatively light backplate and a wide gorget. Tassets were usually very large, rectangular and curved round to follow the line of the rather wide breeches worn at the time. Although the tassets were fashioned from single plates they were still made to simulate those formed of lames, and to this end were decorated with false rivets. They were secured to the lower part of the breastplate by means of straps, or hooks and loops. After the middle of the 17th Century the size of the tassets was generally reduced. Many of the cavalry of the first half of the 17th Century modified their armour, and the most popular style was that of a breast- and backplate worn over a fairly long, wide-skirted leather coat made from oxhide. This "buff coat" was sufficiently strong to turn the edge of a sword although, obviously, it would not give protection against a musket or pistol ball. Since the arms required as little restriction as possible, the sleeves were often fashioned of slightly

and during the English civil wars some were still wearing heavy three-quarter armours which were usually proofed, so that the wearers tended to be confined to rather ponderous movement. The armour for these heavy horsemen, or cuirassiers, usually comprised a fairly substantial breast and back, a very heavy helmet and substantial arm defences. From the waist long tassets, made up of numerous lames, extended to the knees and terminated in a poleyn, and the shin and foot were protected by thick leather boots. At least one regiment of Parliament's army during the English Civil War (1642–48) was armoured in this way—they were known as "Hazelrigg's Lobsters", a scathing reference to the thick protective armour worn and possibly to their red faces, due to lack of ventilation. Among the light cavalry more and more armour was being thinner leather than the main part of the coat. These buff coats became popular after about 1620 and continued in use until the last quarter of the 17th Century.

The policy of abandoning armour continued, and it is generally true to say that in Britain the only troops still wearing armour at the end of the 17th Century were some of the cavalry who retained a breastplate and occasionally a backplate as well. One exception to this general situation was in the production of some particularly thick and heavy armour known as siege armour. This was intended specifically for troops who, by virtue of their engineering work when attacking a defended point or town, usually operated in somewhat exposed conditions. The breastplate and backplate were very substantial and to top it a very heavy helmet was worn. These special armours were not general issue, and were so heavy that they could only have been worn for quite limited periods.

IT was around the middle of the 17th Century that the only substantial British armour factory closed down. Henry VIII was a keen sportsman, taking a great delight in all physical forms of activity. Tilting, or practice combat, was certainly one of his joys and it may well have been this that stimulated his interest in armour and so encouraged him to send to Germany for armourers. Henry persuaded eleven "Almains"—armourers from Germany or the Low Countries—to come and settle in England and in 1515 he established them on a site at Greenwich, just to the south of London. The output of this Royal workshop was, generally speaking, limited to the king and his associates, and it does not seem to have produced armour for general use, although towards the end of its working life the armour produced there was certainly not of top quality. It became the practice for Henry, apart from outright gifts which he made, to issue authorisations

Fig. 50: Half armour by the famous Milanese craftsman Lucio Piccinino, c. 1590; Italian masters excelled in the skill of embossing. Weight 23 lbs. 15½ oz. (Wallace Collection.)

to applicants—probably on payment of a fee —permitting them to have armour made at the Greenwich workshops. Greenwich armours have certain distinguishing features; possibly the most obvious of all is their very broad, square-shouldered outline. This is because the pauldrons tended to be large and were fashioned of rather narrow strips. Many of the Greenwich armours were superbly decorated with etching and engraving, and it is fortunate that a sketch book survives in which are recorded many of the main armours made for members of the court. The notebook was probably compiled by Jacob Halder, a master craftsman at Greenwich until he died in 1607. The drawings are coloured and deal with approximately thirty different armours, of which a number have been positively identified with remnants existing today.

Production continued at Greenwich well into the 17th Century, and the factory was finally closed in 1637.

AFTER the end of the English Civil Wars and the Thirty Years War in Europe, armour was more or less obsolete. A few cavalry units retained it, and pikemen served with the British forces until around about 1680, but from thence forward body armour was largely discarded as a general issue to troops. However, it must not be thought that armour was completely abandoned, and indeed there are a number of

*Below, Fig. 51: Cuirassier's armour with helmet fitted with a slotted face guard, the whole decorated with blueing, etching and gilt trophies. North Italian, c. 1620–35; weight, 59 lbs. 2¼oz. **Opposite**, Fig. 52: Greenwich armour, possibly made for Thomas Sackville, c. 1590–1600. It is decorated with gilt bands and has several additional pieces, including stirrups decorated en suite. (Wallace Collection.)*

references to its casual use during many campaigns in the 18th and 19th Centuries. Marshal Saxe, a famous 18th-Century French general, was firmly convinced that it had a place on the battlefield; his argument was that his experience had shown that many wounds were caused by swords, lances and bullets which were largely spent. He argued that a good quality armour would undoubtedly reduce the number of casualties. There are scattered references in the literature of the period to suggest that some armour saw service in the most unlikely places, such as the forests of North America during the French and Indian wars, and even in the American War of Independence. Indeed, Lord Amherst is shown in a full harness in a portrait painted about 1760, but it is unlikely that this represents combat armour and is probably attributable to a lingering taste for the convention of painting famous men in martial array. The only armour that seems to have been regularly in use during the 18th Century was the siege armour of the type mentioned above; this was employed until well into the 19th Century.

In 1821 the Life Guards of the British Army were once again fitted out with cuirasses, probably because of the great interest of George IV in fashion and military life. The cuirass was of polished steel and the early versions of the breastplate had a brass oval plate fitted at the front, but this was discarded about 1829. The plain style has continued in use until the present day. A number of other European bodyguards were similarly equipped, but despite the fact that these cuirasses were primarily decorative they were strong enough to give some protection; experiments carried out in America indicated that the French cuirass was sufficiently tough to resist the impact of quite high-powered modern rifle bullets.

During the American Civil War (1861–65) a factory was established in New Haven in 1862 for the manufacture of body armours which consisted of a number of plates,

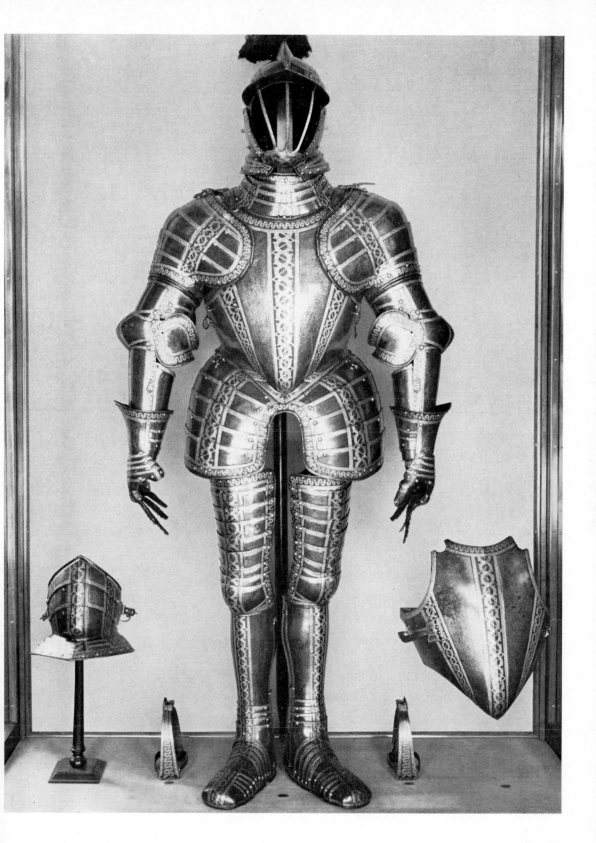

Below, *Fig. 53: The plainer and more usual type of cuirassier's armour, worn with thick boots. German, c. 1630. (Tower of London.)* **Opposite,** *Plate 8: Complete arm from a retainer's armour, still rough from the hammer, made in Flanders or Italy in about 1550. For many years in the armoury of the Earl of Pembroke at Wilton House, Salisbury, it was disposed of in auction at Sotheby's, London between 1921–26. Weight, 4 lbs. (Mungeam Collection.)*

extending from the throat to the groin, which were strapped to the body. These cuirasses were certainly worn in earnest, for one specimen in a Richmond, Virginia, museum was found on a dead soldier in the trenches during the time of the siege. Later, during the Franco-Prussian war of 1870, the French produced a version of the brigandine, or coat-of-plates, with a number of small rectangular plates riveted to canvas. It was in the shape of a poncho with a hole for the head and two straps to hold it in place. It weighed about 5 pounds and its strength was great enough to resist powerful projectiles.

One of the most romantic uses of armour in comparatively modern times was by the famous Australian bushranger, Ned Kelly. He fashioned an outfit of boiler-iron armour, with an ugly but effective helmet with eye-slits, and a crudely made breastplate of two plates from which hung an apron covering the groin. The efficiency of this armour, despite its crude appearance, was surprisingly good, for in 1880 Kelly was able to face, and survive, the concentrated fire of a large number of Australian police, and it was only when he was hit in his unprotected legs that they were able to capture him.

During the First World War (1914–18) a surprisingly large number of experiments in the use of armour were carried out. The French devised quite a number of chest and thigh protectors and a complex defence for the leg, although there is little evidence that they were ever issued. The English were also involved in the testing of armour, and no less than eighteen designs of body shields were produced commercially. There were many experiments in the use of soft armours including padded neck defences, as well as large vests with an inch-thick padding of linen, tissue, cotton and silk. There were also experiments with scale armour, including one uniform jacket which had the entire chest area lined with small metal plates. In 1917–18 the British

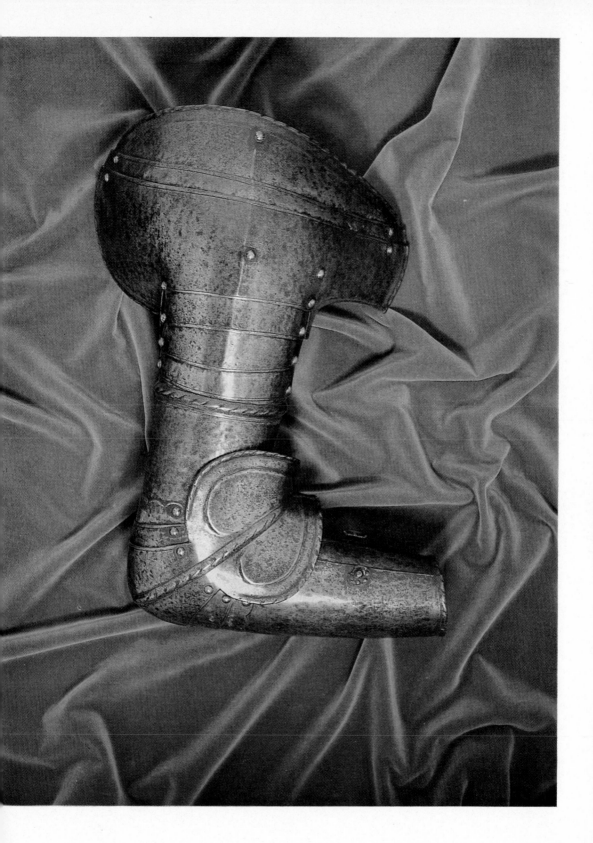

Government produced a corslet known as the E.O.B., which consisted of a breast- and backplate with an abdomen defence; this was fitted with padding and covered in khaki drill. This form of body defence, judging by the result of tests, was extremely efficient. Germany made possibly the

Fig. 54: Armour of James II of England, the face guard modified to display the Royal Arms. On the left arm is a bridle gauntlet, and a buff coat is worn for general protection. Made by the London armourer Richard Hoden in 1686. (Tower of London.)

greatest use of body armour, particularly amongst machine-gun crews. They produced a very substantial defence consisting of a large breastplate with two hook-like pauldrons which went over the shoulders. Secured to the lower part of the breastplate by two long straps were three extra plates which defended the abdomen. These body armours weighed between 19 and 24 pounds.

During the inter-war period the main stream of thought on armour was concerned with its use on tanks and other armoured vehicles. Little experimental work was undertaken except in these fields and the tank, introduced during the First World War, became one of the main assault weapons of modern warfare. Some armour plate was fitted in aircraft and arranged around the pilot's seat so as to offer some protection. In the great Flying Fortress and Liberator bombers of the U.S.A.A.F., gunners were sometimes equipped with splinter-proof overgarments. Apart from these rather limited uses of armour there was not a great deal of interest or use of body defences during the Second World War.

During the Korean campaign in the early 1950s a surprisingly large number of American troops were fitted with bullet-proof clothing, and experiments with modern products such as plastics and bonded materials have aroused renewed interest in armour for the defence of the body. Garments capable of withstanding modern, high-velocity bullets have been produced and issued to law enforcement officers and certain troops; generally referred to as "flak jackets"—a survival from their use by U.S. bomber crews in the Second World War—these armoured jerkins are virtually standard issue to American troops in Vietnam, and at the time of writing British security forces in Ulster are also employing this type of protection in riot situations. At the present time the age-old struggle between attacker and defender seems to be going in the armourer's favour, although for how long is open to speculation.

5

The Evolution of the Helmet

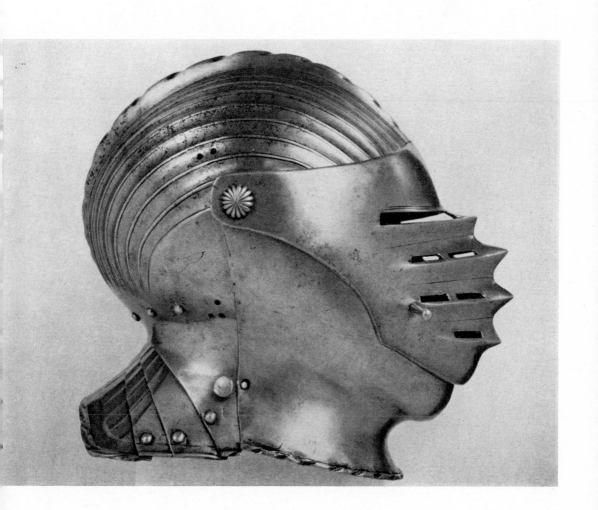

The Evolution of the Helmet

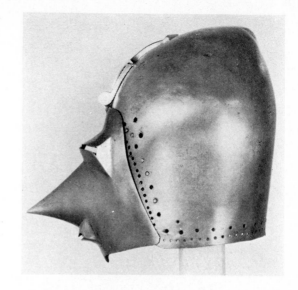

As already described, the particular vulnerability of the head was appreciated from the earliest times, and the helmet is one of the oldest forms of personal defence used by man. In the ancient world the common style was quite simple, being basically conical and sometimes fitted with a neck guard or peak. An early high point in design was the beautiful and efficient Corinthian style; in keeping with the needs of mass production, the Roman legionary helmet reverted to the simpler form of a dome-shaped crown with a flat neck guard or "back peak". This style was also found among the indigenous peoples of Gaul and Britain, and its use by the Romans may have represented the product of general regional evolution rather than an original innovation. For extra strength a peak was fitted above the brow, and two large shaped cheek-pieces were suspended from the temples and tied beneath the chin. This bronze "jockey helmet" continued in use until the middle years of the 1st Century A.D.; and it was at this time, roughly simultaneous with the invasion of Britain under Claudius in A.D. 43, that the legions began to adopt a new style (Plate 3) with a large neck guard, a peak, and wide cheek-pieces. British helmets of this period were

perhaps rather over-decorative, if the surviving examples are taken as typical. The type illustrated in Fig. 18, with its great conical "horns", must have been distinctly top-heavy, and appears to be a rather impractical form of head protection.

The Viking and Saxon helmet can be taken as the first in a continuous line of development in European helmets. Most appear to have been quite simple conical pieces—the shape which occurs in almost every type of helmet throughout the centuries. This shape was obviously of great

Title page, *Fig. 55: Close helmet of Maximilian style, with bellows visor; visor and bevor are hinged at the side, unlike the armet, and the bevor is locked in place by the spring stud visible at lower left. German, c. 1530; weight 6 lbs. 14½oz. (Wallace Collection.)*

Above, *Fig. 56 Bascinet with visor hinged to a bar fastened on the brow—klappvisier; the holes around the edge were for the attachment of lining and camail. German, c. 1380. (Tower of London.)*
Opposite, *Plate 9: Tombs of military men were often distinguished by the addition of some suitable memorial, sometimes by items of armour. In many cases the armour had been a personal possession—as in the case of the Black Prince's tomb in Canterbury Cathedral—but later examples were usually made for the purpose. This fine example of a funerary helmet has some genuine components; gorget and skull are from a 17th century armour, but the rest was made up, probably by a local smith. The crest, depicting a lion's paw holding a broken spear, is of wood and fits over a spike on top of the helmet. (Mungeam Collection).*

importance, for, like body armour, the helmet had to protect the wearer not only by its sheer strength and thickness, but also by deflecting blows. It was important that it offer a good glancing surface and, for general purposes, the conical style was one of the simplest and most efficient ways of meeting this requirement. Although the usual Viking helmet was little more than a simple cone a few more elaborate examples, apparently of Swedish origin, were highly decorated and fitted with face guards; the specimen unearthed from the Sutton Hoo burial ship (Fig. 23) is decorated overall with gilded and embossed scenes on the flaps guarding the neck and face. As mentioned in Signature 3, the evidence for the use of horned helmets by the Vikings is slight, but sufficient to suggest that some were worn. Their symbolic significance is not clearly understood, but it is certain that the concept of the "horned man" had deep and powerful roots in the magical beliefs of the early peoples of Northern Europe.

Details of the Norman helmets of the 11th Century are fairly well documented, although actual specimens are rare. Norman, and no doubt English helmets of the period were conical, and some at least are thought to have been built up on a metal framework with plaques of bone or metal. However, one surviving example now displayed in a Vienna museum is fashioned from a single piece of metal. The swords of this period were primarily slashing rather than stabbing weapons, and it was therefore desirable to provide some form of face protection. The Sutton Hoo helmet has a mask which covers the face completely; since it formed part of a funeral array it cannot be entirely certain that this represents the form in general contemporary use, but if this is the case the design is not very satisfactory—a blow would probably have driven the mask hard into the face. The solution adopted by the Normans was to fit a flat vertical bar to the brow so that it extended downwards over the nose; on some helmets this nasal bar was riveted in place, on others it was an integral part of the helmet. This nasal may have been wide enough to obscure the face and hamper recognition; stories current after the Battle of Hastings (which must remain slightly suspect, as they were recorded by chroniclers writing some time after the event, who may have been influenced by the conditions of their own times) claimed that at one point during the battle a rumour swept the Norman army that Duke William had fallen, and that he had to ride among them and remove his helmet to prove that he still lived. This style of conical helmet with a nasal guard continued in general use until the middle of the 12th Century, but was by no means the only type in common usage; many round-topped helmets, with or without nasals, were also employed during this period.

The fashioning of conical helmets presented the armourer with considerable technical problems, and this may have been the reason for an apparent regression in design.

From about the last twenty years of the 12th Century a cylindrical style of helmet, tapering slightly but with a flat or slightly domed top, was introduced. No doubt simpler to fashion, these helmets must have been less efficient in deflecting blows, on account of the flattening of the top surface. All the foregoing types of helmet were worn until the middle years of the 13th Century, but after about 1220 one particular design known as the *cervèllière* became popular with many knights. This was little more than a metal skull cap; it was fairly close fitting, although one must assume that it either incorporated some interior padding or else was worn over a small arming cap. From the middle of the 13th Century it seems very likely that these skull caps were worn under the coif of mail.

Towards the end of the 12th Century there was a trend towards the fitting of a face guard to all types of helmets; this was usually a metal plate fitted to the front of the helmet and pierced by vision slots and, almost as important, by a series of holes or slots for ventilation. These were essential, as one of the main drawbacks to the use of armour was always the lack of adequate ventilation, with attendant danger and discomfort. The idea of this extra protection was also extended to the back of the helmet, and a neck guard appeared during the first quarter of the 13th Century. The size of the neck and face guards increased and before long the two had united to form a cylindrical, tubular helmet which completely enclosed the head. Until about 1300 most of these were flat topped, probably for the sake of simplicity of construction. This cylindrical form was known as the great helm or *heaume*, and was worn over the coif, which might well cover a skull cap also. The helmet probably had its own internal padding and, in order to hold it firmly in position, it almost certainly had some form of strap or lacing to secure it to the head.

Towards the end of the 12th Century a new type of helmet was introduced which

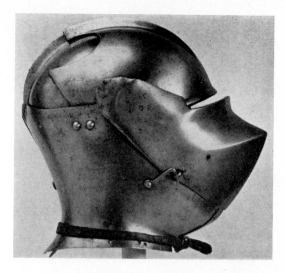

Opposite, *Fig. 57: Pig-faced bascinet with camail attached; the staples and retaining thong are visible. The visor is edged with an engraved brass band. North Italian, c. 1380–1400. (Tower of London.)* **Above,** *Fig. 58: An early armet, with cheek pieces hinged at the top; a reinforcing plate is fitted at the brow and the visor is secured by a hook and hasp. Italian, mid-15th Century; weight 7 lbs. 7 oz. (Wallace Collection.)*

was to remain in service for many centuries; this was known as the kettle-hat, or *chapel-de-fer*. This was basically a dome-shaped metal hat with a very wide brim which frequently sloped downwards, and in general form it closely resembled the steel helmet worn by British troops in both World Wars. These kettle-hats, obviously far more comfortable to wear than a conventional helm, were worn by both knights and common foot-soldiers over a long period and a wide area; in the latter case they were sometimes fashioned from toughened leather rather than metal, but still offered good protection.

From about the middle of the 13th Century the great helm was slightly altered in shape and the crown, instead of being tubular, sloped more towards the top, becoming rather like a truncated cone in shape. The lower plates were now so deep that the helmet actually rested on the shoulders. To ensure a comfortable fit there

was a leather lining, and this could be adjusted by thongs until the helmet rested securely on the top of the head. There is good reason to believe that as early as the beginning of the 14th Century some of the great helms were made with the portion which covered the face separate and pivoted at the sides of the helmet. This offered nothing extra in the way of protection but it did at least ensure that the knight could raise it for better vision and some fresh air. At about the same period, that is the close of the 13th Century, the great helm, together with swords and daggers, was often secured to the breastplate by guard chains. Earlier examples were secured to the belt or the girdle of the surcoat, but from early in the 14th Century the chains were fastened to staples fitted to the breastplate itself. Not only did this prevent the accidental loss of the helm in battle, but the chain also served as a useful suspension when carrying the helmet, and contemporary illustrations show the helmet hanging from the chain thrown across one shoulder. Beneath the great helm the coif and metal skull cap were still worn.

Although the great helm gave very complete protection to the head it did have one slight disadvantage in that the face was now completely hidden. The problem was to "know thine enemy", and it is by no simple coincidence that crests were first fitted to the helmet at about the same time as the introduction of the great helm. These crests were identification devices fitted to an obvious display point—the top of the helmet. The materials used in their construction must have been comparatively light, and whalebone, parchment, and treated leather were all employed in this way. It is at this stage, during the late 12th Century, that heraldry began to develop. The Greeks, Romans, and other ancient peoples had worn crests on their helmets and painted devices on their shields, but the great difference was that these were not controlled. There were no set rules as to their construction, use and adoption by the wearers. Heraldry implies a controlled system with rules governing the devices used by each member of each family, and it is from this period that it began to come into its own. Arms were used on the crests and were later to be applied to surcoats and horse coverings. During the latter part of the 13th and the first half of the 14th Century special panels, or *ailettes*, were worn on the shoulders to display the heraldic signs further.

THE great helm continued in use during this period, as did the kettle-hat, but a new type of helmet began to appear in the 14th Century. It is unfortunate that the same term—*bascinet*—has been applied to three distinct types of helmet: a simple dome-shaped helmet with the sides extended down to cover the ears; a helmet extending down to the shoulders at the back and fitted with a visor, which gave it rather the appearance of a helm; and a tall conical style which only extended to a point just above the ears.

It became common practice to fit a scarf of mail known as a tippet, *camail* or *aventail* to the rim of the helmet to replace the older coif. From about 1330 the most common form of bascinet had come to be a conical helmet extending well down over the ears and reaching almost to the shoulders, with an aventail fastened to the rim, although this latter was occasionally replaced by a plate defence or bevor. From about 1320 onwards the mail was attached by a series of staples—*vervelles*—which passed through holes in the rim of the helmet with a length of cord or thong passing through them to secure the aventail in position.

The great helm was still worn over the bascinet, but it was becoming increasingly common for the bascinet to be the main form

Left, *Fig. 59: Sallet fashioned from a single piece of metal; this type of helmet was worn with a bevor. This example presumably saw service, as several repairs are apparent. German, 1450–60. (Wallace Collection.)*

Below, *Fig. 60: German sallet of form worn by light cavalry. It has a hinged visor and is painted overall with heraldic designs, and dates from about 1490. (Tower of London.)*

designed, with raised flanges to reduce the chances of a point slipping through the slit. At the end of the 14th Century the aventail was often replaced by plate defences. During the 14th Century the great helm became less and less popular, probably on account of the lighter weight and greater comfort and convenience of the bascinet. The helm was increasingly reserved for use at the tournament and joust; some examples from this period are fitted with loops front and rear, so that they could be laced securely into position on the breast- and backplates.

Yet another form of helmet appeared during the 15th Century in Italy, somewhat resembling the Greek Corinthian style. Known as the *barbut*, it covered the head completely except for a face opening; on some, the opening was in the form of a broad T-shape with reinforced edges. A simpler form merely had a wide, parallel-sided opening. Neither type seems to have been popular for long; although some examples of the open-face variety lingered on until the end of the century, the majority seem to have enjoyed their greatest popularity only in the period between about 1430 and 1470.

A type of helmet very popular with both Italian and German armourers of the 15th and early 16th Centuries was the *sallet*—like "bascinet", a term which covers quite a variety of individual designs. The Italian style, for example, was rather similar to the barbut but had a slightly longer tail, often laminated; the brow was frequently fitted with a reinforcing plate. Another late 15th Century version was fitted with a visor which covered the whole face but which was so shaped that when it was lowered it left a gap between the brow of the helmet and the top edge of the visor, replacing the normal sights pierced in the visor itself. These helmets were in use from about 1490.

German armourers produced several forms of sallet around 1460, which had medium-length tails and could be either

of defence. Obviously the protection could be increased by the fitting of a visor, and various forms of these occur almost from the first appearance of the bascinet. During the third quarter of the 14th Century the visors were made detachable. A bar was sometimes attached to studs positioned vertically above the brow and the visor was hinged at the base of this bar; this was known as a *klappvisier*, and seems to have been primarily a German device. Other visors were attached to the side of the helmet on a hinge; the pin of the hinge was secured by a guard chain but when desired the visor could obviously be removed with ease.

During the last quarter of the 14th and the first quarter of the 15th Century the most commonly used form of bascinet seems to have been of Italian origin; this was a tall, egg-shaped, slightly pointed helmet with an interior padding of wool or canvas stuffed with cow's hair. The visor had a pronounced snout, which earned this type of helmet the name "pig-faced bascinet". The sights in the visor were very carefully open-faced or fitted with visors. During the 1470s there appeared what might be termed the characteristic German sallet, with quite a long tail projecting well down over the back of the neck. This tail was sometimes made from a single piece of metal, sometimes laminated.

The *armet* was another new style developed in the early years of the 15th Century. In its Italian form this comprised a skull-piece, usually slightly domed, with a long single tail-piece extending down the back of the neck. Two hinges, one on either side of the base of the brow secured large cheek-pieces which, when lowered, completely covered the face except for a small gap for vision. To guard the open space a visor, pivoted at the sides, was fitted. At the base of the back rib projected a small stud fitted with a large round disc. This was probably designed to hold in position a strap securing a reinforcing plate known as the wrapper, which fitted on the front of the armet and gave extra protection to the face. This rondel was abandoned after about 1520.

A new type of defence known as the close helmet first appeared in about 1500; the main distinction between this and the armet lay in the method of attaching the face protection. With the armet the cheek-pieces were hinged at the brow; on the close helm a shaped bevor, covering the lower part of the face, and the visor, were both pivoted at the same point on the side. The close helmet became extremely popular, and was extensively used both for war and for the tilt. Some were made with a deep roped ribbing at the base which engaged with a ridge at the top of the gorget plate, so that when closed and locked in position it was attached to the gorget, free to rotate but unable to move vertically. Close helmets made at the Royal Factory at Greenwich had a distinguishing feature in the shape of the visor, which had a distinctly indented appearance, curving out to give a rather pronounced point at the front.

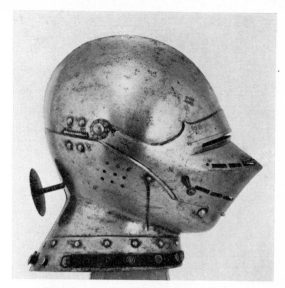

Opposite, Fig. 61: *Italian barbuta, resembling the old Greek Corinthian helmet. This example of c. 1450–70 bears the mark of the well-known Milanese armourer Antonio Missaglia; weight, 7 lbs. (Wallace Collection.)* **Above,** Fig. 62: *Armet of c. 1500, by the Innsbruck maker Hans Rabeiler. Note the characteristic rondel at the back, and the bar to prop open the visor. (Tower of London.)*

As indicated in Signature 4, the tendency during the 16th Century was to discard, lighten and modify armour, and to this purpose the *burgonet* came into common use. These helmets varied in detail, but most had a domed crown extending down to the neck, and a pronounced comb. Further protection to the brow was afforded by a peak which, in the earlier versions, was pivoted at the sides. Two large cheek-pieces, usually hinged at the top rear corner, protected the face; these were closed and secured by a strap and buckle. Extra protection was sometimes gained by the fitting of a *buffe*, a shaped plate strapped to the front of the gorget which covered the face except for a vision space left below the peak; these devices saw service during both the 16th and 17th Centuries. Another type of burgonet produced around the middle of the 16th Century had an adjustable metal nasal; this could be slid up and down in the same way as those on Turkish and Indian helmets.

By the 16th Century the kettle-hat had

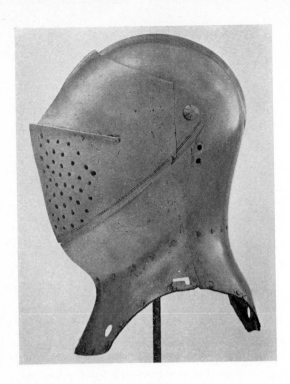

been modified; generally, the brim was narrower than before, and in many cases the crown was made with a comb. This class of helmet is known as a *morion*; the "comb-morion" is distinguished by its extremely high comb and its peak, which is swept up at front and rear. Another version known as the *cabasett* had a narrower brim, and a slightly more conical crown which terminated in a short stalk-like projection. Most morions had cheek-pieces which were laced beneath the chin.

These helmets all remained in common use during the 17th Century; and the burgonet fitted with a nasal was particularly popular. A long, laminated neck guard was usual, as were two simple cheek-pieces, and this version was known as a lobster-tailed burgonet, or "pot". During the 1630s a modified face guard comprising three bars uniting at the chin was introduced on the English version of the burgonet; this is the form popularly associated with the famous Parliamentary cavalry regiments which were raised and led with such devas-

tating effect by Cromwell during the English Civil Wars. Popular among the pikemen of the time were morions with wide, slightly down-sloping brims sweeping up to a peak at front and rear and fitted with cheek-pieces. Close-fitting metal caps, *secretes* or "skulls", were worn during the English Civil Wars by officers, who had discarded helmets in favour of the wide-brimmed hats currently popular in both the Royal and Parliamentary armies. The armour of the heavy cuirassiers frequently included a close helmet fitted with a visor fashioned from a series of heavy bars.

Another version of the close helmet, which seems to have been mainly of Italian origin, was in use in the early years of the 17th Century under the name of *Savoyard*, or *todenkopf*—"death's-head". Its distinctive feature was a visor quite unlike those on other contemporary close helmets, being fashioned in the form of a rather grotesque face with large eye holes and, on some examples, a grinning mouth. This fashion for grotesque armour was not new; there had been a vogue during the early part of the 16th Century for helmets made in the shape of animal, human or bird masks. Some of these helmets were fitted with steel moustaches, noses and side wings, or with curving horns. One helmet in the Tower of London was labelled for many years as having belonged to a king's jester. It was, in fact, made by one of the greatest armourers of Innsbruck, Conrad Seusenhofer; the visor is fashioned as a facial mask and there are two curling horns fitted on the sides. An intriguing feature is that the face bears a striking resemblance to the Emperor Maximilian I, who presented this armour to King Henry VII; an endearing detail is a small "dew drop" suspended from the Emperor's nose! There is good reason to believe that the helmet was also fitted originally with a pair of spectacles. It is little wonder that this droll helmet should have been ascribed to Henry's jester, Will Sommers.

In general terms it may be said that the 17th Century saw the end of the widespread use of helmets. Certainly siege helmets were still worn—as mentioned in Signature 4—and these were essentially burgonets with particularly thick crowns and peaks and very substantial interior padding. Another quite practical form which survived for a time was known as the "spider" helmet; this was basically a burgonet to which were fitted a number of pivoted bars which, when not required, could be folded up over the crown. In action they could be dropped down to form a sort of loose cage dangling around the crown and peak.

The great majority of European armies, however, discarded helmets of all kinds in favour of wide-brimmed feathered hats, and later, three-cornered hats. This situation continued throughout the 18th Century,

although there was a re-adoption of helmets in certain light cavalry units. By the middle of the century a number of these units were equipped with quite substantial leather helmets; the colonial wars led to the discovery that the tropical sun had a very deleterious effect on these leather pieces, and this brought about the limited introduction of tin helmets. These were often fitted with a comb, to offer slightly better protection against a down-swinging sword cut. The end of the 18th and the beginning of the 19th Centuries saw a gradual re-introduction of helmets, and the French were

Opposite, Fig. 63: Great bascinet, popular for foot combat. This one may well have been made in the Greenwich workshops, c. 1515. (Tower of London.)
Below, *Fig. 64: Close helmet with grotesque visor, the point shaped as an eagle's head. Augsberg, c. 1530. (Wallace Collection.)*

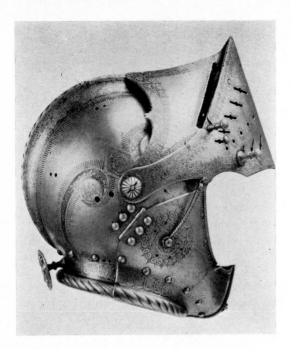

Above, *Fig. 65: An armet, almost of the close helmet type, made in Augsberg c. 1535. The visor is raised and supported on the side bar; etching, including a simulated spiked collar, decorates the surface.*
Opposite, *Fig. 66: Made in Greenwich, possibly by the Master, Jacob Halder, this finely decorated burgonet has a falling buffe attached by hooks and hasps. It is decorated with deep etching, and is part of a complete armour—see Fig. 52. English, c. 1590–1600. (Wallace Collection.)*

THIS position changed drastically shortly after the outbreak of the First World War. In place of the rapid, wide-ranging manoeuvres of the 18th and 19th Centuries, warfare was petrified into the static stalemate of vast trench systems. Trench warfare was no new development; as a specialised technique for approaching fortified points in periods of siege the basic principle had been in use for centuries, but never before had the entire armed might of nations been condemned to this peculiarly squalid and harrowing type of operation. Modern artillery now had the ability to fling shells to explode in the air above the glorified rat-runs, showering the men below with a variety of murderous projectiles. The troops exposed to such bombardment naturally suffered severely from head wounds and progressive military thinkers, particularly in Germany and France, devoted their energies to devising some form of protection.

French cuirassiers were probably the only troops who went into the First World War equipped with any form of helmet and armour, and even these were totally unsuitable for modern operations. Machine-guns and heavy artillery soon showed that cavalry had little, if any, place on a modern European battlefield, and these troops—those who survived—were sent to the rear to await the break-out which never came. It was, however, among the French troops that General Adrian first explored the possibilities of designing some form of head defence. According to tradition he was impressed by the tale of a wounded man, who pointed out that his life had been saved by an improvised helmet—a curved mess-tin which he had fitted inside his hat! Folk-lore or not, General Adrian certainly designed a form of *secrete*, similar to that of the 17th Century, for fitting inside the French trooper's kepi. Though crude, these skull protectors were apparently effective, and noticeably reduced the incidence of head wounds. Large numbers of

possibly the most deeply involved in this new trend; in the late 18th Century their Dragoons were issued with fairly substantial helmets of steel and brass, often decorated with an outside turban of animal skin. The basic design of this helmet remained unaltered, and indeed survives to this day in the form of the ceremonial helmet of the French *Garde Républicaine*.

During the 19th Century the design of the helmet oscillated between purely decorative, partially decorative and partially protective functions; but, in fact, the protective qualities of most of the helmets of this period were negligible. By the end of the century their use was limited almost exclusively to cavalry units, and was based entirely on decorative considerations.

these metal domes were stamped out in February and March 1915, and the results were so impressive that other armies soon followed the French example. The basic French pattern was gradually developed; a small crest was fitted, and a down-sloping brim, until it formed a light helmet with adjustable lining and chin strap. This Adrian helmet was adopted by both the Italian and Belgian armies as well as the French, although comparative tests showed that it was not as ballistically efficient as the British model, and penetrations by projectiles were not uncommon. Numerous experiments with visors were carried out, although these never appear to have been general issue.

The British soldier exchanged his soft cloth cap for a steel helmet at about the same time. Apparently designed in 1915 by a Mr. Brodie, it was, in effect, a development of the old "kettle-hat" —a shallow, bowl-shaped crown with a wide brim fitted with an extra metal rim round the edge. Experiments with visors were carried out, but these were only used under special circumstances; it is interesting that British designs were usually based on the use of mail, possibly in the interests of flexibility. These were often issued to tank crews, who apparently required a high degree of facial protection—the early tanks featured unguarded engines mounted in the middle of the crew compartment of the vehicle. The basic British helmet design was adopted by the American forces, who continued to use it until 1942 when it was replaced by the well-known pattern which has now spread over much of the world.

German troops began to receive the heavy "coal-scuttle" helmet in place of their largely decorative leather headgear in time

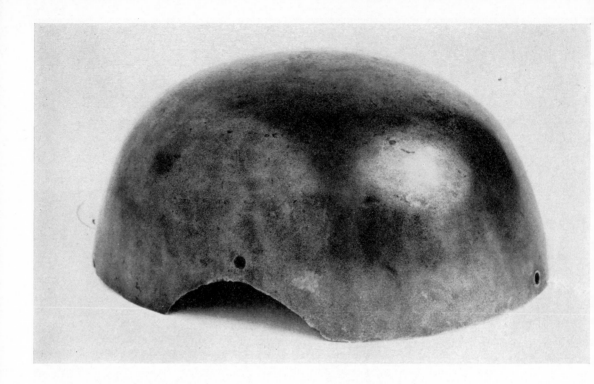

for the first battle of the Somme in the summer of 1916. The *stahlhelm* was in fact the heaviest and largest of all First World War helmets, being very deep in the crown with a large, sloped neck guard and a narrow frontal peak. Two projecting ventilation spigots were fitted at the temples; these also formed part of the mounting for a strong frontal reinforcing plate, which slotted over these two lugs and was held in position by a strap passing round the back of the helmet.

There has been little significant development of the helmet since the First World War. The British Army continued to use the familiar "tin hat" until after the close of the Second World War, although the modified pattern now in use was gradually introduced from 1944 onwards. The original style, manufactured in millions, is now in use by many overseas armies. As mentioned above, the U.S. forces exchanged their British pattern helmets for a new design in 1942; a sound compromise between protection and convenience, it is still in use by America and many other nations. Two smaller, lighter versions of the German *stahlhelm* were introduced before and during the Second World War; these disappeared from Europe after 1945, although a limited re-introduction in some West German units has been noted in recent years. The many other patterns of helmet currently in use by the world's armed forces are all basically similar, deep bowl-shaped designs with narrow flared rims which generally offer good protection to the neck and lower skull. Their prototypes may be found in hundreds of medieval illustrations and monuments; the lessons learned by hard experience four, five and six centuries ago are still entirely valid. Only in the field of raw materials has there been any sign of significant innovation; in some designs steel is giving way to sophisticated plastic compounds whose strength-to-weight ratio would have delighted the old master-armourers.

The Tournament: Warfare as Spectacle

6

The Tournament:
Warfare as Spectacle

In all primitive cultures, survival depended in the last analysis upon aggressive courage and violent skills. Until comparatively recent times a man's worth was generally measured by his performance in combat, and in many ways this attitude has persisted into the present day. It is therefore natural that displays of warlike skill should have played a part in many civilisations. One of the earliest examples of this type of ritualistic bloodshed was associated with the basically practical activity of hunting; and among the Egyptians, Sumerians and Assyrians the hunt became the "chase", with the hunter emphasising his skill and courage by riding down and slaying the lion, the most noble prey of all. Many contemporary sculptures depict the kings and princes of the day mounted in their chariots and followed by admiring subordinates, racing along the fringes of the great reed-beds and slaying the lion with their great bows. The use of the bow and arrow in these hunts, weapons with which the monarchs of that area often achieved a legendary skill, probably ensured that the royal hunters faced no great danger.

As in so many areas of human behaviour, it was probably the Romans who first developed the idea of exhibitions of skill in arms into an organised form; the Greek festivals of games, from which the Romans no doubt took the basic idea, were essentially athletic rather than warlike. In time the spectacle became such a feature of Roman life that many details have fortunately survived. Not only were they demonstrations of skill, cruelty and horror, but also an important political weapon for keeping the population—the Roman mob, whose latent strength every ruler regarded with a healthy fear—in a state of happy disinterest, their minds and energies sated to an astonishing degree with the vicarious excitement of the arena. The cost of mounting these spectacles was enormous, but no matter how difficult or desperate the circumstances might be, the organisers apparently regarded the payment of astronomical sums to be a completely necessary part of a career in public life. Under Augustus sixty-six days—more than two months of the year—were given over to races, horse trials and theatricals. Under his successor Tiberius the annual figure rose to eighty-seven days; and by the middle of the 4th Century A.D. there were no less than 175 holidays, ten of them set aside for gladiatorial displays.

Title page, *Fig. 69: Silvered and engraved armour made for Henry VIII, probably by Italian makers in c. 1514. This armour has a helmet of the armet type and a skirt of plate—*tonlet. *The horse armour is Flemish, c. 1514–19. (Tower of London.)*

Opposite, *Plate 11: A model of King Casimir III of Poland (1333–1370), with his standard bearer. (Archer Collection.)*

In Rome the most magnificent building devoted to games and warlike demonstrations was, of course, the great Circus, a stadium which could accommodate 180,000 or 190,000 spectators. Chariot racing was one of the most popular events in this great arena, as were ordinary horse races, sometimes with the additional feature of hazardous trick riding, and leaping from horse to horse. Weapon displays on horseback, and picking up prizes from the ground while galloping at full speed, were also frequent items on the programme. During the period of the Roman Republic, military displays were often mounted in the Circus, in which troops decked out in special parade armour demonstrated various spectacular movements and manoeuvres.

Gladiatorial combats as public spectacles seem to have originated in Etruscan Campania, but apparently the practice did not reach Rome until the 3rd Century B.C.; during the Republic they were only held at private funerals. In 264 B.C. it is recorded that only three combats were held, but by 200 B.C. the figure was 25, and by 174 B.C. the number of displays had risen to 74. The nature of these demonstrations was radically altered in 105 B.C. when two Consuls sponsored a display as a public event, whereas on all previous occasions they had been essentially private functions.

Fig. 70: A satisfactory conclusion to a course at the tilt. This illustration of 1480 shows a number of interesting details such as the enveloping saddle, the frog-mouthed helm, horse trappers and crests.

This new feature encouraged the demand for trained swordsmen and gladiators, and training schools were established and rapidly proliferated. The Emperor Augustus (27 B.C.–14 A.D.) claimed that in eight spectacles which he mounted, over 10,000 contestants had fought. Surfeit rather dulled the public taste for simple combat, and the promoters tried to stimulate interest by including various ethnic groups not previously seen in the arena, each using their own native methods of fighting— Britons fought in chariots, Greeks in close phalanx with spears, Thracians were known by their small, round shields, and so forth.

The majority of gladiators did not take up the profession from choice; in their ranks were to be found convicted criminals, prisoners of war, slaves and a very few volunteers. In the unlikely event of a gladiator surviving three years in the arena, he was presented with a wooden sword as a symbol of his freedom. The life was brutal and hideously dangerous, but nevertheless a successful gladiator could hope to gain considerable rewards. The sponsors and promoters paid large sums of money, and Roman society followed the careers of notable gladiators in the same way as 20th-Century society follows the careers of professional boxers. For their brief period of glory they were often the toast of the rich,

Fig. 71: By the time of Henry VIII (1509–1547) the tilt was higher and there had been changes in armour and saddles— here the frontal plates provide extra protection. (Tournament Roll of Henry VIII).

fêted and pampered wherever they went, with many opportunities to turn their popularity to advantage. Part of the fees was spent on the tools of their trade, and surviving fragments of armour found at Pompeii suggest items of high quality.

The night before the games were due to open the contestants were given a free banquet, and afforded every possible luxury and licence—in sharp contrast to modern training practice! On the opening morning

Fig. 72: For the Rennen, *run with pointed lances, armour was strengthened with additional pieces—note the great vamplates on the lance and the all-enveloping* Renntartsche *on the left side of the body. (Tower of London.)*

the gladiators paraded around the amphitheatre in their full fighting rig, and probably saluted the Emperor with the oft-quoted phrase, "Hail Caesar, we who are about to die salute thee". The weapons were examined by scrutineers, and the proceedings opened with mock "warming-up" fights. Then came the signal, on horns and trumpets, pipes and flutes, for the first of the serious combats to begin. The combinations were many and various, but a popular and often-depicted form was that between *retiarii* and *myrmillones*. The *retiarii* were usually unarmoured and relied on speed and agility, being armed with a net —the edges weighted to ensure that it opened out when cast—and a trident. *Myrmillones* wore partial armour including a large, wide-brimmed, visored helmet; a laminated guard on the right arm; a greave on the left leg; and a large *scutum*. This group fought with the sword. Armour for the arena was often elaborate, decorated with plumes and even with precious metals, as were the weapons. When one of the contestants was wounded or pinned down he laid down his weapon and raised a finger of the left hand, but his fate was determined almost entirely by the spectators. If they approved of his performance they waved something white, or gave the "thumbs up", and his life was spared. If he had displeased them—or if, as was frequently the case, their main interest was in seeing blood spilt—the thumb was turned down, and the victor struck the final blow. To ensure that there would be no bluffing the organisers had a ghastly system whereby apparently dead contestants were touched with a hot iron; if there was any reaction then the appropriate steps were taken.

The appearance of animals in the arena apparently dates back to 186 B.C., when the first such exhibitions was held in Rome. Animals were not only exhibited but were hunted, fought and killed in the arena by a group of men known as *bestiarii*. As with the gladiators, the palate of the mob soon became jaded, and the Empire was scoured for prime or unusual specimens; and species of animals were seen in the arena of Rome which would not be seen again in Europe until the 16th and 18th Centuries. Lions, tigers, bears, giraffes, ostriches, rhinoceros, hippopotami, apes, many different species of deer—all were dragged into the hideous slaughter, as animal was forced to fight animal or man.

For 400 years or more the relish of the Romans for their "games" was unabated; and with the increasing decadence of their society, so the spectacles they demanded became more degrading. The original themes, the display of military skill or prowess in the hunt, gave way to the most unspeakable spectacles of perversion and sadism. Some attempts were made to lessen their horror, and the Imperial gladiatorial schools were abolished in 399 A.D. In 404 gladiatorial games were forbidden in Rome, but they did not cease completely, and St. Augustine speaks of them at least ten years afterwards. Games involving the slaughter of animals persisted until much later, and are known to have taken place as late as the 6th Century. With the fall of the Roman Empire organised spectacles became far less common and there are few records of similar events for the next few centuries.

I T is not until the 11th Century that references to warlike games again begin to appear; but the philosophy behind them was entirely different from the motives of the Romans. The medieval war games were essentially a test of skill between more or less equally matched opponents, and although death might occur, it was not an expected result. The earliest form recorded, certainly in the 11th Century, was the tournament or tourney—probably derived from the French word *tournier*. Tourneys were miniature wars, with large groups of warriors taking part. These mock battles were not always limited to a set field or en-

closed space and there are records of tournaments ranging over quite considerable areas of countryside. In contrast to the tourney, the joust involved only two combatants. Distinctions were made in the form of the contest—there were "jousts of peace" and "jousts of war". The joust of peace, or *jouste à plaisance*, was fought with blunted weapons; but in the *jouste à outrance* sharp weapons were used and the bout could, in theory, continue until the death

Fig. 73: Side view of the same armour—made in Innsbruck in circa *1490—shows the queue which supported the lance, and the spiked screw on the breastplate which located and fixed the* Renntartsche. *(Tower of London.)*

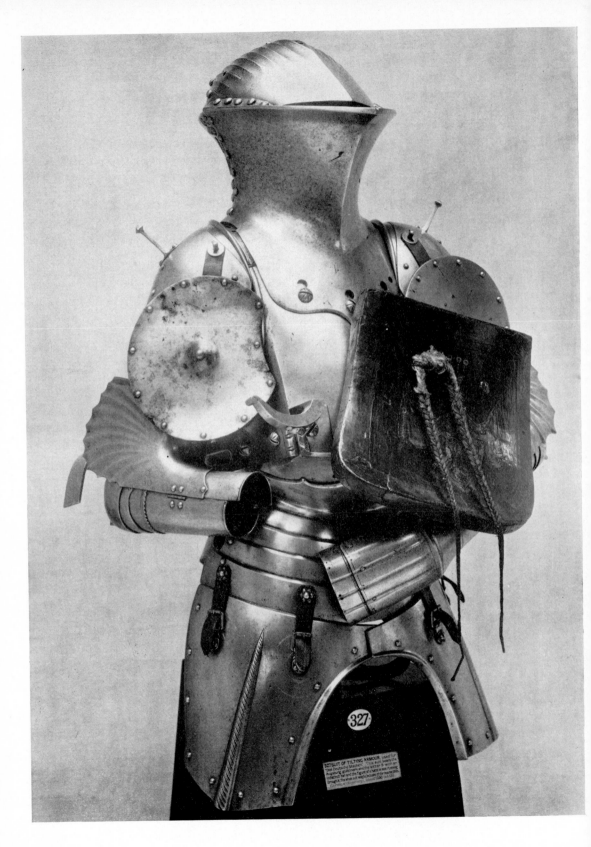

327 SUIT OF TILTING ARMOUR, used for *Das Deutsche Stechen*. This suit bears the Augsburg guild mark and the armour impresses a reinforced top and the figure of a hero in the running tongue. The whole suit weighs over 90lbs (c.1580)

of one of the contestants. The Marshall or umpire had the right to stop the fight at any point, so that death was not inevitable in these bouts. There are early references to a type of combat known as the Round Table, but apart from the obvious connection with the Arthurian legends there is little in surviving accounts to indicate exactly what form it took, although one or two references seem to suggest the use of blunted blades.

Far less dangerous than either the tourney or the joust was the quintain, which was mainly a device by which the warrior might practise his aim and speed. At first the quintain seems to have been simply a target at which the contestant struck as he galloped past, but later it became more sophisticated. An arm, pivoted at the centre, carried on one end a target and on the other a suspended weight. As the rider struck the target he had to avoid the other end as it swung round just as he passed by. For the unwary rider a severe clout was his reward for any lack of concentration or skill, with the added possibility of a severe fall.

In England the tournament is said by William of Newbury to have appeared during the reign of King Stephen (1135–54) and he claims that it was of French origin. In theory, as already described, these were mock combats; but tempers and lives were lost, and it is reported that at one meeting held near Cologne in 1240 no less than sixty of the participants were killed. So damaging were these scarcely limited outbreaks of warfare becoming that in 1228 Pope Gregory IX had issued a Bill forbidding the holding of tournaments—apparently with little effect. In England, Henry III issued a prohibition on tournaments without special permission, and a similar edict was issued during the reign of Edward II. At

this time there were in England five authorised tournament sites—simply open spaces of a suitable size, fenced in with some form of barrier.

In 1274 Edward I, on his way home from the crusade, passed through France, and while there was invited by the Count of Châlons to take part in a tournament. During the mêlée the Count attempted to drag the King from his horse, but was himself dismounted. Tempers frayed and hard blows were exchanged; before long a body of English archers went into action, nothing loth, and what had started as a tourney finished as a battle, with dead on both sides.

In 1278 a tournament was held in Windsor Park, and the Roll of Purchases is still in existence; it is recorded that thirty-eight men took part, including some from overseas, and armour and weapons were provided for them. Since the swords were fashioned from whalebone the armour was light and made of leather. The spectacle must have been very colourful, for the armour was gilded and silvered and crests were fitted to the armour of both man and horse. Around the horses' necks were chains of small bells. Similar jousts and tournaments were held in honour of special occasions, such as visits from nobility or weddings. At first the honour of being allowed to take part in the tournament was considered sufficient reward, but gradually prizes, some of great value, began to be offered. In a royal tournament held in London in 1390 by Richard II in honour of his Queen, sixty knights jousted with rebated lances. Some extremely valuable prizes were given; on the Sunday the best lance received a crown of gold and another received a rich gold clasp. On Tuesday, when the squires were the contestants, falcons and horses were offered as prizes.

In jousting the number of courses run, or blows given with various weapons, was at first only three, but as time went on the number increased until it was as many as twelve. There was also an increase in the

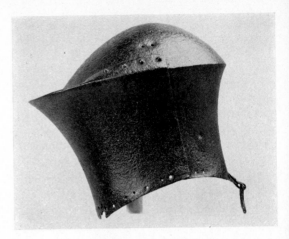

Tilting helms. **Left,** *Fig. 75: An English helm weighing over 20 lbs., complete with the slotted metal straps or* charnels *which secured it to the body armour, front and back. This piece dates from* c. *1490.* **Above,** *Fig. 76: An English helm fashioned from two pieces of metal only, with holes to accommodate the laces of the interior padding. Made in* c. *1515, this helm weighs 16 lbs. 10 oz. (Tower of London: Wallace Collection.)*

number of rules regarding the use of weapons, the type of weapons and the form of combat. On the whole the general tendency was towards an amelioration of the violence, an improvement of manners and a lessening of injury.

There seems little doubt that tournaments were originally fought with conventional armour and weapons, and consequently casualties were inevitable. At the Council of Clairmont, held in 1130, the tournament was forbidden; and although this ban was largely ignored the tournament did not become respectable until 1316 when Pope John XXII rescinded the ban. Even to the hardened warriors of the 11th and 12th Centuries it must have seemed somewhat futile to risk life and limb in mock combat, and some time in the 12th Century the first steps were taken to reduce the risks by fitting the lance with a blunted head. In place of the point a crown-shaped, three-pronged fitting, the coronel, was attached

to the end of the lance. In general the object of a joust with rebated lances (that is those fitted with a coronel) was to splinter the lance or to knock the opponent from the saddle, both results needing a good, direct hit. This trend towards greater safety was emphasised, and it is highly likely that special forms of armour were developed at an early date. These were probably slightly more extensive than the normal piece, and they could be made thicker; the greater weight was of less importance since quick movement was not quite so imperative in the lists as it was on the field of battle.

During the 14th Century the great helm, which by then was very substantial, was largely reserved for tilt and tourney, and a special form was evolved known, from its shape, as the frog-mouthed helm. This helm appeared late in the 14th Century and was very securely fastened to the breast- and backplate by slotted bars (charnels) fitted at the front and back. The crown of the frog-mouthed helm was only very slightly domed, so making it difficult for a lance point to obtain a purchase. Perhaps more important were the shape and angle of the slope; the gap left between the dome and front plate was so designed that the wearer could only see through this slot when leaning slightly forward. The edge of the skull plate was almost level with the lower front plate, so that when the knight leant forward in his saddle as he came into a gallop he was in a position to sight his opponent. As the moment of impact drew near the knight straightened and immediately the slit in the helmet was almost completely obscured. Loss of vision was of little importance then, for momentum and the horse's training would have kept him on course. This design did mean that the chances of an accidental strike through the gap were negligible. This very safe and substantial form of helmet continued in use almost to the middle of the 16th Century. Despite its massive construction the great helm was occasionally fitted with a reinforcing plate on the left-hand side, which had to take the greatest number of knocks.

D URING the 15th Century further precautions were introduced into jousting, for there must have been a considerable risk of two heavy horses, probably moving fairly fast, colliding one with another. The system of introducing a fence separating the two riders was introduced, possibly in Italy; the earliest references suggest that this took place early in the 15th Century. At first the fence, known as the tilt, was little more than a cloth demarcation barrier, but later a more substantial fence was introduced. Riders started from either end and rode left side to left side with the lance held across the horse's neck. Combats carried out across this fence were most often with rebated lances, and the winner was computed on the number of lances broken,

or on marks awarded for the point of impact. Obviously it was more difficult to place a strike on the helm and, consequently, such a hit counted for more than a blow on the larger area of the body. Normal field armour was pressed into service although there are references, early in the 15th Century, to extra pieces being screwed, bolted, or attached by some other method to the basic field armour. A French manuscript of the middle of the 16th Century specifies a special joust armour which comprised a cuirass with a lance rest and buckles for the attachment of the helm. There was a special gauntlet, the *manifer*, for the left hand, which was very substantial and not unlike an elbow gauntlet. It had a very long and substantial cuff extending well up to the elbow, and at the end was shaped to fit the angle of the arm when holding the reins. A much smaller gauntlet, probably of leather, was used on the right hand, and a polder-mitten protected the rest of the arm. This had a small pauldron for the shoulder together with a round disc, a *besagaw*, which covered the armpit; and hanging from the shoulder was a wooden shield.

In the 14th Century a German style of joust, known as *Hohenzeuggestech*, was run with the aim of splintering lances. The horse was fitted with a special saddle which had the seat raised well up so that the knight was able almost to stand on the stirrups. This position enabled him to get maximum weight and grip on the lance. The legs of the riders were protected by a very substantial wooden front to the saddle which curved up and round his thighs. This form of joust appears to have fallen from fashion about the middle of the 15th Century.

Gestech was the form which found the greatest following: this was run with an ordinary saddle, and the object was either to unhorse the opponent or to break the lance. Armour for the *Gestech* consisted

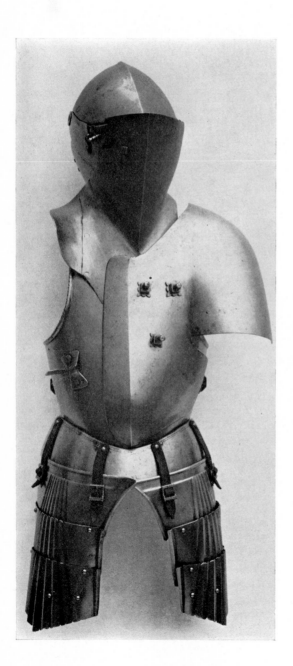

Fig. 77: Italian tilt armour, showing the extra plates bolted in position. A buffe *covers the lower part of the helmet, and a* grand-guard *protects the left side of the body. This armour dates from c. 1580. (Wallace Collection.)*

of a frog-mounted helm screwed to the breastplate, which was itself extremely substantial. On the right-hand side of the breastplate was fitted a very large lance rest, as well as a backward projecting hooked bar known as the queue. This device held the lance very securely in the correct position, ensuring a very substantial blow. The riders' thighs were protected by fairly normal tassets, although these were quite short. Since there was little danger of injury to the back, the backplate on these *Gestech* armours was normally little more than an "X" for support. The arms were protected by small pauldrons, while at the armpits were fixed round plates, the besagews. Some of these *Gestech* armours have on the shoulders a large, upward-projecting steel peg, which was intended merely as a convenient support when carrying the lance to and from the joust. On some of these armours the arm defences can, in fact, be locked into the correct position for couching, or holding the lance. Most of the manifers were completely rigid, although some were laminated at the back of the fingers. For the right hand there was no metal gauntlet, a leather glove being considered sufficient since the main defence was in the form of a large, conical plate, the vamplate, fitted to the lance just in front of the grip. This vamplate first appears on lances in the 14th Century.

Another form of armour designed specially for the tilt was very different; this was intended for the *Scharfrennen*, in which the main object was, again, to splinter the lance or unhorse the opponent. Despite the fact that the name appears early in the 15th Century little is known about the armour designed for it, except that it seems to have been a light half-armour with a sallet. By the latter part of the 15th Century a special armour had been devised which usually featured a cuirass similar to that for the *Gestech*, except that the front section and leg defences were more substantial and generally extended to the knees. Attached to the breastplate was a large bevor which was surmounted by a very solid one-piece sallet with just a single vision slit. Extra defence for the body from the neck to the waist was afforded by the *renntartsche*, fashioned from a combination of wood, leather and metal, and attached to the breastplate by means of a screw and butterfly nut. This piece was shaped to the body and followed its general outline.

On some of these tilting armours an ingenious spring-loaded plate was fitted on the breast of the armour; when this was struck by a lance a mechanism was operated which caused the pieces to fly apart. This device removed the possibility of any argument as to the validity of a hit.

Not all tournaments and jousts were fought on horseback, a certain number of combats being fought on foot using a variety of weapons. From the end of the 15th Century it was common practice for the combatants to be separated by a wooden barrier over which they fought. As with the other armours, until the beginning of the 16th Century normal field harness was used, but with a great bascinet. Early in the 16th Century a special form of foot combat armour appears, the most distinctive feature of which was a large skirt-like defence extending to the knee and comprising a series of hoops; this was known as the tomlet. There is also in the Tower of London, one foot combat suit of Henry VIII which completely covers the body; in place of the normal skirt or tasset defences, hoops completely encircle the thighs so that, in effect, the entire body is enclosed in a steel shell.

In the 16th Century it was common practice to construct a normal field armour and supply with it a number of extra plates which could be attached to convert it to a harness suitable for the various forms of tourney, foot or mounted. More elaborate garnitures had extra helmets, whilst others

Fig. 78: *The very substantial helmet and breastplate on this armour weigh more than 31 lbs. On the left shoulder is the tilting-targe used for the Italian tilt. German, c. 1590. (Wallace Collection.)*

merely had interchangeable visors; there was also a large reinforcing piece which extended from the centre of the breastplate right round to the arm, known as the grand guard.

Tilting probably reached its peak during the early part of the 16th Century, but it was then gradually abandoned and by the end of the 17th Century it was largely forgotten. Certain styles of the tilt and tournament lingered on for another century or so, and there were one or two revivals. In 1839 one such revival was made at Eglinton in Scotland, when it was planned to recreate all the glamour and glory of ancient times; but alas, on the day, the heavens opened and the bedraggled ladies and knights watched a display in which enthusiasm and inexperience united to produce a near-fiasco.

Horses obviously played an extremely important part in title and tournament, and a good steed was treasured by a knight. In fact most knights owned a small string of horses each for some special purpose; the largest and most expensive was the well trained "destrier", which was a fairly sturdy animal. Stamina and strength were important for the destrier had to carry a substantial load when the knight was fully armed. These animals were apparently reserved for the tilt, although their use in war was not unknown, but more often the knight rode a slightly smaller horse known as a "courser". For general riding, and popular with the poorer troops, was the "rounsey".

In battle the horse was an obvious target, since a dismounted knight was far less effective, and his steed was in constant danger from archers and foot-soldiers. Armourers were able to offer some protection, and there are references to horse armour at an early date. Mail and scale armour were both used in the Ancient World, but seem to have been abandoned following the collapse of the Roman Empire, although this is by no means universally

Above, *Fig. 79: Steel framework of a German horse muzzle dated 1561 and bearing a German motto:—*"Wenn Gott will, so ist mi zil"—"As God wills, so is my aim." (*Wallace Collection.*)

Right, *Plate 12: Tournament clash between mounted and dismounted knights. The horse wears a typical barding, with heraldic motif repeated from the shield.* (*Archer Collection*).

certain. There are references to trappers of mail and quilted material as early as the 13th Century; these enveloped the horse, reaching nearly to the ground. In the 14th Century coats of plates are mentioned, and these were probably made in the same style as for men. Plate defences, of metal and leather, occur in the latter part of the 13th Century; on the chest was the *peytral* and on the flanks were the *flanchards*. The body defences were completed by the crupper and a neck guard of laminated plates or mail, the *crinet*. The horse's head was guarded by the *chanfron*, which was a shaped metal plate which covered the entire front of the head and, on later examples, the ears as well. Smaller versions reaching only to about the eyes were also fitted, and these were known as half-chanfrons. Some of the full chanfrons had a projecting spike on the forehead. Although not part of the defences, the saddle was a vital part of the knight's equipment and its shape was a matter of concern, not only for its comfort but also for its efficiency. Both saddle and stirrups were designed to allow the knight to ride with his legs straight, for this meant he was able to use his entire weight when delivering a sword blow or taking the shock of a lance thrust. Most saddles had the front faced with steel as extra protection and some had the rear section, the cantle, curved round to enclose the hips of the rider, holding him firmly in the saddle. This feature became less necessary in the latter part of the 15th Century when light, hollow lances (*bourdonnasses*) were introduced for the tilt. Their method of construction ensured that they shattered immediately on impact, despite their large and rather cumbersome appearance.

Horse armour was generally discarded during the second quarter of the 17th Century, and the majority of surviving examples date only from the 16th Century (see Figs. 69–71). Cloth trappers, usually bearing the owner's arms, were in use as early as the 13th Century, and no doubt

added a splash of colour to the otherwise sordid and depressing medieval battles. Romantic and glamorous they may seem in the paintings of Uccello, but in fact they were harrowing affairs in which mutilation and life-long injury were commonplace, and little or no medical attention could be expected.

Fig. 80: German tilt armour with a mitten-gauntlet, manifer, *as well as reinforces at elbow and shoulder.* Circa 1580–90. *(Tower of London.)*

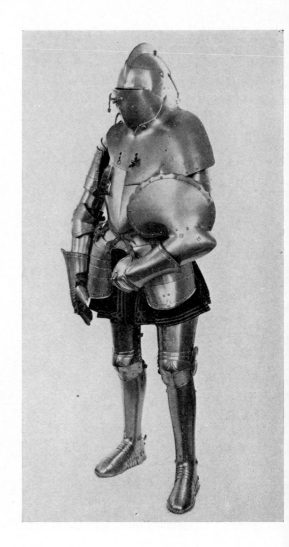

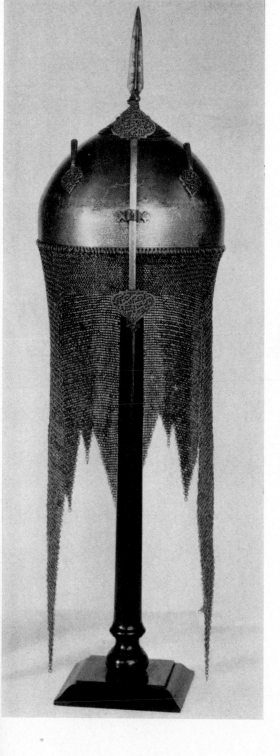

Oriental
Armour

Oriental Armour

Title page, *Fig. 81: Fine Persian helmet with inscriptions from the Koran inlaid around the rim; the flattened sections at the ends of the nasal bear Arabic prayers, and the mail curtain terminates in characteristic points, which hung over the shoulders. (Wallace Collection.)* **Opposite,** *Plate 13: Persian helmet with sliding nasal, two plume holders and an inscription including some gold inlay. There is a mail fringe of heavy links, and the helmet weighs 3 lbs. in all. Late 18th/early 19th Century.* **Below,** *Fig. 82: Two of the four plates of a Charaina – the smaller fitting under the arm. The surface of this 18th Century Persian piece is decorated with chiselled foliage and overlaid gold work. (Wallace Collection.)*

THE development of European armour follows a clearly defined line, and it is relatively easy to follow the changes from very simple beginnings. There is a sense of continuity, as the armourer developed his craft and skills until he was able to enclose a man from head to foot in a complete shell of steel. The variety of helmets, indeed of all pieces of armour, made throughout Europe was quite considerable and the variations on any given theme were very numerous; but, in general, any piece of armour can be dated to within a few decades on design and shape. In the Orient, using the word in its widest sense, the same clear line of development is lacking; with certain exceptions the shape of a Persian or Indian helmet of the late 19th Century differs but little from one dating from the 17th Century or even earlier periods.

This continuity of design is in no sense indicative of a lack of ability on the part of the Asiatic craftsmen, for their command of metal-working was considerable. In the field of decoration their skills and techniques often surpassed those of the West. The study of Oriental armour raises certain problems, for the available sources of information are far less numerous than in Europe. One immensely valuable source of

knowledge has been the study of funeral brasses, which show the changes in armour over the centuries, but Asia lacks any equivalent monuments. From the 10th Century on, in Europe, there are quite a number of illustrated manuscripts, engravings, paintings and sculptures all contributing some knowledge, but in the East the ban imposed by Islam on the representation of the human figure had serious effects on the recording of life in ancient times. This ban does not, of course, apply to the whole of Asia for, as was inevitable with almost every religion, Islam did throw off splinter groups, and not all sects followed the prohibition. Much information can be gained from the many very delightful miniatures from Persia and India, and a few early portraits of rulers have survived.

Again, in the West distinctions between national styles are, if not obvious, at least apparent; usually German and Italian armour styles can be discerned without difficulty. However, across the tremendous land masses of the East there was a constant surge of invasion and conquest with consequent absorption of new cultures. Sometimes the culture of the conqueror was imposed on the subject, but in other cases the reverse occurred. This fusion means that national styles (indeed the very term "national" is perhaps inapplicable in these conditions) were modified, and it is often extremely difficult, particularly with the later items of Oriental arms and armour, to specify the country of origin; the distinction between Persian and later Indian armour is often very fine. Similar blurring occurs with Turkish armour, for the Ottoman Empire extended over vast areas of Asia Minor, North Africa and the Balkans, and the constant interplay of different cultures resulted in armour which exhibited Turkish features but was, perhaps, made in Egypt.

Information concerning the craft of the Oriental armourer is extremely limited, as the receipts and inventories which are of such tremendous use in the researching of European development are also lacking. Fortunately some pieces of Asiatic armour are dated, but here again there is a minor pitfall, for Islamic countries use a chronology different from that of Western Europe. In Western culture the years are counted from the birth of Christ but in Islam dates are calculated from the flight of Mohammed from Mecca to Medina in 622 A.D. This event is known as the *Hijra*, and Islamic dates are given as A.H. (the year of the *Hijra*). Thus any date given on an Oriental piece is some 622 years earlier than its equivalent date under Western chronological style. There is, in fact, a slight difference and the relationship of dates is not quite this direct, although the result so derived represents a good working figure.

There are certain other major differences between the armour of the two continents; in general terms, plate armour has predominated in the West from the 14th Century, but in the greater part of the Orient plate armour, in the Western sense, never became universal. Mail was common to most forms of defence and continued in use in the Orient long after it had been abandoned in the West. As a reasonable generalisation it can be said that in Europe armour had been discarded by the end of the 17th Century, but in countries such as Japan, North Africa and India troops were fighting in armour well into the later part of the 19th Century.

In the East there was a far greater emphasis on the use of what might be termed segmented defences, built up of units each made up of smaller units. They used mail, scale, laminated armour and, most common and widespread of all, lamellar armour. This may be described as a form of scale armour; although it varies in detail at different periods and in different areas of the world, it is basically a system of overlapping plates, lacing sometimes to a basic garment, sometimes merely to one another, to form a

Opposite, *Fig. 83: Another Persian helmet, but of grotesque and decadent form. The embossed nose of the "face" has been accommodated by a bend in the nasal, so that it will not actually slide into position. There are poetic inscriptions and some applied gold decoration. This is a 19th Century piece, as is the subject of Fig. 84* (**above**), *a complete cuirass of five plates with the original padding. Gold patterns and inscriptions decorate the surface, which is dated 1809, and opens down the front. (Wallace Collection.)*

flexible but efficient form of defence. The scales are normally laced together in horizontal strips and these are arranged to overlap in a variety of styles to form a complete garment. Sculptures of ancient Assyria (see Fig. 6) suggest that the Assyrians used this form of armour both in long and short types of tunic. The shape of the actual lamellae vary considerably, being rectangular, square, clipped, long and narrow, or rectangular with a semicircular top. Plates such as these have been found in graves in Europe, Hungary, Sweden and in central Asia.

Many of the Eastern countries have, at varying periods, used a basic form of laminated armour somewhat similar to the Roman *lorica segmentata* (see Plate 3) with body defences made up of overlapping metal

strips. As was the case among the warriors of Scandinavia, many of the early Oriental illustrations show a form of splinted defence for arms and legs made up of a series of parallel metal bars secured to some form of base garment.

PERSIA was one of the most important centres for arms production in Asia and the work of Persian craftsmen was highly regarded. Persian smiths were to be found domiciled and working in areas as far apart as India, Russia and Arabia. In the ancient world Persia had been one of the major powers. Under Xerxes, a great army had invaded Greece in the 5th Century B.C.; contemporary descriptions indicate that few of his troops wore armour, but by the time of Cyrus the Younger Persian soldiers are described (by Xenophon) as wearing brazen armour and helmets, and mention is also made of the horses being armoured as well. Discoveries at Dura Europos, a town on the river Euphrates, suggest that a Persian soldier of the 3rd Century A.D. wore a round-topped helmet not dissimilar from those to be found over much of Europe at the time, and a mailed shirt. It was on the same site that one of the most interesting of early illustrations of armour was found; dating from the 2nd Century A.D., it shows a mounted warrior with his horse completely covered by some form of trapper, whilst he is protected on legs and arms by laminated armour and on the body by a combination of scale and mail. On his head is a tall, conical helmet.

Laminated defences, if one may rely upon certain carvings, persisted until the 3rd Century A.D., as did a dome shaped, thimble-like helmet. By the 7th Century it appears that mail and splinted armour had become very common. Another interesting development dating from about the same time was the fitting of a curtain of mail to the rim of the helmet. This mail had two eye holes but otherwise completely covered the face. This form of facial defence was rarely used on European helmets, although a few examples have been found in Sweden and Russia.

Between the 8th and 10th Centuries lamellar armour seems to have regained favour and the evidence indicates that the warrior of this period wore a long lamellar tunic reaching well below the knees, whilst the head was guarded by a domed-shaped helmet. By the latter part of the Middle Ages, the 14th and 15th Centuries, contemporary miniatures show the arms fitted with a form of vambrace consisting of a double-hinged plate and some simple round guard to the elbow. Legs were commonly guarded by thick fabric or mail, with heavy boots, although metal greaves were sometimes worn. Round-topped helmets are all

Opposite, Fig. 85: Helmet, shield and arm guard decorated en suite *with silver and turquoise; Persian, 19th Century. (Wallace Collection.)* **Below,** *Fig. 86: Detail of chiselling on a Persian arm guard; Persian armourers did not observe the general ban on representing the human figure, imposed by Islam.*

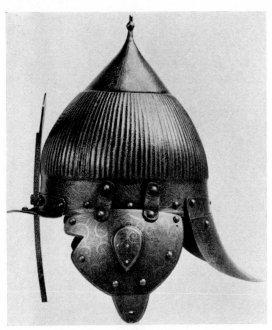

fitted with aventails and some also have additional cheek guards over the mail.

Apart from the aventail, which on occasions covered the entire face, visors seem to have been very rare among the Persians. There is one helmet preserved in the Kremlin armoury which has an embossed mask covering the face. During the 15th Century some helmets made in Persia had extremely exaggerated points drawn out from the conical top. The wearing of feathered plumes in the helmets became increasingly common from the first half of the 15th Century.

From the 16th Century onwards miniatures show Persian warriors wearing conical helmets to the top of which is fitted a tall spike, or occasionally a plume holder. Besides the main central holder two small ones were mounted on either side of the brow. Suspended from the base of the helmet was the usual mail with two long,

pointed extensions at the front which hung down over the chest. Since few details of the armour are shown it can be assumed that the main defence was of mail worn beneath an outer garment. In addition to the body armour of lamellar construction several effigies and miniatures show a circular metal plate on the chest and these were also found on many of the Turkish illustrations.

Another form of plate defence for the body was the *Char Aina*—"four mirrors." This defence comprised large plates for chest and back and two smaller ones to cover the sides. They were usually rectangular and plain although circular and fluted ones are known. These forms of body defences remained more or less unchanged until the final abandonment of armour during the latter part of the 19th Century.

Late Persian helmets had a fairly deep dome, a feature which distinguishes them from those of India, with a separately-made socket fastened at the top into which screwed the spike or extra plume holders. Another common feature found on Persian, Indian and Turkish helmets was the sliding nasal, similar to those found on the European burgonet. A bar of square section, with each end flattened into a leaf shape, passed through a securing socket on the brow of the helmet. This could be raised or lowered according to taste and when in position extended right down to the chin and afforded some protection against the sweep of a sword in exactly the same way as the European model. The aventail was fixed to the rim of the helmet by a series of small holes drilled around the edge, through which links passed to engage with the aventail. Oriental mail was frequently not riveted as in Europe, but merely butted, that is the two ends are pushed together— a system which tended to reduce the defensive qualities of the mail since it was far more liable to split and tear. It was of course a quicker and cheaper method of production. Some of the Persian helmets were fitted with a pair of curved horns near the top of the cone. With these helmets there was usually a shield and at least one arm defence, all being decorated *en suite*. This form of arm protection was a vambrace extending as far as the elbow with a strap to secure it at the top of the forearm, and a series of splints connected with mail which strapped round over the wrist. The back of the hand was protected by a glove or mitten of mail. The whole of the arm piece was usually lined with some form of thinly padded, or quilted, material; such pieces were known as *bazuband*.

The similarity between the early forms of armour devised by the various Asiatic peoples is quite striking. In the case of the Turks figures depicted on early illustrations have many points in common with Persian figures of similar dates. There is, too, a resemblance, superficial perhaps, to some European armour. In the 9th Century a Turkish figure is shown wearing a tunic which could well be of mail with a coif, while the helmet is basically the same as a Norman *spangenhelm*. During the Middle Ages mail was very popular with the Turks, although they frequently combined mail with small plates. In the Metropolitan Museum, New York, there is a very complete Turkish armour of the 15th Century. It has a fairly low-crowned helmet fitted with an aventail which is basically the same as the Norman coif except that instead of covering the head it is suspended from the helmet's rim. Body defences comprise a number of parallel horizontal plates covering the shoulders in a narrow band and broadening out to encircle chest and thorax. The shoulders and upper part of the arms are protected by mail while, from just above the elbow, an arm defence similar to that of the body, with a number of narrow horizontal parallel plates, covers the rest of the arm as far as the tips of the fingers. Laminated defences extend as far as the waist and from the waist to the knee; the mail hauberk is fitted with a series of lines of separate plates and these extend round to the back of the body as well as the front.

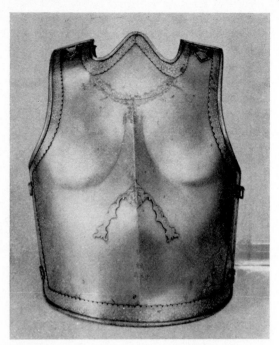

Above, *Fig. 90: Cuirass made in India early in the 19th Century, approximating the European style of the late 16th Century and decorated with applied gold work.*
Opposite, *Fig. 91: Rajput warrior's equipment of the late 18th/early 19th Century. The tunic is a "coat of a thousand nails" with plate reinforcements, and the arm guards resemble those of Europe. A straight-bladed sword—*khanda*—hangs from the cross-belt. (Wallace Collection.)*

The hauberk is fairly long, reaching to just above the knees which, in turn, are protected by cup-shaped discs. A small greave extends from just below the knee to the top of the instep and the feet are protected by mail.

From the end of the 15th Century the Turkish helmet was generally tall with a fluted, conical skull, but later examples were more rounded and plainer. Fitted at the front was a small peak through which passed a sliding nasal bar. From the sides of the helmets were suspended large cheek pieces not dissimilar in style to those of the Romans. Some of the Turkish helmets were also fitted with the long face guard of mail found on Persian helmets.

Many members of the Turkish cavalry were equipped with large circular plates fitted on breast and back, the two pieces being connected by mail interspersed with a series of plates covering the rest of the body. Most of these discs are fluted with radiating lines. This style of armour is often associated the Janissaries, who were originally special body guards for the ruler. This group was founded in 1360 and was composed of captured Christians who had been converted to Islam. Usually captured as children and raised from boyhood in an atmosphere of spartan, almost mystical asceticism and self-denial, these celibate warriors eventually lost their exclusivity as the rules of their closed community were relaxed. In some ways they resembled the Praetorian Guard of Rome, for they were a very privileged group accorded certain rights denied to others, and indeed they, like the Praetorian Guard, became the controllers of the Imperial throne. The Janissaries became more and more involved in politics, and it was not until 1836 that this group was finally disbanded.

Somewhat similar in formation to the Janissaries were the Mamelukes, who were a bodyguard formed from among Turkish slaves and used by the rulers of areas in the Middle East. Most, apparently, wore a dome-shaped helmet with mail shirt and leggings. Beneath the mail shirt, as in Europe, were probably some padded defences. A form of mail brigandine or jack was particularly favoured by these warriors, in which a mail shirt was decorated or disguised by fitting it between two layers of rich material. During the 15th Century the helmet of the Mameluke was large enough to fit over a turban and the deep brim was recessed to avoid covering the eyes. Most are fluted, and much of the surface was often decorated with inscriptions or patterns. A nasal bar, usually broad and flat, gave some protection to the face. Towards the end of the 15th Century the turban helmet was gradually replaced by a type which resembled those of the Turks, with a rounded skull in place of the older conical form and with a peak and sliding nasal bar. Ear guards were also attached on either side of the bowl. The mamelukes eventually became the main power in Egypt; their leaders ruled the country until their control was finally broken by the French in 1798.

Further south, in the Sudan, the most common form of defence was mail, and hauberks are quite common. Generally speaking the mail was made of butted links and the hauberk had a round opening at the neck and short sleeves reaching to the elbow. Like the earlier Norman hauberk the skirt was split to allow the wearer to ride on horseback whilst still affording some protection to the legs. The abundance of mail in North Africa led to the growth of the legend that much of it had, in fact, been captured from crusaders and handed down from father to son ever since—but like so many good stories, it is quite erroneous.

VERY little is known of the early history of Indian armour. It is extremely likely that the invasions by the Turks, Arabs and Mongols influenced its developments and it probably followed broadly on the Persian and Turkish styles. Turkish armours of mail with additional plates woven in were common amongst the Indians, and many of their "four mirrors" were decorated with brass edges.

Early Indian mail was always made from wire of a round section with the ends riveted together, but during the later period—18th and 19th Centuries—it was not as well made and the rings were merely butted together. On a few helmets the face was protected by a complete flap of mail, vision being through the gauze-like effect of the links. Many of the mail coats dating from 17th Century India are unlike the earlier hauberks and are strapped and laced at the front, rather like a coat. Quilted armours are quite common in certain parts of India, especially in central areas and the Rajputan. The padding was of material and cotton wool and was frequently faced with crimson or green velvet. For additional strength some of these padded garments had metal plates fastened at various points on the chest and thighs. Many of

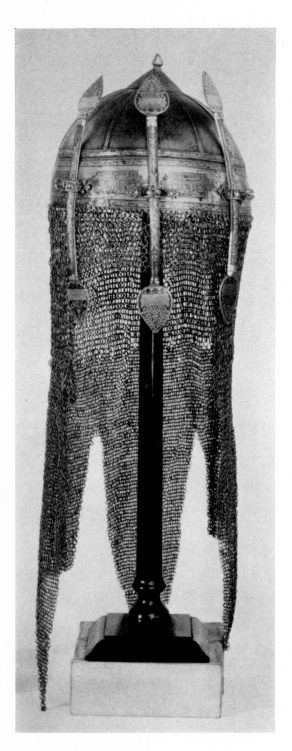

of these fabric armours were decorated overall by patterns made by the domed heads of reinforcing nails; indeed, such garments were known as "coats of a thousand nails". Indian armourers were among those Asiatic craftsmen who were stimulated by contact with European traders to copy their style of armour. A number of examples exist which are, in effect, native copies of European breast and back plates; some are joined by hinges on one side, and on the breast plates there is a central ridge and frequently an indication of muscles, rather reminiscent of the Ancient Greek style.

One or two armourers even attempted to copy European helmets, and there is, in the British Museum, a silver gilt helmet from Southern India with a characteristic shape and the stalk on top of the crown which is found on so many morions. The peak is fitted with a large anchor-shaped nasal which would, in fact, protect the greater part of the face. The most common helmet of India was the *kulah-khud*, which is basically the same as the Persian style, differing in one or two details. Generally speaking the Indian helmet is far lower-crowned than that from further North and in place of the spike found on both Persian and Turkish helmets, there is usually a central plume socket in addition to the two mounted close together at the crown. There is another distinction in the manner of securing the nasal. On most Turkish and Persian helmets the nasal could be adjusted by loosening a screw which passed through the bridge holding the nasal bar, and then re-tightening it. Most of the Indian helmets have a far simpler device which allows the nasal to be either up or down. In the up position it was secured by a small swivel link which engaged with a hook mounted at the base of the nasal.

Armour was obviously used a great deal throughout Asia but probably the commonest form of defence was the shield. Almost invariably the shield was round, whatever its area of origin. Early Persian shields appear to have been fairly light, probably of wicker, as were those of Assyria. From the 13th to 14th Century more substantial ones are shown on the miniatures; these consisted of a central steel boss around which circular, concentric rings of cane and thread were fitted. However, from sometime in the 16th Century onwards, they tend to be produced completely of steel, but decorated in exactly the same style as the plate armour. Most Persian shields tend to have a very pronounced lip at the edge, often with a thin moulding of iron or brass. Four small bosses were fitted near the centre and the entire surface was often decorated with figures or patterns or quotations from the Koran.

Indian shields were basically of the same pattern and examples are fairly common; some were produced in steel but a large number were fashioned from thick hide from suitable animals such as the buffalo or rhinoceros. Some hide shields were left plain whilst others were covered with black lacquer or with paint and decorations. A quality of hide greatly prized by Indian shield makers was its transparency, and some makers left a small part of the shield plain and unlacquered so that the owner might test the translucency. Almost all shields, whether of Indian or Persian origin, have four bosses mounted around the central point. These were slightly domed and were often decorated, but were basically securing devices which held in place four metal loops on the inside of the shield. To these loops were fastened a padded cushion and a pair of thongs which were gripped by the hand; the fist rested on this cushion, which absorbed any shock of a blow taken by the shield.

The Indian armourers probably produced the largest single armours ever made anywhere in the world, for the Hindus, in particular, placed great reliance upon the shock effect of elephants, and armours intended to cover the whole of these great

Fig. 93: Engraving of 1804 showing Egyptian Mamelukes—the mounted warrior closely resembles Indian and Turkish warriors of the period.

beasts were produced. The structure of these was basically the same as those made for men, with lamellar armour threaded and reinforced by mail and draped over the entire body and head of the elephant. Despite the awesome appearance of these beasts, they were in fact very vulnerable, especially to the effects of fire; and the impact on an army of fear-crazed elephants stampeded into retreat by an enemy's fire could be catastrophic.

Although knowledge of the history of arms and armour throughout most of Asia is at best fragmentary, this is not so in the case of Japan. Thanks to a variety of circumstances an enormous amount of information survived and from statuettes, paintings, prints and carvings and actual specimens buried in dolmens, it has been possible to build up a very complete picture of the evolution of Japanese armour. To an eye accustomed to the generally smooth outlines of European armours those of Japan seem large, cumbersome, and fussy, and their mode of construction tedious. Despite its somewhat impractical appearance Japanese armour formed an efficient defence, as indeed it need to be, for Japanese swords were among the sharpest and most efficient in the world.

It seems that the earliest of Japanese armours were largely made up of plates set in a rigid framework, but as early as the 4th Century the standard of workmanship was extremely high. Although this type of armour continued to be made up until the 8th Century, another style made its appearance during the 5th and 6th Centuries A.D. when, presumably via China and Korea, the construction of lamellar armour was taken up by the armourers. The earlier form had a pair of shoulder guards, superficially resembling those of a Roman *lorica segmentata*, extending to the elbow, and the cuirass was made from a rigid framework filled in with a series of plates. From the bottom of the cuirass hung a skirt of loops, whilst the collar was made in two pieces. Vambraces were reminiscent of the Persian style. The helmet was composed of a bowl made of horizontal plates riveted together, and to cover the neck and sides of the face a laminated neckguard reaching to the shoulders. When lamellar construction reached Japan the smiths kept the same basic fashion but substituted strips of lamellar armour for the loops and plates of the earlier style. The new helmet was made with a peak and a bowl constructed of a number of horizontal rings alternating with tapering vertical plates, topped off with a crest-holder.

During the latter half of the 7th Century and the whole of the 8th Century Japanese armour was varied in style and construction with mixtures of laminations and lamellae. The scales were all covered with coats of lacquer and the lacing was varied in colour and style. By the 12th Century the so-called "great armour" had been developed, which included a helmet with a hole in the top of the crown through which the hair of the warrior was passed; later, when hair styles changed, the hole became purely ornamental. To prevent a sword blade cutting through the lacing securing the neckguard there were two sweeping turnbacks at the cheeks. The helmet was lined on the inside with soft doeskin and secured to the head by a long cord. Facial protection was achieved by a moulded metal mask, lacquered, usually, in black and red. This was made in three sections—chin, nose and brow pieces. To make the warrior as fiercesome as possible the face masks were often embellished with beards, moustaches, wrinkles and grotesque features.

The Japanese warrior, resplendent in armour, faced much the same problem as the Western knight, that of easy recognition in battle, and he solved it in much the same way. To the peak of the helmet great, upsweeping U-shaped crests were fitted, and small pennants were flown from the back of the helmet or from a small stick fixed in a holder at the front of the helmet. To Western eyes another solution, although essentially practical, seems a little strange, for many *samurai* carried flags secured to the back of the cuirass.

The entire 16th Century was occupied by civil wars and is known as the Age of Battles; and under the stimulus of war the armourers developed and improved their product. In general the tendency was towards simpler, easier to produce models and hence there was greater use of plates. Many great nobles wore armours which were copies of earlier styles, and it is indicative of the history of Japan that armours made after 1568 are referred to as "modern" —*tosei*.

From the middle of the 15th Century many Japanese armourers began to sign their work and study of the surviving armours reveals that the Myōchin family was one of the most prolific and skilful of them all. Since the possession of an armour made by one of the great craftsmen was considered a work of prestige the "masters", the chief armourers, issued certificates of authenticity with their products, and many of these still exist.

Naturally there were many variations of all parts of the armour, with combinations of mail, lamellae, splints and plates. When the Portuguese traders introduced firearms in the 16th Century there were further complications, since armour now had to be thicker and stronger to resist the new weapons. There was also some rather fantastic and grotesque forms of helmet and horse armour pieces produced—some with a very distinct touch of Disneyland about them!

The Japanese, with their delight in detail, made special arrangements for the care and transport of their armour. Except for the cuirass, which might be a single plate, the greater proportion of their armour was of lamellar construction which meant that it could be collapsed and folded away into a comparatively small space. No *Samurai's* household was complete without a special box in which to keep and transport the armour. These chests were usually mounted on six small wooden legs and were normally covered with thick black lacquer, a form of decoration in which the Japanese seem to have delighted.

Like the sword makers, armourers suffered an eclipse when the Emperor Meiji amended the older feudal system and created a standing army on the Western pattern in 1868. There was a brief reappearance of the old glory, with *samurai* wearing their armour and using their swords, when a revolt against the Emperor broke out in 1877. A few armourers continued in production, until the 1940s, but in general the drabness of modern war had replaced the ancient glamour.

Fig. 94: Uniform—Ting kia—of 19th Century Chinese court official; numerous plates are riveted on the inside of the long tunic, and the helmet has a silver skull. (Wallace Collection.)

British
Uniform:
The Early
Years

17ᵗʰ Regiment of Foot.

1742.

British Uniform: The Early Years

Title page, *Fig. 95: A book of instructions for Foot Guards, 1745, includes a number of explanatory plates; this illustrates the correct response to the order* "Club your Firelock." *The belt with sword and bayonet, the cartridge box and the long gaiters are all characteristic of the period.*

Left, *Plate 15: This is a page from a bound volume of plates completed in 1742 and known as* "*A Representation of the Cloathing of His Majesty's Household and all the Forces upon the Establishment of Great Britain and Ireland.*" *Each plate shows the uniform of one regiment, both infantry and cavalry. The 17th Regiment of Foot later became The Leicester Regiment, and this soldier wears the typical long gaiters and collarless coat of the period.*

Right, *Fig. 96: The seal of Edward I (1272–1307) shows the three leopards often described as three lions, on the king's shield and horse trapper; they first appeared on the Great Seal of Richard I in 1198.*

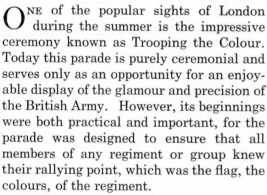

ONE of the popular sights of London during the summer is the impressive ceremony known as Trooping the Colour. Today this parade is purely ceremonial and serves only as an opportunity for an enjoyable display of the glamour and precision of the British Army. However, its beginnings were both practical and important, for the parade was designed to ensure that all members of any regiment or group knew their rallying point, which was the flag, the colours, of the regiment.

Primitive warfare had no need of such fripperies, for each member of a war band would have been known to the others. With the Red Indians of North America all members of a war party were volunteers from the same tribe. In general each tribe tended to have its own particular style of painting for war—the Dacotahs, for instance, normally had one half of the face painted red and the other half black. As civilisation developed and towns grew the old personal acquaintanceship gradually faded, and it happened that men from the same town could find themselves grouped with fellow citizens whom they had never seen before and would probably never see again. It therefore became essential that they should have some means of distinguishing these colleagues from the enemy. One of the systems used was the standard, a rallying sign which could be used to lead an army into action and indicate the direction in which the attack should be made. One of the best known of all such standards was, of course, the Roman eagle which, apart from displaying the signs of victories and credits gained by a legion, also encouraged a feeling of group identification; the standard came, in certain ways, to personify the legion. The story related by Caesar in his *Gallic Wars*, of the standard bearer who leaped from the boat when the rest of his legion hesitated, dismayed by the wild looking Britons, is well known. The risk of their standard's capture was sufficient to overcome their momentary fear, and they leapt to the attack.

Effective though the banner was, it had its limitations, for once the battle was joined and confusion reigned it was often difficult to see the banner let alone recognise it. In such battles as Hastings there was probably no great difficulty in distinguishing friend from foe for, apart from the fact that the majority of Normans were mounted and clean shaven and the British were largely infantry and well bedecked with moustaches and long hair, there was, of course, a language difference. In other less clearly defined battles the problem was no doubt alleviated by a chain of recognition in that the leader of one section of the army or battle would be well known to his main officers who, in turn, would be recognised by their subordinates, who would be known to their own particular group of soldiers. No doubt in battle half an eye would be kept on the leader so that instructions could be given and appropriate action taken. However, with the gradually increasing coverage given by armour the problem was further intensified. Facial recognition after about the early 13th Century became impossible, for the head was completely enclosed by a barrel-shaped helm. It became imperative that some form of easy recognition be adopted before a fatal mistake occurred. It was in these conditions that the formula of heraldry was born, and from these simple beginnings was to develop a complicated and involved science.

No doubt the original choice of a badge by any one person was very much a matter of personal preference; landmarks, battles, local customs, physical features, legends were all utilised for some of the original emblems. Once selected the emblem—for probably in the beginning it was no more than a simple device—could be applied to any convenient surface. Shields were obvious places on which to display this emblem and indeed the Greeks, Romans and Normans, among others, are shown in various illustrations bearing devices on the shield. Selection and use of such badges seems to have been quite haphazard and possibly varied from battle to battle. Under the laws of heraldry, once the emblem had been selected it became the "trade mark" of a particular family. It might be modified as a result of marriage or some other event,

Fig. 97: By the 14th Century heraldry had developed into a far more complicated system, as in this representation of Hartman von Kroneberg, which shows a great crest fitted to the top of his helm.

but basically it remained with that family. However, as the number of people claiming the right to use these emblems increased, more complex and involved devices had to be evolved. Even so confusions arose and quarrels broke out between families over the right to bear a particular badge. So complicated did the situation become that in 1483 the College of Heralds was constituted as the final authority to examine and settle such disputes. The use of these personal arms became, in effect, a mark of property and was placed on pewter, cutlery and weapons as well as being worn as a badge by retainers of the family. Here then is what may be described as one of the first forms of uniform, the use of heraldic devices.

Nobles often recruited bodies of men and dressed them in a form of uniform bearing the family badge—livery—and this practice reached its peak during the Wars of the Roses. During this period most of the fighting was done by the retainers of the various noble families. King Henry VII proclaimed the Statute of Liveries; by forbidding the wearing of livery the king was seeking to sweep away the last of these personal armies. Some idea of the size of the problem may be gained from the report that when the Earl of Warwick attended a Great Council of Westminster in January 1458 he brought with him a retinue of some 600 men each of whom was dressed in a red jacket which was decorated with part of his coat of arms, the ragged staff.

Similarly, troops provided by towns or villages, as required by various statutes, were sometimes equipped with coats which were also of the same colour or pattern. In 1470 it was reported that each of the men from Canterbury wore a red coat with a white rose on it. Red was not the only colour used, for as early as the reign of Edward III there were references to jackets of white bearing the red cross of St. George. This style of coat was also worn in 1480, certainly by artillery men.

One of the first groups to wear the King's

Fig. 98: This cuirassier, illustrated in a book of 1632, wears a long scarf or sash as a means of identification. Tied crossways round the body over the breastplate, it was coloured according to the order of the commanding officer.

Livery as its uniform were the Yeomen of the Guard, whose prime purpose was to guard the king, although they also served as a nucleus of the army in time of war. In 1470 their uniform was apparently green and white, but at the coronation of Henry VIII in 1509 the Lord Chamberlain's records show that they were each issued with several yards of red cloth. When Henry VIII met King Francis I of France near Guynes, in 1520, each sought to outdo the other in the glamour and colour of their respective retainers' uniforms. Pictures of the time show Yeomen of the Guard wearing coats of red with puffed sleeves decorated with bands of black, and with the Rose and Crown on breast and back; the breeches and hose seem to have been a matter for individual choice. Although one would have thought it a most impractical colour for war, white seems to have been very popular, and accounts of the Great Muster of London in 1539 make frequent references to such coats. Queen Mary seems to have favoured white although in 1556 the City of Reading dressed their levy of men in blue coats with a red cross device. In order to retake the town of Calais the City of London raised a force of 1,000 men, equipped with white coats charged with red crosses.

During the last quarter of the 16th Century red gradually began to predominate as far as British soldiers were concerned, but there were as yet no official regulations from the Government about the choice of colour. Certain orders specifically state that coats were to be of such colour as "You can best provide".

From the early part of the 17th Century a simple and cheaper method of distinguishing friend from foe was adopted, and this was the use of a scarf. Frequently the colour of the scarf was based on some colour used in the arms of a leader. This sash, or scarf, was either wound round the neck,

Left, *Fig. 99: A Gentleman Pensioner of 1687, typical of most officers of the period, with full-skirted coat and heavily decorated turn-back cuffs.* **Below,** *Fig. 100: This rather depressed-looking gentleman is a Yeoman of the Guard of the same period. His uniform, complete with the Royal Cypher on the breast, is basically the same as that worn today.*

tucked into the belt, or worn as a sash across the breastplate. The "scarves" were, in fact, more correctly sashes, if the one at the Victoria and Albert Museum is any indication, for it is nearly 9 feet long. This means of identification continued in use well into the middle of the 17th Century.

One serious problem facing all troops engaged in the English Civil Wars (1642–48) was the fact that both sides tended to wear the same coloured coats. Strangely enough the Roundheads, usually accepted as being dour and less colourful, seem to have used a larger variety of colours than the Royalists, who limited their choice largely to red, white or blue and perhaps green. Among the colours used by Parliamentary troops may be noted orange, grey, blue, green and even some purple. These standard coats were primarily worn only by the ordinary troopers; officers, both commissioned and non-commissioned, supplied their own equipment and dress and were, presumably, far more varied. During this period there occur oblique references to the use of lace on some of the military uniforms. Embroidered badges too were beginning to make their appearance, indicated by such references as the taking of prisoners at the siege of York who had crosses embroidered on their coats. The Provost Marshal had his men distinguished by crossed swords embroidered on their coats. The overall conclusion is that the traditional red coat was beginning to predominate. Any uniformity of colour seems to have been limited to the long coat, for there is little evidence to suggest that breeches, socks or shoes were, in any sense, uniform. The same was true of the headgear, for although broad-brimmed felt hats seem to have been very popular there are also references to some form of cap, and obviously many men on both sides wore some form of helmet. In the case of the cavalry it would probably have been a burgonet, and for those on foot it would have been a morion or pikeman's pot. Most of the evidence suggests that

what uniformity there was applied primarily to the infantry, since the cavalry was, in general, recruited from the wealthier members of both sides. Many riders were almost certainly still dressed in their ordinary everyday wear and there seems to have been no attempt to standardise dress.

Obviously, with this common use of similar colours on both sides, some additional means of identification was essential —hence the need for the scarf or sash. Again both sides seem to have varied their colours although, in general, red seems to have been more popular with the Royalists both as a scarf and as a hatband, whilst Parliament preferred the orange, tawny colours taken from the Earl of Essex's coat-of-arms. Even with the use of such coloured scarves mistakes no doubt arose, but there was an additional safeguard known as the field sign. This could be anything conveniently to hand, such as a bunch of leaves or a piece of white paper, anything which could easily be tucked into a hatband or under a sash, or attached to the coat in some way. Presumably orders of the day must have been passed along giving details of this field sign so that it would be known to the troops. It is also reported that a reverse procedure was adopted; Prince Rupert issued instructions during the campaign around Bristol, that officers and soldiers were not to wear any neck bands or handkerchiefs around the neck.

It is also during this period that the first references appear to the introduction to another feature which was to become general throughout the British Army. "Facings" were extra lines of colour seen, normally, at the lapels and cuffs, and which were made by lining the jackets with material of a different colour so that as the lapels and cuffs were turned back the inside colour became visible. These facings were to become one of the main distinguishing features of the various regiments during the 18th and 19th Centuries. When the New Model Army was created further steps

Below, *Fig. 101: An officer of the Norfolk Militia in 1759, wearing the skirt of his coat buttoned back, and the boots which replaced the old long gaiters.* **Opposite,** *Fig. 102: Bandsmen's uniforms were usually very ornate; this coat was worn by a drummer of the Royal Artillery in about 1750.* (*National Army Museum.*)

seem to have been taken and red became more or less the general colour for all troops, although facings varied from regiment to regiment.

With the Restoration and the return of Charles II in 1660 a reorganisation of the army was obviously essential; many regiments were disbanded and others were retained in what became, in effect, the British Standing Army. Among those to be retained were, of course, the horse guards and the foot guards. There were three troops of Horse Guards, the King's, The Duke of York's and the Duke of Albermarle's. The King's troop appears to have have been dressed in red with blue facings, and there is a mention of gold lace being fitted to the coats. The Dukes' troops were distinguished by the absence of lace on their jackets, and a further distinction was made between the troops by the feathers in their hats—the King's troop had white feathers, as did the Duke of York's, whereas the Duke of Albermarle's troops had no feathers but wore a crimson ribbon. When General Monck died in 1670 there was some renaming of the second and third troops; the second became the Queen's Guards and the third the Duke of York's. Again, there were distinctions between the three regiments, and by now the use of facings and lace was firmly established.

It was during this period that a new type of soldier was coming into general service with many Continental armies and was also being introduced into the British forces. With the appearance of gunpowder explosive projectiles of various kinds were developed and amongst these was the grenade, or, as it was known then, the grenado. In this period they were essentially metal cases holding a charge from which projected a length of slow match fuse; the fuse was lighted and the grenade thrown. For this weapon it was desirable to have strong men who could throw long distances, and such troops derived their name from the grenade and were known as

Grenadiers. These specialist groups were to form an essential part of most regiments from then on. Presumably for reasons of convenience, Grenadiers were issued not with the conventional broad-brimmed hat, but with a peculiar fur cap; this was a cylindrical fur hat with a lining which hung down over the fur. Most other soldiers of this period wore a black felt hat with a low crown and a fairly wide brim. The style of wearing the hat varied quite considerably; the brim was sometimes worn pinned up at one side, sometimes at both sides, and

Below, *Fig. 103: In 1768 a Clothing Warrant decreed that Grenadiers' caps should be of black bear skin with a metal plate at the front bearing the "King's Crest". On the back was a grenade motif, with the regimental number; this example is of the 97th Foot.* **Opposite**, *Fig. 104: Uniform of an officer of the 7th Light Dragoons, c. 1786. The 1768 Warrant stated that Light Dragoon coats "may be without lace or embroidery", but the Colonel had the option of having the button holes decorated if he wished. (National Army Museum.)*

sometimes with the sides arranged to form a triangular, three-cornered hat, and this latter was to remain popular for some considerable time.

In the early 1680s when companies of Grenadiers were added to each regiment distinctions were made between various regiments by such means as the colour of the buttonholes. For example, the King's troop Grenadiers had red coats lined with blue, the button holes being blue with yellow tufts. The Queen's troop had red coats lined with blue, but the coat loops were green with yellow tufts. The third troop, the Duke of York's, had all yellow button loops.

Towards the end of the 17th Century references suggest that it was becoming more or less normal practice to issue full uniforms including coat, breeches, shirts, shoes, stockings and a hat. A further change which took place around this time was the replacement of the wide collar which had been worn by most of the infantry. In its place a neck scarf or cravat came into general use. In the same period sashes were worn by most troops, and there was a continuation of the idea of wearing sashes coloured to indicate the various regiments; the foot guards, for example, had white sashes with blue fringes, while the Royal Scots wore all white sashes.

Uniforms were beginning to get more and more elaborate and complex, and by the 1680s many officers were wearing coats decorated with silver and gold lace as well as scarves of gold and silver taffeta with fringes of gold and silver, and even the privates' hats were laced with silver and decorated with ribbons.

James II created a number of regiments which were to become well established, one of the first being the Fusiliers. At the time of their inception they were intended as guards to watch over the artillery trains. Naturally such slow-moving columns were particularly vulnerable to ambush and surprise attack, and it was intended that the

Fusiliers, armed with flintlock muskets, should serve as a selective defence force. Their uniform is described as being a red coat with yellow lining, worn with great breeches and stockings.

True uniformity was still a long way off, since the Colonel—the commanding officer —was the proprietor of the regiment. He received certain allowances, and from this money he was expected to supply all the uniforms and equipment of his troops. Inevitably there were variations and discrepancies, and sometimes downright swindles, perpetrated under this system. Some, to save money, bought cheap material and shoes and often reduced the ornamentation to a minimum. Fortunately for the British soldier there arrived on the scene during the reign of James II that great organiser and general, John Churchill, Duke of Marlborough. It was Marlborough who introduced the sealed pattern scheme whereby tenders were invited for the supply of uniforms, or indeed any of the equipment of the army; examination was carried out of the various samples submitted, and one selected. The chosen sample was then sealed and became the pattern on which all other orders had to be based.

In 1707 a Royal Warrant set up the ''Board of General Officers'', which was composed of a group of Colonels; one of their tasks was to supervise the supply of equipment, and the patterns selected as described above were ordered to be kept at the office of the Controller of Accounts at Whitehall. The Board of General Officers also drew up regulations controlling the scale of supply of uniform, stipulating how long certain items should be expected to last. It is interesting to note that among the regulations laid down by them in 1708 is one which states that Sergeants, Corporals, Drums, Trumpeters and Hautboys were to wear the same type of uniform as the ordinary foot-soldier, but of a generally better standard all round.

Opposite, *Fig. 105: The coat of a common soldier of the 1st Foot Guards,* circa *1790. Normally this coat was worn open from the breast down; it has blue facings.* (*National Army Museum.*)

At the beginning of the 18th Century the general infantry uniform consisted of a long coat reaching roughly to the knees and with fairly wide skirts. There were two large pockets situated well below the waist, and large, wide, folded-back cuffs. Down the front a number of buttons and the corresponding buttonholes were decorated with lace ribbon, whilst the edges of pockets, cuffs, and so on would bear the various facings of the regiments. The legs were protected below the breeches either by thick stockings or spatterdashes, which were long gaiters buttoned up at the side and tied at the knee. The hat was generally in the three-cornered style, although the Grenadier cap had been somewhat modified by this period and the tapered cloth bag fitted on the inside of the fur lining had been stiffened so that it was strong enough to stand on its own. A number shown in pictures of the time are fitted with quite high front sections, some of which bear the king's cypher, and others are decorated with a small embroidered grenade. The soft cloth section was often supported by a stiffened front panel and this might well be decorated either with the arms of the colonel or the badge of the regiment and its name.

With the advent of the Hanoverian succession a number of minor changes took place, such as the introduction of the arms of Hanover including the white horse—a feature incorporated into the insignia of many of the regiments of the period, whose use continues even today.

Basically the uniform changed but little, although the grenadier or "mitre" cap with its embroidered badges was now firmly established, albeit with regimented differences. Most were fairly tall, with a little tuft at the crown and a peak which was folded up, and bore on the front flap the white horse of Hanover. Coats were fairly long and wide-skirted, the majority of them red, lined of course with a different coloured material. Beneath was worn a waistcoat which also appears to have been red; both stockings and gaiters were worn by various regiments. Cuffs were very large, folded back and decorated with the lace appropriate to the regiment. For the ordinary infantryman the main distinction lay in the use of a three-cornered hat rather than the mitre cap.

WITH the accession of George II slightly more definite evidence becomes available as to details of the uniform, for during his reign a number of official decrees or warrants were issued by the authorities stipulating dress requirements. In 1742 *"A Representation of the Clothing of His Majesty's Household and all the Forces upon the Establishments of Great Britain and Ireland"* was officially published; this book consists of a number of paintings showing men of all the various regiments. In 1743, 1749 and 1751 further clothing warrants were issued, but it must not be assumed that the details given therein necessarily applied to each and every regiment. In many cases variations were tacitly accepted and true uniformity was as yet some distance in the future. One very interesting feature of the warrant of 1742 is

that it specifies that, in future, no change may be made to the uniform of a regiment by the Colonel without special permission of His Majesty or the Captains General. As far as can be judged the general fashion was still a large, loose coat, but the cuffs had become far more elaborate, many of them being decorated with buttons and laced buttonholes. The inside lining was still of a different colour. It was during this period that it became common practice to fold back and hook up the skirts of the coat, probably to reduce the inconvenience when marching. The old greatcoat was, as per regulations, cut down after being worn for a year to make the waistcoat, and in almost every case the waistcoat is, therefore red—there are one or two exceptions as with all these generalisations. The breeches, too varied in colour; Royal regiments such as the Foot Guards wore blue breeches, but the majority were red. A wide belt encircled the waist, and another crossed the shoulder and was held in place by the waist belt, which was buckled over it. The shoulder belt supported a pouch, probably of leather and usually decorated with the crown and "G.R." From the waist belt hung a suspension frog which secured the bayonet and the small sword (or "hanger") which was still carried by the troops of this period. From the shoulder belt were suspended a pricker—a sharpened piece of metal—and a small brush, which were used by the infantryman to clean the touchhole of his musket. On the march the men's legs were protected by brown gaiters, probably made of canvas or some hard-wearing material, which fastened down the side with small black buttons. For ceremonial occasions and parade wear they also carried a pair of white gaiters. In the case of the infantry a cartridge box was fastened to the waist belt by means of a strap.

During the second half of the 18th Century there were considerable changes in the uniforms worn, and new styles of coat, hat, and indeed all other equipment

appeared. From 1768 a new general uniform was adopted by the British Army. Many Grenadier companies replaced their old mitre cap by a fur cap of somewhat similar shape but with a metal plate in front instead of the older embroidery. Further distinction was made by the Grenadier officers wearing epaulettes on each shoulder, whereas other officers wore only one on the right. Waistcoats and coat linings of buff or white replaced the older colours; the one exception was for members of Light Companies, who retained red waistcoats. These new-style troops were equipped with uniforms which reflected a concern for practical usage rather than for mere finery. In place of the long, wide-skirted coat they wore a jacket finishing just below the waist. Officers of Light Companies, like those of the Grenadiers, wore epaulettes on both shoulders. Footwear was also more varied, with some troops wearing boots reaching nearly to the knee whilst many others wore a half-gaiter covering the shoe and reaching to mid-calf.

The campaigns fought in thickly wooded country during the American War of Independence were responsible for a general simplification of uniforms, and braiding and loops were often removed, although many units retained decoration around the button-holes. Equipment was also simplified, and it was decided that infantry had little real need for a sword; these were withdrawn from service, leaving only the bayonet to be carried on the belt.

Opposing the British forces was an army which had no uniform to speak of; many soldiers were still wearing their everyday work clothes, and were recognisable as troops only by the weapons they carried. Some wore uniforms, for there had been colonists serving in the militia units in North America and these, presumably, continued to wear their uniforms although the badges of King George were certainly removed. Many of the other forces wore the hunting shirt recommended by their commander, George Washington. In 1775 Congress selected a brown uniform, but in 1779 it was finally decided that the main colour would be blue, with white linings for the infantry. Cuffs, collars and lapels would be varied in colour according to the home territories of the regiments.

With the peace of 1783 British troops were withdrawn from the new United States of America, but in a very short time they were to be committed to the long and bitter wars against Napoleonic France. As a result of these protracted campaigns and the new ideas engendered, uniforms were to undergo even more radical changes in Britain and Europe.

Fig. 106: Although the long-tailed coat was modified early in the 19th Century to a shorter coatee, the tails were retained on the uniforms of many staff officers. This is the coatee of a Lieutenant General of the Army Staff, circa 1813. (National Army Museum.)

9

British Uniform Since 1800

British Uniform Since 1800

I F there is any thread of general development to be discerned in the history of uniforms during the 18th and 19th Centuries it is the change from florid extravagance to drab practicality. The American War of Independence (1775–1783) undoubtedly played a part in starting this trend, for in this conflict the British fought a new type of war against a determined, resourceful enemy who ignored European conventions. As a result a new approach was developed, a more flamboyant attitude was evolved and this was reflected, to a degree, in uniform styles.

During the American War French troops had fought against their traditional enemies the British, and contributed towards the successful conclusion of military operations in North America which led to the birth of the United States. It may be that some of the ideas of personal freedom common among British and Colonials alike were taken back to France and contributed, in some small measure, towards the spread of liberal thought. In 1789 the French Revolution broke out; every established tradition and convention was questioned and fortunes were turned upside down. In face of all expectations the ragged, ill-equipped French Revolutionary armies survived the attacks of Austria and Prussia and even inflicted defeats on them. A tremendous sense of pride and achievement was engendered, and the leaders realised only too well that anything which could

Keith's Soldiers Assistant.

Soldier under Arms.

Fig. 109: Uniform coatee of a Captain of the Amounderness Militia, c.1813, with high collar and single rows of buttons. (National Army Museum).

enhance this feeling was to be welcomed. A sense of "belonging" was desirable, and a common uniform could be a tremendous help in achieving this feeling. The appeal of a uniform depends to a degree on its appearance, and as many of the new leaders lacked the inhibitions and "taste" of the "aristos", they delighted in frills, fopperies, fashion and self adornment. Even the great Napoleon had his moments, and his coronation costumes evoked protest from his brothers. This increased opulence in military fashion was not limited to the French; troops of émigrés and foreign legions added some rather bizarre features to the ranks of the British Army.

In 1798 Napoleon led his troops to Egypt, and was very taken with the mysterious East; and although the campaign which had begun so brilliantly ended tragically, the French did not forget it. Mamelukes, the military rulers of Egypt, apparently caught the French imagination, and many of their

drummers and bandsmen, among others, were decked out in versions of the Egyptian dress.

The French armies, flushed with success, took even greater pleasure in dashing uniforms and, under Napoleon, French control spread further and further across Europe. More and more small states and principalities were called upon to contribute troops to Napoleon's armies, and consequently the brilliance and colour of the uniforms became even more varied. It is impossible to generalise on French uniforms of the Napoleonic period, for the diversity of colours, facings, fittings and extra adornments in the way of epaulettes, feathers, buttons, belts and straps is staggering. Tunics and coats were of every shape, style and colour; green, red, yellow, white, and almost every shade of blue from a light sky blue to near-black. Apart from tunics of a single colour there were, of course, many combinations; red coats with gold trimmings, blue with fawn, yellow and red, blue and red, white and green, and so on *ad infinitum*. Trousers were equally diverse, sometimes of the same colour as the tunic, equally often of a completely different colour. Epaulettes, lace, braid, facings, stripes, coloured patches, folds, embroidery and innumerable patterns of buttons decorated coat and trousers. Footwear was only a little less diverse, for many of the troops had boots reaching to the knee, while others had button gaiters up to the thigh; some had half-gaiters, and still others were fitted with high boots reaching well up to mid-thigh.

Headwear had always been a favourite uniform accessory, and French-inspired styles were later to be adopted by many other armies. At the outbreak of the Revolution most of the French infantry favoured either a tall fur mitre-cap, a cocked bicorne hat or a leather helmet with a fur crest, not unlike that worn by some British troops. During the Egyptian campaign a form of helmet called a shako first began to figure in the illustrations of the period. These were of many shapes, but probably the most common was the bell-top form which widened gradually from the brim to the crown. A small peak gave some protection to the eyes and a chin chain was secured at either side by a large, circular boss. Decoration comprised any combination of plaited cords draped across the front, badges, and a range of plumes, tufts and pompoms which beggars description. Some of the plumes stood over twelve inches tall whilst others, although shorter, had a diameter of three or four inches. Another popular item of headgear was the *bonnet à poil*—a tall bearskin particularly favoured by such groups as the Grenadiers of the *Garde Imperiale*, *Chasseurs à Pied* and *Grenadiers à Cheval*, although similar patterns were also worn by troops from some of the German States, among others.

Cavalry uniforms were even more glamorous than those of the infantry; units such as the Cuirassiers wore heavy breast and back plates and a helmet of steel and brass with a peak and high comb, decorated with a red plume and horse hair crest. Carabiniers had a similar shaped helmet but with a much higher crest of red or white. One group of light cavalry, the Hussars, were considered particularly dashing; some wore the bell-topped shako but others wore a high-crowned cylindrical version. The feature which particularly distinguished this group was the extra fur-trimmed jacket, or *pelisse*, which hung from the right shoulder, derived from the wolf skins which the original Hungarian riders were said to have carried. Across the front of their tunics were loops of braid connecting lines of ball-like buttons.

From distant Poland Napoleon included among his forces some light cavalry who fought with lances. Apart from their lances this group were distinguished by their peculiar hat, known as a *tschapka*. Its origins lay in a cloth cap of the 17th Century, but by the end of the 18th Century it

had acquired its distinctive form, which was a flat-topped, four-sided cap with a small peak, and once again the inevitable cords and plumes.

Opposing the French armies on many fronts, at various times, were Prussians, Austrians, Russians and Spaniards, and in many cases their uniforms were as spectacular as those of the French. Many favoured bell-topped shakos which were surmounted by sundry plumes, some of which were long and thin, while others were extremely thick and short. Most of the troops, both infantry and cavalry, were equipped with belts which passed over the shoulders. These belts, often double, held the cartridge box and bayonet or sword—frequently both together. In the case of cavalry a single cross belt was often fitted with a spring clip which engaged with a ring fitted to the stock of a carbine.

Fig. 110: Short tailed coatee of an officer of the 14th Light Dragoons, c.1838, with the very high collar of the period. (National Army Museum).

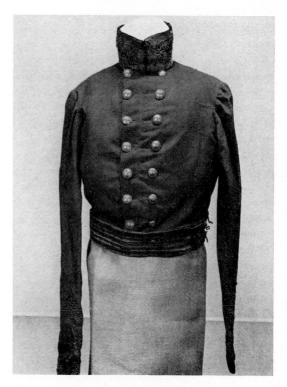

CONSISTENTLY opposing the French for twenty years, in one part of the world or another, were, of course, the British forces. In the years following the American conflict their uniforms had undergone certain changes which had generally been towards simplification. The earlier long-tailed coat had largely been replaced by a shorter skirted one which now buttoned to the waist. For the infantryman lapels were abolished in 1797, so that he now wore a single-breasted red jacket. From the shoulders padded wings stood out; his legs were covered by long, overall lined trousers reaching to the ankles, and in place of the long gaiters most troops wore a much shorter "spatterdash" covering the foot and extending a short way up the leg.

Below, Fig. 111: Full dress tunic of a Captain (crown and star on the collar) dating from c. 1856. It has a single shoulder cord, and the buttons bear the number of the 34th (The Cumberland) Regiment. (National Army Museum). Opposite, Fig. 112: NCOs and men of the 2nd Duke of Cornwall's Light Infantry in full kit, c. 1890, including two pouches each holding 50 rounds. The total weight carried in the Slade-Wallace pouches and knapsacks was about 50 lbs.

Some of the infantry of the line and marines wore what was essentially a top hat, whilst the Scottish troops had a low-crowned feather bonnet, but in 1800 a new style cap known as the shako was adopted. Made of japanned leather, it was cylindrical, flat-topped and fitted with a small peak, while a coloured plume was mounted centrally at the front. A lighter version, made of felt, soon replaced the heavier model and in 1812 the so-called Waterloo pattern was introduced. Although the crown was lowered a false front gave it the appearance of being as tall as the earlier version. Plumes were retained and the plaited cord draped across the front was, for most of the infantry, white, but for officers crimson and gold. Most of the infantry, both regular and volunteer, wore wide double cross-belts made of white leather, supporting a cartridge box and bayonet.

English cavalry uniforms, like those of the French, tended to be rather more picturesque, and the Dragoon Guards wore a helmet not greatly dissimilar from the French pattern. It had a horse hair plume, a peak, and a crest of bearskin with white cockades. Light Dragoons favoured a smaller metal helmet with a lower bearskin crest, but in 1812 this was replaced by a bell-topped shako with tall horse hair plume. A shako was also worn by the Hussars, but the hat which became characteristic of this group was that known in Britain as a busby. Originally from Hungary, the Hussars had worn a cap not unlike the early mitre cap, with a central cloth bag, and trimmed with fur. The fur section was made taller, the coloured bag was allowed to flop down from the centre, and a tall, feathered plume was mounted centrally at the front. Picturesque, but impractical, these fur caps were often replaced by a more conventional shako.

At the beginning of the 19th Century a new colour, green, made its appearance amongst the uniforms of Great Britain. During the American War of Independence

the British forces had been impressed, often at the cost of high casualties, by the efficiency, accuracy and tremendous power of the Americans' long-barrelled Pennsylvanian or Kentucky rifles. This, and other factors, induced the British authorities to consider the introduction of riflemen into the permanent establishment of the British army and in 1800 the 95th Regiment of Foot was raised. These troops were fitted with green uniforms, the idea being that they would be used for forays, scouting and skirmishing and therefore needed to be as inconspicuous as possible.

With the ending of the Napoleonic wars in 1815 the natural tendency would probably have been towards further simplification, but at that time the effective ruler of England was, of course, the Prince Regent, and this plump gentleman had an outstanding interest in matters sartorial. He extended this interest to military costume, and when his coronation took place in 1821 he indulged to the full his civilian taste for elaborate clothing. One of the lasting results of his interest was the reintroduction of the cuirass to the British Household Cavalry. Although the French cavalry had retained the cuirass during the late wars,

British cavalry had abandoned body armour in the early 18th Century, and that issued to the Household Cavalry was essentially ceremonial rather than practical. As Prince Regent, George had ordered the Household Cavalry to wear a steel helmet decorated with gilt laurel leaves and with a tall, exaggerated bearskin crest which made the helmet very top heavy.

George IV may well have been condemned by many of the troops for his introduction of picturesque if somewhat impractical uniforms, but he must be credited with the introduction of official Dress Regulations. These were first issued in 1822 and set out in detail the uniforms to be worn by officers of each regiment; unfortunately the details of other rank's uniforms were not included, which means that the picture is incomplete. Even though Dress Regulations specified what should be worn it is by no means certain that the named regiments adhered strictly to the regulations, and a number of variants are to be seen in the illustrations of the period. Dress Regulations have been issued subsequently at irregular intervals, right up to the present day.

During the reign of William IV, short though it was, a surprising number of alterations were made in details of the uniform; this monarch appears to have had a marked preference for red—it seems to have been his policy to convert all units to red. In 1835 the tall feathered plume previously worn with the infantry shako was abandoned, and in its place a ball made of worsted wool was substituted.

In 1830 another important change had taken place; the lace, that is the coloured embroidery on the uniform or shako of the infantry, was fixed as being gold for regular officers and silver for officers of the militia (see Plate 17). The militia was a system of local second-line defence which was established constitutionally after the Restoration in 1662, and consisted of troops who were summoned by ballot to serve in the militia for a specified period of time. Normally limited to home service, they could voluntarily transfer for service overseas. The method of selection varied; in general it was by ballot, but it was possible, in certain circumstances, to pay a substitute to serve.

As far as British uniforms were concerned it is probably true—as far as any generalisation is true—to say that they reached their peak in colour and glamour during the first half of the 19th Century, and from thenceforward the trend was towards a simpler style. The reasons for this were complex, but practicality was one very important factor.

Below, *Fig. 113: Mounted drummer of the 6th Dragoon Guards, wearing a white metal helmet. The 6th Dragoons normally wore white plumes on the helmet, and at the horse's throat. Circa 1900.* **Opposite,** *Fig. 114: Sergeant of the 3rd Grenadier Guards, c.1901; the tunic buttons are arranged singly, whereas those of the Coldstream Guards are in pairs, the Scots Guards in threes, the Irish Guards in fours and the Welsh Guards in fives.*

In 1844 the old, rather top-heavy bell-topped shako, introduced in 1815 and modified in 1839, was replaced by the so-called Albert pattern shako which, in some ways, was not dissimilar from the old Waterloo pattern. It stood some 7 inches tall had a leather top, and besides the conventional front peak had a small rear peak. Other ranks wore an ordinary leather chinstrap but the officers' model had a gilt chin chain with links decreasing in size towards the centre. A large worsted ball, the top two-thirds white and the remainder red, was fitted centrally at the front of the crown. The Albert pattern shako was to remain in service until 1855 when a slightly different pattern with a lower crown was adopted. It retained the peaks at back and front, but this time the back tapered towards the crown and the chin strap was of black leather. This pattern remained in service until 1861, when another new type was introduced; it was basically similar, although with a lower crown, and the outer covering was attached to the cork base by sloping lines of stitching. This shako had been in service for some eight years when it was replaced by a similar pattern which lacked the stitching and back peak, and had in its place braid around the top and down the sides. In place of the old leather strap a metal chin chain of interlocking rings was fitted.

I N 1854 the Crimean War broke out; this futile, tragic fiasco was the first major conflict in which Britain had been involved since Waterloo. Russia stood alone against the unlikely combination of England, Turkey and France. The campaigns came as a rude shock to the militarists of the period, for much of the equipment and organisation, never before put to the acid test of active service, was found to be unsatisfactory. Shakos tended to fall apart in bad weather, and the undress cap, which was of a simple pill-box shape, was most often worn in its place. The distinction

between full dress and undress was essentially that between ceremonial and working. Modifications were made to the tunic and many of the trimmings were abandoned, leaving a basic red tunic without the regimental facings.

Experience gained in the Crimea was confirmed in the second great conflict of the mid-19th Century, in what was probably the first of the "modern" wars. In 1861 the

*Below, Fig. 115: Drum Major of the Seaforth Highlanders, c.1900; he wears an ostrich-feather bonnet with five tails, and a sporran of black and white horsehair. **Opposite**, Fig. 116: Lt. Col. A. D. Neeld, 2nd Life Guards, who served in the South African War of 1899-1901. He wears khaki uniform and holds a khaki helmet, although a white helmet with a khaki cloth cover was also worn.*

irreconcilable differences between the Northern and Southern States led to the outbreak of the American Civil War, 1861–65. Exuberant local patriotism led to the formation of many units and of these a number adopted colourful costumes based on foreign fashions, including some very picturesque versions of the French Zouaves, with baggy red trousers and short jackets, and a turban-like headdress. Alas, the rigours of compaigning soon emphasised the impractical nature of such fancies, and led to a general simplification until both sides had adopted very similar uniforms. These consisted of light blue trousers, and a jacket with skirts reaching roughly to mid thigh; in the North the tunics were dark blue and in the South a lightish grey. Again, both sides adopted very similar styles of headdress; the two most popular were the kepi, a low-crowned version of the British or French shako, and the wide-brimmed campaign hat.

In 1870 the Franco–Prussian war broke out with results that were disastrous for the French. Despite the pseudo-Napoleonic splendour encouraged, indeed positively forced upon his country by Napoleon III, the Prussians, by virtue of better equipment, better planning and greater skill, triumphed on every front. Probably feeling that imitation was the sincerest form of flattery, many nations copied certain features of the Prussian uniform. One of their common helmets had been fitted with a top spike, and in 1876 the British military authorities experimented with a cork version of the Prussian helmet. In 1879 the pattern was officially adopted, being known as "helmet, universal home pattern". For the general infantry it consisted of a cork body covered with dark blue material or, in the case of light infantry and rifle regiments, a dark green cloth. For officers the front peak was edged with brass; on either side were two bosses, in the shape of the Tudor rose, and to one the end of a linked chin chain was permanently fitted. This chain terminated with a single link which could be fixed over a hook on the opposite boss; alternatively, the chain could be draped across the front and up to a hook attached to the top boss, into which screwed the spike. The pattern designed for the artillery differed in having a cup and ball fitting in place of the spike. This helmet was not universal wear and certain regiments, such as the Fusiliers, Hussars, Lancers and Highland regiments, retained their own special style of headwear. A white-covered helmet of basically the same pattern as the 1879 model was worn by troops overseas.

By the turn of the century the British infantryman had a more or less standard uniform, which consisted of a red tunic with coloured cuffs, cloth epaulettes, dark blue trousers, boots and white webbing straps. There was at this period a move towards the abandoning of bright colours on active service. It was in India and Africa that the change was flourishing, for around the middle of the 19th Century certain troops in India, which was then a British possession, had taken to dyeing their uniforms a mud colour to afford some natural protection and camouflage. During the campaigns in South Africa the khaki colour was found to be far more satisfactory than the conspicuous red jacket and, in 1880, troops arriving from India to take part in the Boer War of 1880–81 were issued with khaki although the traditional red jacket was retained for home service. After 1886 khaki became the officially approved uniform for active service, and was used throughout the Boer War of 1899–1902. In some ways the Boer War paralleled the Crimean campaign, for in both the power of Britain was defied. In South Africa a group of fiercely independent farmers inflicted defeat after defeat on the mighty armies of Britain. Final victory came to the British, but at a heavy cost, and there were strong demands for military reforms.

British Army uniforms were now basically

of two kinds, with a colourful dress uniform and a plainer, more practical everyday pattern. On special parades and other occasions British troops appeared in all their glory, with the officers resplendent in golds, reds, bearskins, busbies and helmets. The Dress Regulations of 1900 contain eleven full plates of photographs illustrating some twenty different types of headdresses worn by the army. The total number was greater, for there were many variations on the main types.

In the same regulations there are twenty-four plates showing some of the many styles of jacket worn by the different regiments on parade or in the mess. There are no less than seventy-seven different patterns of lace to be used on uniforms illustrated in the 1900 Regulations. In truth the term "uniform" applied to military wear in the British Army was positively ludicrous—for dress was anything *but* uniform. Many regiments had special claims to exclusive

features and such rights were jealously guarded; authority usually bowed to demand and accepted the distinction. Sometimes it was an odd patch of colour, the right to a special lace or the wearing of an extra badge, as with the Gloucestershire Regiment. It was accepted that these extra distinctions gave a soldier a certain feeling of loyalty to the regiment.

Khaki was eventually approved as a general issue, and in 1902 the army officially adopted a universal service dress, although the full dress was still retained. In place of the leather or webbing gaiters worn earlier a new leg protection was adopted; in an apparently retrograde step, puttees were introduced. These were essentially khaki

Fig. 117: Men of a Royal Artillery Ammunition Column, including a Sergeant Major, gunners, trumpeter and driver. All wear field caps with chinstraps, of the sealed pattern of 1894.

bandages which were bound around the top of the boot and part of the way up the calf. Simplification was also undertaken as far as headdress was concerned and a type of cap known as the Broderick—which, having no peak, rather resembled the British sailor's cap—was issued. At the front was a red segment of material to which was attached the badge. It was extremely unpopular, and by 1905 the khaki general service peak cap was being worn by other ranks.

THE outbreak of World War I in 1914 forced upon the authorities a number of changes; khaki became standard for the British forces, with the soft field cap, generally with the wire former removed to give it a softer, non-reflecting surface, being used for the first 18 months or so. Subsequently, of course, the steel helmet became standard wear in the battle area, whilst the field service cap was normal behind-the-line wear. This move towards drabness was reflected in the uniforms of the other European powers; in 1914 both Germans and French had, on occasion, ridden into battle clad in their ceremonial uniforms. The French cuirassiers were basically no different from their ancestors who had ridden into action at Waterloo, but the machine gun and artillery provided bloody proof that the cavalry was largely obsolete in modern warfare, and the last traces of glamour disappeared from the battlefield. There were few major changes in uniform during the four years of conflict, although one new form of headdress made its appearance. In the confined quarters of the tank, introduced in 1916, it was difficult for troops to wear any sort of stiff headgear, and a beret was issued to tank crews. The Germans generally discarded their *pickelhaube*, or spiked helmet, and adopted a peakless cap.

After peace came in 1918 a war-weary world set about reducing its forces, and there were major cuts in all armies. Amalgamations and disbandments meant that many of the famous regiments of the British army disappeared. Ceremonial dress made its reappearance in the 1920s, but the general service uniform remained largely unaltered until 1938, when the so-called battledress was introduced. This consisted of khaki trousers, secured at the ankle by small webbing gaiters, and a loose fitting blouse. Numerous pockets were fitted to the uniform, including a patch pocket on one trousers' leg. Headgear was the field service cap which had been worn during the South African campaign and featured in the 1900 dress regulations. In theory this cap could be opened out to become a "balaclava" type headdress. Not all colour disappeared from the military scene, and in Britain a special walking-out dress was approved in 1936 for the coronation of

Fig. 118: General The Right Honourable Sir Redvers Buller, Commander in Chief in South Africa. His headdress, known as a busby, is of black Persian lamb. Distinction was made between the Rifle Brigade and the Rifle Regiments, which wore a red and black plume (as here) and black ostrich feathers respectively.

George VI, although it had been available to troops at their own expense for some time. It was basically an all-blue uniform, with a peaked cap bearing regimental distinctions in the form of coloured bands.

World War II saw a more general adoption of the beret, with certain distinctive colours—the newly raised Commando units, hard-hitting raiding groups, wore green, while the airborne troops took an intense pride in their maroon beret. There was also a general issue of khaki berets, although the Royal Armoured Corps retained their traditional black.

By the time World War II ended in 1945 the process of simplification had made great strides, and special forms of garment had been designed for most purposes. The widespread use of airborne troops had led to the introduction of coverall garments, to ensure that their equipment did not become entangled with the parachute lines. The camouflaged smock, "poncho", or complete combat suit was in general use among specialist troops. Special combat clothing for use in desert, jungle and Arctic terrain had been designed and issued. This process

Above, *Fig. 119: The unpopular and short-lived Broderick cap of c.1902, resembling a naval cap or the German* feldmütze. *The flash at the front was red.* **Right,** *Plate 18: Hospital Staff coat of* circa *1815. The buttons are gilt: eight on the chest, two on each sleeve, one on each cuff and three on each tail. A single metal epaulette was worn on the right shoulder. (Jeffcoat Collection)*

of simplification and practical design has continued over the last quarter century, and the modern fighting man's combat dress is completely practical, lacking all superfluous extras, and is produced only in those colours which enable him to blend into his surroundings. Generally speaking the only touch of flamboyance which survives is to be found in the head-gear worn when not actually on the battlefield; the coloured berets of specialist formations, and the bonnets of Scots regiments, are retained in the British forces of today, and the former practice has, indeed, been copied by many other nations. Airborne troops of several armies are distinguished by red berets, and the famous green berets of the United States Special Forces are copied directly from the Commandos of the Second World War.

Fortunately almost every country in the world retains at least one group of soldiers whose prime function is to look good. In France there is the *Garde Républicaine*, who wear much the same uniform as the cuirassiers who charged into battle on the field of Waterloo. Britain's Household Cavalry and Foot Guards retain their famous ceremonial dress and function, alongside their more serious rôle as élite units of the combat forces. America has the West Point Cadets, and Greece the skirted Evzones; and many of the new nations have established presidential guards, in emulation of European units whose traditions and battle-honours stretch back for centuries. Trained to perfection, and uniformed in styles which recall the glamour of old wars and dead empires, all these formations are employed in providing a spectacle for admiring crowds; for spectacle has now entirely disappeared from the ranks of the fighting regiments.

War has always been, and still is, a bloody, degrading business, but at least in the past it looked exciting. Today, with the brave colours and gorgeous display replaced by mud-coloured garments of stern practicality, it has been stripped down to its basic ugliness; the illusion of glamour, so necessary to fallible humans, has gone, and what remains is not splendid, but merely terrifying.

Fig. 120: Soft stitched cap of the First World War—this one bears the date 1918. Worn behind the lines as an alternative to the steel helmet, it was comfortable and practical—but a far cry from the finery of Wellington's armies, who marched over France and Belgium just a century before.

The Volunteers

10

The Volunteers

Title page, *Fig. 121: Officers of the City Imperial Volunteers, c.1901. Third from left is General Trotter, commander of Home District forces; he and the officer next to him wear round forage caps, while others wear the khaki-covered helmet and the slouch hat. Note the shoulder chains of the officer second from right.* **Left,** *Plate 19: Leather helmet of the Norfolk Yeomanry (The King's Own Royal Regiment.) Raised in 1901, it consisted of four squadrons with King Edward VII as the Honorary Colonel; in 1905 he became Colonel-in-Chief. At the same date the title of the unit was confirmed as the King's Own Royal Regiment of Imperial Yeomanry.* **Right,** *Fig. 122: Norfolk Yeomanry helmet, with black skull bearing a brass cross marked with the W.R. cypher, and black horsehair crest. This helmet dates from c.1831–37. (Winsbury Collection).*

THERE have always been volunteers—men who undertook military service without compulsion or pressure—but these were usually individuals; and the idea of large numbers of them joining together to form units is a fairly new concept. From the time of Ancient Greece until the Middle Ages it was understood that every freeman was available for service if the need arose; all might not be called, but they were liable. While a young Rome was struggling to survive and expand, all citizens were expected to serve in the ranks of the legions; but as her empire grew this duty was increasingly resented, and mercenaries made up a larger and larger proportion of the forces.

In Western Europe the growth of the feudal system led to a clearly defined statement of obligation. In return for protection and land a tenant was bound to serve his master, be he baron or king, for a set period in time of war. When William the Conqueror landed in England he brought with him an army largely composed of volunteers who were hopeful of fame and fortune. After his success William rewarded them

with parcels of land and, in return, they did homage to him, promising to be his men. Naturally there were changes in the system over the centuries, but the principle remained the same; when the king called, his tenants rendered service.

The basis of calculation was the knight's fee—a piece of land which was considered to be of sufficient value to support a knight on active service for forty days; in fact the size of a single knight fee varied from place to place, but the holder of a large number of fees was obliged to ensure that he provided an equivalent number of knights. In 1256 Henry III ordered that the holder of every knight's fee was to be knighted, so increasing the military strength of the nation; there was an option, in that those who did not want to accept this honour could be excused on payment of a fine. Later the feudal obligation to serve was commuted to a payment of a fixed sum known as "scutage", and the amounts collected were used to pay mercenaries. References to this payment first occur around the middle of the 12th Century, but it was almost certainly in

29th To the Left Face.

32nd Charge Bayonets.

Figs. 123 and 124 illustrate a series of engravings showing various movements of the musket, from an encyclopaedia of the late 18th Century; they are typical of a spate of works dealing with the military arts written during this period.

operation prior to this date. In Magna Carta (1215) a clause stipulated that scutage could only be imposed upon the consent of Parliament.

Whilst the knights were assembled on the basis of land holdings the greater part of the foot soldiers were raised by the *Posse Comitatus*, which meant that every male between the ages of 15 and 60 years was liable for service when called out by the sheriff, who was the king's local representative. The forces so levied were limited by law to service inside the country and were not liable to serve overseas unless there was a dire emergency—although some monarchs tended to cry emergency rather quickly!

In 1181 Henry II proclaimed "An Assize of Arms" which was later enlarged and confirmed by Edward I. The standard of equipment was regulated by a man's worldly wealth; a holder of a knight's fee was to have armour, helmet, shield and lance, as did those who held chattels or rents worth 16 marks. In 1285 the Statute of Winchester reflected the change of values, and Edward I went into greater detail; owners of land or goods worth £15 or 40 marks were to have armour, sword, dagger and a horse, but if the value was £10 or 20 marks then he was excused possession of a horse. At the other end of the scale those with means of £2–£5 were to have bows. To ensure that there was no evasion of responsibility two constables for each locality, known as a "hundred", were appointed to view the arms and report. These regulations remained in force until 1558, when Phillip and Mary altered the scales and details of equipment. Persons with an estate worth £1,000 had to keep, among other items, six horses for light cavalry use, equipment for three demi-lances, forty almaine rivets, pikes, long bows, arrows and harquebusses —a substantial arsenal. Those with goods between values of £10 and £20 had to supply a long bow, a sheaf of arrows, a steel cap and a halberd. Again, commissioners were appointed to view and check the supply of arms and armour for the local forces. Servants of those bound to supply harquebusses were ordered to practise shooting at a mark.

Whilst the *Posse Comitatus* might provide a substantial home defence force the problem of raising armies to serve overseas remained, and one answer adopted by all rulers was the hire of mercenaries. That this expedient could be a handicap is shown by another clause of Magna Carta, which demanded that when peace came all foreign soldiers "who are come with horses and armour to the prejudice of the people" shall leave the kingdom.

A surviving muster roll of the army which Edward III took to France in 1346 gives the daily rates of pay—earls 6/8d, ordinary knights 2/-, mounted archers 6d, Welsh footmen 3d, and the rest 2d a day. Some idea of the expense of war can be arrived at, for the total strength of the force is given as 31,294 with another 16,000 in the supply columns and shipping. Although the army here described was not truly mercenary in the usual sense of the word, it is reasonable to assume that the rates of pay for such troops would have been within the same range. In 1349, following the Black Death, the English Parliament drew up the Statute of Labourers; this set down that a reaper received 2d a day, a master carpenter 3d, and a journeyman 2d, whilst most foot soldiers received 6d plus a share of any loot.

True mercenaries were commonly obtained from Belgium; Brabanters and Flemings figure prominently in contemporary accounts. In Britain they were seldom a great problem but on the Continent they were a constant menace, for once they had been paid off they often became outlaw bands, preying on the countryside. During the numerous Italian campaigns many so-called "free companies" were formed; these consisted of a leader of note around whom gathered a group of mercenaries. One such group under Ruffin, or Griffith, became immensely wealthy by ravaging France

28th. To the Left Face.

31st. Shoulder Firelock.

Louis XVI's Swiss Guard remained loyal to him, and paid with their lives. On many battlefields Swiss mercenaries faced troops of German mercenaries known as Landsknechts; these groups, noted for their flamboyance, were considered to be as good as the Swiss, and retained their popularity throughout the 16th Century.

During the 15th Century France made a military innovation which was to be followed by most other European powers, for Charles VII (1422–1461) created a standing army. He raised 15 companies of cavalry (some 9,000 men) on a permanent basis, and paid them a wage. So successful was this step that in 1448 he raised a force of 16,000 infantry on the same basis.

during the period when the French King John was held prisoner in England. According to Froissart, who wrote an account of the wars in France, there were in 1361 16,000 mercenaries on the rampage—a high figure, although all medieval figures are somewhat suspect. One of the most famous of leaders was the Englishman Sir John Hawkswood, who led a band of *condottieri*—Italian mercenaries—of some 3,000 men. He was especially remarkable for his rise from common beginnings, being originally a yeoman of Essex, and ending his career as a power in Italian politics. He was also a man of honour who kept to his sworn agreement, unlike many mercenaries who cheerfully changed sides to suit their pockets.

In the 15th Century Switzerland became the supply centre of mercenaries who gained a reputation for courage, skill and loyalty. In 1480 Louis XI of France took 6,000 of them into his service, a union which was to last until the French Revolution when

IN Britain the old muster system was still in force, and under Henry VIII there were frequent summons. According to the Chronicler John Stowe, in 1539 the City of London mustered 15,000 men, "besides whifflers and awayters". Such musters were supervised by the Lord Lieutenant of the County, an office introduced by Henry VIII. At this time the only permanent standing force were the Yeomen of the Guard and a few troops maintained in Ireland, and it was these Standing Forces in Ireland that were to play an important part in the train of events which led to the English Civil Wars, 1642–48.

Parliament removed the right of impressment from Charles I, and took it upon themselves. They declined an offer from the King to raise a force of 10,000 volunteers to serve in Ireland, fearing that such an army would be used by the king for his own purposes. Events moved inexorably towards a final confrontation, and Parliament took over the command of all forces and fortified

Fig. 126: Black leather helmet with white plume and white metal fittings. A brass cross bears the device of a mounted knight in white metal and the number IX, while the scroll reads PRO ARIS ET FOCIS *and FMR—for Fifeshire Mounted Rifles. Circa 1865. (Winsbury Collection).*

places, giving orders that the king's commands were to be ignored. Open rebellion first occurred outside the gates of Hull, and in 1643 Charles I raised his royal standard at Nottingham—although, ominously, the wind blew it down. He then sent out his orders to the Commissioners of Array which, in effect, called out the local forces to support the king. In the beginning the forces of both King and Parliament depended largely on the Trained Bands, which had been established in 1572 when groups of picked men were ordered to be trained and equipped at public expense. Parliament were fortunate in having the support of the London Trained Bands, which were very efficient, but the Royalists had to recruit most of their regiments and start their training from the beginning, paying them from their own pockets. Many Royalist arms were acquired from the Trained Bands, although in some areas the authorities prevented their seizure by storing them in well-defended centres.

Parliament were fortunate in their supply position, and also in the drive of their officers; a complete overhaul and replanning led to the creation of the New Model Army, with the cavalry holding pride of place, manned by volunteers. It was undoubtedly due to the New Model Army that Parliament won the Civil Wars, and it was on this foundation that the later British Army was based.

With the restoration of Charles II in 1660, certain changes in the nature of the army were obviously necessary. Despite the rejoicing with which the king's return was greeted, Parliament and the country still bore the scars of the later wars, and viewed armies with suspicion. Obviously the king needed some troops, if only for a ceremonial bodyguard, and reluctantly Parliament accepted an establishment of five regiments. Britain now had a small standing army, and despite some alarms and excursions from the French and Dutch, the country lay safe behind the defence of the Channel.

The standing army was committed to various campaigns in Europe, but danger at home seemed non-existent until the Stuart uprising in 1745 generated great concern. The militia had continued in being, but the general lack of urgency had led to a decline in readiness, and when it was needed it was found to be in a very parlous state. A report made some little time before the invasion reported that Chester Castle was defended by 75 men who lacked ammunition or stores, and that in the whole of Lancashire there were only three inexperienced regiments of foot. Obviously, in this period of danger, something had to be done; the local authorities were given a more or less free hand to raise groups of armed men, and number of associations for defence were

Royal Victoria Rifles.

5 St Martins Place
3.ʳᵈ June 1853

Sir,

You are requested to attend a General Meeting of the **Royal Victoria Rifle Corps** to be held at the Oriental Hotel Vere Street Oxford Street on Monday the 6ᵗʰ day of June 1853 at the hour of 7 o'Clock, in the evening M.T. for the purpose of electing (by ballot) three acting Captains of Companies: the corps being now recognized as a Volunteer Corps under the Act 44 Geo 3.ʳᵈ Cap 54

I am, Sir,

Your obedient Servant,

Sir J. Phillippart

Geo. F. ___ Hon. Secretary.

N.B. The Subscription for 1853 & 4 must be paid previously to voting.

created. Northamptonshire claims one of the first, which was raised in 1744. This Northamptonshire group, in their official application, undertook to clothe and mount themselves at their own expense.

In April 1746 the Battle of Culloden spelled the end of Prince Charles' hopes, the need for volunteer units disappeared, and with grateful words of thanks from His Majesty King George the various associations were disbanded. However, the country had had a salutary shock, and it was felt that some reform was called for; and in 1757 a Militia Act was introduced which transferred the responsibility for the force to the local government officials. All men between 18 and 50 years, liable to serve, had to be listed on returns made by the local parish officials. From this list a certain number were selected by the Lord Lieutenant, by ballot, and were required to serve for three years. Training was vigorous, and throughout the year one day a month was given over to training; additionally, a full muster was held twice a year. The heavy demand on people's time made it rather unpopular but it did result in the production of a far more efficient force. In 1758 another act allowed volunteers to join the Militia in addition to those who were impressed by the ballot. In July 1759 the London Militia turned out and mounted a great review in Hyde Park before the King.

T HE Seven Years War between France and England ended in 1763; once again the immediate threat which had encouraged the growth of the Militia was removed, and once again most of it was allowed to run down. However, in 1773 the Boston Tea Party and other ominous rumblings stimulated the authorities to consider the position once again, and in 1778 Militia commanders were authorised by an Act to form volunteer companies. In 1779 an Act authorised the formation of a force of volunteers of 30,000 men in addition to the standing companies.

Opposite, *Fig. 127: Notice No. 1, calling members to a meeting to elect officers, on the reconstitution of the Royal Victoria Rifles as a regular Volunteer Corps. Printed on light blue paper, 8 by 10¼ inches.* **Above**, *Fig. 128: Shako of London Rifle Brigade, with a plume of cock's feathers, c.1870. The white metal badge incorporates a shield of City of London Arms. (Archer Collection).*

Just as the volunteer force was beginning to grow in stature and recognition the crises were resolved; peace came in North America, and Europe's problems seemed to fade into the background.

The lull was to be of short duration, for in 1789 the French Revolution broke out, and once again Britain lay in danger from her traditional enemy. It was soon apparent that conflict was almost inevitable, and in 1794 an Act authorised the formation of volunteer units. That the volunteers had a part to play in the defence of Britain was proved, somewhat hilariously, in 1797, when a force of several hundred French sailors and marines landed near Fishguard in Wales. The local Yeomanry were summoned, and the ill-prepared French force offered to discuss a truce; but Lord Cawdor, the local commander, demanded unconditional surrender and the French, rather surprisingly, agreed.

In 1797 there was a great birthday review of the Volunteers in Hyde Park, and a large number marched past His Majesty, who was reported to be much impressed by their military bearing. All over the country military enthusiasms blossomed, and the growth was further stimulated in 1803. The peace of Amiens had apparently ended the Napoleonic wars as far as Britain was concerned, but it was little more than a temporary truce, and in 1803 it became apparent from Napoleon's preparations that he was seriously considering an invasion of England. The number of volunteer units multiplied enormously, with every armed branch represented; there were even a few artillery volunteers.

The usual procedure in forming a unit was to call a meeting at which the chair was taken by some local notable. A resolution was put to the meeting that a local force should be raised, and on the formal adoption of this resolution a letter was sent to the Lord Lieutenant of the County. The offer was then passed on to Whitehall, and if it was felt that there was a need and that the company would be of reasonable efficiency, the offer was accepted and the people duly notified. After the formation had been officially approved by the Home Office the men usually elected their officers; then came the vital question of uniform, and since, in many cases, the volunteers undertook to provide their uniforms at their own expense, the choice was wide open.

The development of almost every Volunteer Unit of the Napoleonic period followed broadly the same course. The story of one small parish in London is fairly typical. On 18th July 1803 a meeting was held under the chairmanship of the Marquis of Titchfield which considered and approved a resolution that the parishes of St. Andrew and St. George should form a division, and three officers were nominated as lieutenants. It was reported to the meeting that £2,000, a very large amount in those days, had been collected voluntarily. Next there was a local meeting held in the workhouse on 27th July 1803; the very important matter of uniform was discussed and approved, and the motion reads as follows:

"Scarlet regulation jacket with blue collar and cuffs but without facings, yellow buttons, a cap with a yellow gilt star in front and regulation feather, white Kerseymere breeches with covered buttons of the same and full black cloth gaiters with black leather buttons. N.B. The waistcoat is no part of the uniform as the Regulation Jacket covers the waistcoat."

A signing-in book was made available for members of the public, who had until 15th August to enrol; those who joined could either pay £5 towards the cost of the uniform, or they could claim it free, or make a partial payment. On 25th October 1803 the official return was given as—One Lieutenant Colonel, one Major, one Adjutant, seven Captains, seven Lieutenants, six Ensigns, twenty-two Sergeants, fifteen drums and four hundred and twenty-six privates—a grand total of four hundred and eighty six. Numbers varied slightly, but generally stayed within the region of 480 to 500.

Volunteers were under military discipline, and again the records of this same St. Andrew and St. George Volunteers report that on 19th December 1803 there was a court martial of Thomas Saylor, a Drum Major, for disobedience, drunkenness and neglect of duty, etc. He was found guilty;

although the court agreed that some expressions used to him were wrong and uncalled for", he was nevertheless reduced to a fifer. Similarly, on July 12th 1804, it is reported that a Sergeant and a file of men left London to visit Farnham in Kent, to collect a deserter. He was brought back, tried, found guilty, and sentenced to 125 lashes. The records state that he was taken out and strapped up ready for his lashing but that the Major, in consideration of his past good behaviour, pardoned him. A certain amount of high spirits was evident among the local volunteers, for another plaintive statement on 7th July records that the inhabitants of Holborn had complained that after drill a number of the members fired their muskets in the street, and strict

orders were given that in future the officers were to ensure that any spare cartridges were to be taken away from the men. Shooting competitions were arranged, and on 3rd December 1804 one of the officers presented a sword which was to be shot for by the N.C.O.s and Privates on 20th and 21st December. The rules were set down on a printed slip and the sword was, in fact, won by a Sergeant whose shot was nearest the centre.

The Volunteers maintained their vigilance throughout the Napoleonic period, but in 1814 the threat seemed to be over and most of the units were officially stood down; the ballot for the Militia was suspended in May 1816. Although the Militia and Volunteers had been disbanded the Yeomanry—the mounted volunteers—were left untouched. Obviously mounted units were more capable of quick movement, and their value was enhanced by the fact that the Yeomanry tended to come from the more politically stable elements of the population. They could be called upon to serve as riot control units should the need arise.

Opposite, *Fig. 129: Cloth proficiency badge, as defined in "Regulations of Volunteer Force 1881", for wear immediately above the left cuff by members who obtained 25 points and above at ranges up to 800 yards. Red border, silver stars and rifle, 4 by 2+ inches.* **Below**, *Fig. 130: A group of the Eton Rifle Volunteers, with Enfield rifles; note the shakos and cross belts.*

One of the most tragic instances of their use was the so-called Peterloo Massacre, when eleven people were killed and many wounded by troops, including Yeomanry at a meeting held in Manchester on 16th August 1819. Similarly in 1830, when there was some unrest over the Reform Act, the Yeomanry were again called upon to serve.

There were always supporters of the Volunteer system; the Duke of Wellington was one, although the Commander-in-Chief of that time, the Duke of Cambridge, was opposed to them. A number of Volunteer units had continued to serve after the official stand-down in 1814, by converting themselves into rifle clubs so that they might legitimately continue to meet and practise shooting. One or two were, in fact, reconstituted as official volunteer units in 1852; but it was the events of the following few years, with the outbreak of the Crimean War in 1854, the Indian Mutiny in 1857, and the belligerent attitude of Napoleon III of France—who threatened to sack London and avenge the defeat of Waterloo—which really stimulated the renewed growth of the volunteers.

In 1859 the Government sent out a circular sanctioning the formation of Rifle Volunteers Corps under the Act of 1804. Besides the Rifle Volunteers, Artillery units were approved where appropriate. There was some controversy as to which was the first unit to be formed, the two chief contenders being the Victoria Rifles and the 1st Devonshire; if the test of precedence is to be accepted then the Devonshire group were accepted first by the authorities. The Army List of the period gives 94 groups of Rifle Volunteers, 62 Artillery, 21 Engineer and, surprisingly for a country so devoted to riding, only 16 Light Horse or Mounted Rifles groups. Enthusiasm for the volunteer movement was overwhelming, and units continued to spring up all over the country. There was some opposition from such characters as Sir Robert Peel, but the Royal accolade was given in March 1860 when a

Opposite, *Fig. 131: A member of the Eton Rifle Volunteers, wearing a spiked helmet bearing the badge shown in Fig. 152; the uniform was light grey.* Above, *Fig. 132: Top, Red and blue cockade of the Imperial Yeomanry, worn on the turned-up brim of the slouch hat. Left, Cap badge—with slider—of the Bristol University Officer Training Corps. Right, cap badge of the Cambridge University O.T.C.*

Royal Levee was held. No less than 3,200 officers were presented to Queen Victoria and Prince Albert, and contemporary reports comment on the variety of uniforms. It had been recommended early in the formation of the movement that the uniform should be simple; a blouse was suggested as being the best solution, and grey was a recommended colour. At the levee every shade of grey was represented, and there are references to a large number of coloured facings. Reports say that the shako was the commonest headgear, but a great variety of horsehair feathers, plumes and pom-poms were fitted. One group who stood out particularly were the officers of St. George's Guards, with their black helmets and white plumes.

As the volunteer movement became more firmly established and better organised definite rules and regulations were set down; and section 20 of the Volunteer Regulations of 1881, which deals with uniform, states that application for permission to change the colour of the uniform would be favourably considered "provided the change was to scarlet"; the Regulations also stipulated that when a corps was allowed to adopt scarlet tunics or frocks, that is patrol jackets, the facings authorised would be similar to those worn by the senior regiment "of the regular force belonging to the same district brigade". Artillery volunteers would wear scarlet and the Engineers blue cord on their tunics or braid on their "frocks". Artillery volunteers would also wear a scarlet, and Engineers a blue band and button on the forage caps. All volunteer regiments were to wear on the sleeve an Austrian knot; those in green were to have a light green knot, those in blue a scarlet knot, and those wearing scarlet a black knot, except for the Engineers. The Regulations stipulated that the corps clothed in green should adopt green facings of the same shade as their tunic or as that of the Austrian knot, and no change would be permitted "except in this direction". Rifle volunteers corps wearing a busby were to have the lower feathers and horsehair of the plume of light green if the corps wore green, or else of the colour of the facings when they were clothed in scarlet or grey.

Further recognition and encouragement of the volunteer movement was accorded in July 1860 when Queen Victoria attended a shooting competition organised by the National Rifle Association, founded in 1859, on Wimbledon Common. The Queen graciously fired the first shot and scored a bulls-eye—hardly surprising, as the rifle was mounted on a fixed rest and had previously been carefully sighted. The enthusiasm for the volunteers remained amazingly high, although there were a certain number of changes in common with

the regular forces, in designation and organisation.

IT was with the outbreak of the South African War in October 1899 that the volunteers met their greatest test. The Boers fought a campaign unlike any that the British forces had faced since the American War of Independence; in attempting to deal with this new technique the old fashioned methods of warfare proved inadequate, and Britain suffered heavy losses and many defeats. Heavy casualties, mainly from disease, created a manpower shortage and the authorities reluctantly agreed to recruit volunteers for service in South Africa. They called for men who could ride, and these volunteers were formed into the Imperial Yeomanry. The Government was not inclined to pay them, and it was set down that each member of the Imperial Yeomanry would provide his own horse and equipment. With active service in South Africa came a general adoption of khaki for the Yeomanry, and many adopted the slouch hat with one brim turned up, rather like that favoured by the Australians. In the case of one unit known as Lovat's Scouts, a patch of appropriate tartan was fixed to the upturned brim, as well as stiff hair plumes. Besides the Imperial Yeomanry units, groups of which were attached to various regiments, there were a number of separate Yeomanry units which were formed and paid for by some rich patron.

It was decided that infantry units should be raised on the same principle, and the City Imperial Volunteers were formed; this formation was made up of units of volunteers from the existing bodies. In all some 26,000 volunteers were to serve in South Africa before the end of the war. One of the oldest of the Volunteer Units, the

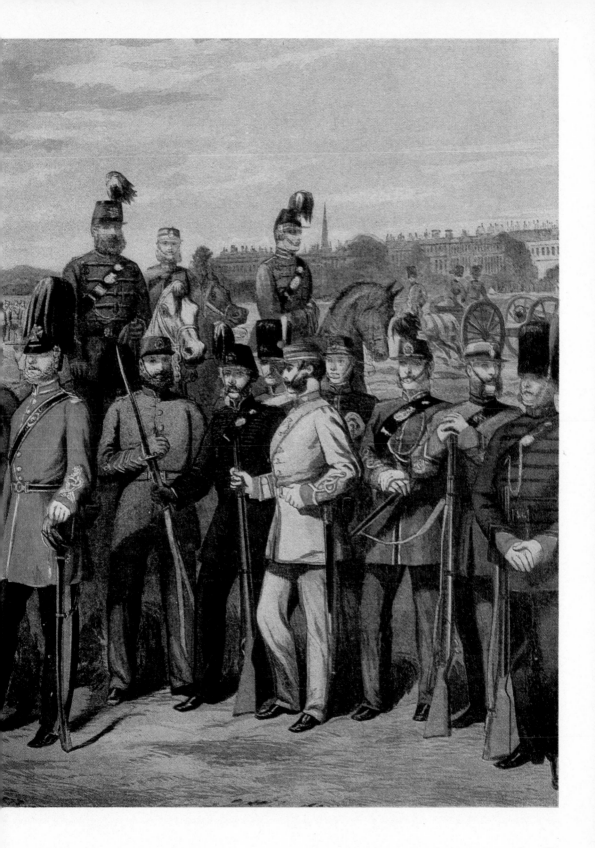

Honourable Artillery Company, also sent troops to serve in South Africa.

South Africa had taught the British some very hard lessons, and it was natural that there should be many questions raised. In 1907 a committee under the chairmanship of Lord Haldane presented a full report setting out plans for a new style army. Among the suggestions he made was that there should be an Expeditionary Force of regular troops backed up by a Territorial Force of volunteers who would be relied upon for Home Defence. Every infantry regiment was to be made up of five battalions; 1 and 2 were the main regular units, 3 consisted of special reservists, and 4 and 5 were to be composed of Territorial volunteers. This new system meant the end of the volunteers in their old form, and naturally the arrangement had a mixed reception; but, in general, the old spirit survived, and many battalions were soon up to strength.

During the First World War Territorial Forces served with distinction in all theatres of operation, and many were officered by men trained in various Officers' Training Corps established, under an army order of 1908, at public schools and universities. In 1916 the old, tacitly understood liability of every man to serve the king was made legal by the introduction of conscription.

In May 1940 there was another great burst of enthusiasm for volunteering, for the success of the German armies in France and Belgium made the invasion of Britain seem inevitable. An appeal was made for the formation of groups to defend the country—the Local Defence Volunteers—and the response was overwhelming, if somewhat chaotic. Organisation slowly developed and the force, soon renamed as the Home Guard, played a small but vital part in the conduct of the war.

Fig. 133: Officers of the Worcestershire Imperial Yeomanry wearing the hackle— the small bunch of feathers on the side of the slouch hat.

German
Uniforms

11

Vor Verdun.

„Meine Herren, unsere Gegner haben den Kanzler noch immer
nicht verstanden, — reden wir noch ein bischen lauter mit ihnen!"

German Uniforms

T HE emergence of Germany as a single nation was a comparatively recent phenomenon, and notably short-lived; less than a century elapsed between the foundation of the unified German Empire, and the division of the country in 1945. It is true that under the Frankish leader Charlemagne the geographical area roughly corresponding to modern Germany was unified, but it fragmented after his death in A.D. 814, and a succession of weak heirs and external threats quickly erased the results of his genius. During the Middle Ages there were attempts by various monarchs to control and unite the semi-independent states, but these met with little success. Otto I (936–973) had himself crowned as Holy Roman Emperor; but, as has been succinctly remarked, is was not Holy, it was not Roman, and it certainly was not an Empire.

It is often said that the German race is militarist by nature, but history has shown that sheer survival forced the adoption of a warlike attitude; the small German states learnt that survival in the turmoil of constant interstate squabbling demanded that they be strong and willing to fight. This period of chronic petty warfare is referred to as the *Faustrecht*—"the rule of the fist".

In 1275 Rudolf of Hapsburg was made Emperor, and he did succeed in imposing some measure of control over the troublesome kingdoms. In 1356 all the states

Title page, *Fig. 134: Leather infantry* pickelhaube *with Bavarian badge and leather chinstrap. At the side is a red, white and black metal cockade; the peak has a metal rim, and the spike is detachable.*
Left, *Plate 21: Lithograph, 10½ by 8¾ inches, dated 8th April 1916, depicting a German general addressing his officers. The caption reads:* Before Verdun —"Gentlemen, our opponents still have not understood the Chancellor—Let's speak to them a little louder".

Above, *Fig. 135: Officer of Hussar Regiment von Malachowski, c. 1770. The jacket is yellow, the trousers white and blue, and the pelisse blue. (Archer Collection)*

Left top, *Fig. 136: Guards star helmet plate worn by,* inter alia, *the Prussian* Garde du Corps. **Below,** *Fig. 137: Prussian* Garde du Corps, c. *1880, with eagle crests mounted on their helmets; the uniform was basically white with red decorations.* (*Archer Collection*)

finally reached an agreement and it was decided that in future an Emperor would be chosen by the princes of the seven chief states, who would subsequently be known as the seven Electors. Although the agreement apparently indicated a degree of union, the true effect was to perpetuate the internal divisions. Over the centuries the disruptive splintering continued, until, by the 18th Century, there were somewhere in the region of 1,750 independent states in the area—most of them little more than large estates, but each ruled by a titled person. Some rulers claimed royal status, others were satisfied with dukedoms, while still others were known as Margraves; but whatever his title, each obstinately asserted his independence.

One of the largest and most powerful states was Prussia, which could well be called the foundation upon which Germany grew. It was here that the ruling class known as the *Junkers* had established their position, a warlike group with the philosophy that to do battle was the highest destiny known to man. The man originally responsible for Prussia's predominance was the Great Elector, Frederick William, who ruled between 1640 and 1688. In 1675 he defeated the Swedes and liberated his country from their rule. His son, Frederick, was not satisfied with his title and sought the style Frederick I, King in Prussia, which he received in 1701—a fine distinction, since West Prussia was under the rule of the King of Poland. Subsequently the title was changed to the more conventional King of Prussia.

The uniforms of Prussian troops were generally cut to give a full, rather loose appearance with wide, folded-back cuffs which reached nearly to the elbow. Head-dress usually comprised a cocked hat, a mitre cap or a bearskin. A French style was adopted when the Great Elector ordered his palace guard to wear the long sleeveless tunic favoured by the French Musketeers. Regulations governing all aspects of military dress and discipline were a common feature of Prussian thinking—a feature which has persisted to this day.

Military fashions have, over the centuries, been influenced by many fancies, but surely one of the strangest occurred in 1717. The Elector of Saxony was much taken by some splendid vases in the Palace of Charlottenburg owned by Frederick William I of Prussia. An exchange was arranged, and nearly six hundred dragoons and cuirassiers were passed to the service of Frederick in return for the vases. Since these were of a blue and white pattern the newly acquired Prussian troops were clothed in uniforms of the same colours, and were known as the "China Dragoons".

Frederick William I succeeded to the throne in 1713, and had soon extended the borders of his country; he devoted much time and care to the expansion of his army. During his reign—1713-1740—the numbers rose from 38,000 to 80,000, and among other ideas Frederick conceived the plan of raising a regiment of giants. From all over Prussia his agents sent, by threat or bribery, all the men they could find who were over six feet tall. The numbers rose from 1,200 to 3,000, including some men nearly eight feet tall. Frederick's Giant Grenadiers wore a blue coat reaching to the knee, with breeches, waistcoats, cuffs and collars of red. Originally red stockings were worn, but these were later replaced by white gaiters with brass buttons.

In 1740 Frederick the Great became King of Prussia, and despite his early anti-militarist sentiments he soon evinced a strongly aggressive attitude which was expressed in the conduct of war and the design of military finery. His troops were decked out in glamorous uniforms with generous lace trimming, silver being his favourite. In 1741 he introduced groups of Uhlans into his cavalry—a feature of the German cavalry until the First World War. In the same year another new unit was formed, distinguished by a badge which was to become famous, and was, indeed, to be copied by many other nations. The Von Ruesch Regiment of Hussars adopted a silver skull and crossbones badge which, combined with their black hussar uniform, gained them a wide reputation. (This combination of a silver death's-head on a black uniform was perpetuated during the Nazi era in the uniform of the tank troops, the natural heirs of cavalry traditions.) Yet another striking innovation was the soft hussar cap known as the *flugelmutze*, a felt cap with a long, loose flap which was worn either wrapped around the cap or dangling down the back. Other hussar regiments in the Prussian cavalry wore uniforms of blue and white, green and red. Frederick the Great took a very active part in the War of Austrian Succession (1740–48) and, as a result, added Silesia to his kingdom. In 1756 he was involved in the Seven Years War, and won some outstanding victories.

During the Napoleonic Wars Prussia, Austria and other German states suffered various defeats, and contingents from many of them served with the French forces. In 1808 there were many changes in the uniforms of the Prussian army, including a fairly general adoption of the shako, many being fitted with very striking plumes and cockades. Generally their tunics were waist-length at the front with short tails; blue was the most usual colour, although many of the Chasseurs and Riflemen wore green. Many cavalry units also wore the shako, but formations such as the cuirassiers wore crested helmets resembling the French style. One or two regiments retained the older style of cocked hat with a tall feather plume.

WITH the defeat of Buonaparte at Waterloo in 1815—a defeat to which Blucher's Prussians contributed—peace came to Europe once more, and a great Congress was held at Vienna in an attempt to straighten out some of the enormous and complex international problems which faced the Continent in the aftermath of war. A confederation of thirty-eight independent German states was created, in which Prussia was deliberately denied a leading position. This attempt to curb Prussia's power was ineffectual; under Bismarck, the Iron Chancellor, the country's influence in European affairs increased enormously.

Some criticism was levelled against the very colourful uniforms worn by the Prussian troops, and it was planned to make them far more practical and less restrictive. Tunics which reached to mid-thigh largely replaced the waist-length jacket, and loose-fitting trousers reaching to the ankle proved more acceptable than the tight-fitting style. In 1842 the shako was replaced by a tall,

domed leather helmet with a peak and neck-guard and surmounted by a tall spike. A further embellishment was the coloured cockade worn on the right side of the helmet, on the lug to which the chin scales were fitted. In 1843 the helmet was made a little more glamorous by the addition of a horsehair plume for parade and ceremonial occasions; most of the infantry wore black plumes, with the Guards in white and bandsmen in red.

In 1864 Bismarck welcomed the opportunity to test the army in battle and the Prussians, aided by the Austrians, attacked Denmark. The campaign was speedily and efficiently concluded. The alliance with Austria was short-lived; in 1866 the erstwhile friends were at war, and within seven weeks the Austrians were suing for peace. The following year Bismarck created a North German Federation, which, in effect, made Prussia the ruler of the greater part of Germany.

The Franco-Prussian War of 1870 was an overwhelming disaster for the French, who had been encouraged by Napoleon III to think of the Second Empire as a reincarnation of Napoleonic France. Prussian arms soon demolished this fantasy, and swept all before them. As a result many countries copied parts of the uniform of the victorious army—a practice still in evidence today. The spiked *pickelhaube* was given a lower profile; in 1867 it had been altered by the replacement of the square peak by a round one. Most of the troops were also wearing jackboots with the trousers tucked in the top. In addition to the Prussians, units from Bavaria and Saxony also served in this war; their uniforms naturally varied, but many wore a hard, shiny headdress in the shako style, with a small oval cockade on the top. This shako had also been adopted, as early as 1854, by the Prussian *Jäger* and *Schützen* battalions—the Rifle and Sharpshooter units.

After the supreme victory of 1870 the German Empire became a reality, and in January 1871 it was formally declared. It was officially a federal union of twenty-five states with a central seat of government in Berlin; Bismarck became Chancellor and the King of Prussia became the Emperor. One of the first fruits of this union was the standardisation of all the armies involved, with the common adoption of the Prussian pattern. Local distinctions were preserved in badges and trimmings, and in 1897 a round cockade of concentric circles of red, white and black—the national colours—was made common wear on the right side of the helmet, balanced by a similar cockade in regional state colours on the left. For ceremonial wear the *pickelhaube* was fitted with horsehair plumes, and, from 1892 onwards, a cloth cover was issued for use in the field. Originally this bore the regimental number, but subsequently it was left quite plain. A standard field service uniform was adopted in 1907 and was in general issue within a few years; of a slate grey colour, with regimental distinctions of various colours and designs at cuff and throat, this was the uniform in which German troops went into action on the outbreak of the First World War in 1914.

The uniform proved to be efficient, but too elaborate for general wear in the squalid static warfare which soon scored the Continent with a vast trench system from Switzerland to the sea. The fussier details of cuff, collar and tail distinctions were abandoned for wear in the field, and a simpler and rather looser-fitting tunic was issued. The tan leather of belts, boots and equipment gave way to black; and in the closing stages of the conflict, when strategic materials of every type were in desperately short supply, the high jackboots gave place to an ankle-length boot worn with cloth puttees. So poor was the quality of this issue that it was generally said that the boots were made of cardboard and the puttees of paper. In the field of headdress the changes which occurred during the war were more obvious and immediate. The leather *pickelhaube* with its metal furniture was replaced progressively; shortened or reversible spikes were fitted, and substitute materials—pressed felt, metal alloys and even papier maché—were used in the construction of the headgear, in an attempt to conserve stocks of leather. In 1915 the steel "coalscuttle" helmet replaced the *pickelhaube* for use in the field. For undress and out-of-the-line wear the Imperial German troops had the *mütze*, the "porkpie" cap which figures in illustrations of uniforms as early as the 1800s. For "other ranks" this was a rather ugly cap with no peak, a soft cloth crown and slightly stiffened band of a colour appropriate to the unit and arm of service. On the crown was a metal rosette, in national colours, while the band carried a state or regimental rosette. For officers, both commissioned and noncommissioned, better quality versions for this cap were issued, with a black leather peak and a chinstrap (see Plate 21.)

Two parade helmets of the Imperial German era merit special mention; of these

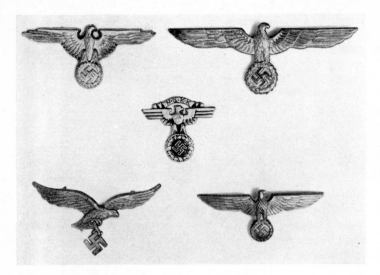

Left, *Fig. 140: Metal cap eagles of the Third Reich.* Top left, *Waffen-SS and final pattern Allgemeine-SS;* top right, *Navy;* centre, *National Socialist Transport Corps (NSKK);* bottom left, *eagle from peaked cap of a senior Luftwaffe N.C.O.;* bottom right, *Army.* All are in white metal alloy except the naval eagle, which is in yellow alloy.

Below right, *Fig.141: Cloth eagle badges of the Third Reich.* Top left, *grey thread on green, Army enlisted man's breast eagle.* Top right, *pale grey thread on black,* Waffen-SS *man's sleeve eagle.* Centre, *silver bullion thread on dark blue,* Luftwaffe *officer's breast eagle.* Bottom left, *silver bullion on dark green, late pattern Army officer's cap eagle.* Bottom right, *yellow thread on dark blue, presumed Navy senior petty officer's cap eagle.*

the most spectacular was that of the Imperial Body Guard, the *Garde du Corps*. This helmet was a metal version of the *pickelhaube* made from an alloy of zinc and copper and fitted with a sweeping neck guard. On parade occasions the high dome supported a gorgeous flying eagle in place of the less elaborate spike. The Saxon Guard Cavalry wore a somewhat similar helmet except that instead of an eagle a crouching lion surmounted the dome, holding in its paws a shield.

From 1914 to 1918 Germany had little occasion to mount spectacular parades and ceremonies, for the nation was fighting for its life. Eventually, after a terrible war of attrition, the Allies' greater industrial potential and the belated entry of America into the war brought about Germany's ruin, and in November 1918 an armistice was signed. It seemed the end of German hopes and ambitions, and the remnants of the once-magnificent army were disbanded, fragmenting into a large number of small marauding bands who indulged in street fighting with communist "soviets", *Freikorps* service against the Bolsheviks in the East, and straightforward banditry. Given the circumstances of complete social collapse which attended the Armistice, the victors agreed that a small national army

should remain in being for security reasons; the numbers and composition of this force were rigorously restricted, and its uniform and equipment were generally speaking those of Imperial Germany.

IN the turmoil of the 1920s and 1930s a new force began to grow in influence, which seemed to promise a return to national order and self-respect; and under the hypnotic influence of Adolf Hitler the people began to embrace his new ideology of National Socialism. One reason for his success was the *Sturm Abteilungen* or SA, a political army which he used for physical and mental blackmail of friend and foe. He was shrewd enough to realise that a uniform is enormously effective in fostering a feeling of common identity, and he encouraged his SA men to buy and wear a brown shirt, breeches, jackboots and a round kepi-style cap. On the left upper arm was worn a Party brassard—a red armband with a white disc charged with a black swastika, an ancient symbol which has been identified on surviving stone-carvings as far apart as Tibet and Peru, and is thought to have been a sun emblem, of benign influence. It is ironic that the right-facing or reversed swastika adopted by the Nazis is generally associated with darkness and ill-omen—a reversal in the natural course of the sun across the sky.

As Hitler's power increased, so did that of his revolutionary army, the SA; it grew to a vast organisation of 3,000,000 men, and under leaders such as Ernst Roehm its militancy and strident demands for a say in the direction of the new political structure became first an embarrassment to Hitler, and then a threat. He was now moving in high circles, seeking to acquire the backing of the High Command and various respectable political forces, and his beer-hall toughs had become a liability. It was even suggested in 1933 that when Hitler achieved real power the SA should become the prime fighting force of the new German Reich—not a suggestion designed to attract the co-operation of the High Command. On June 30th 1934 matters came to a head; while the Army stood ready in the background, various picked groups of police and party officials carried out raids on the SA leaders, arrested them, and dragged them off to summary execution. The rank and file were disarmed, and became from that moment on a useful but toothless regional organisation which was used for many tasks, including recruiting and civil defence co-ordination.

One of the main weapons used by Hitler in this purge was the *Schutzstaffeln*, or SS. This had been formed from within the SA in 1922–23, as a totally reliable body guard for the leader. For a long time the size and influence of this group, distinguished by black uniform caps, was minimal; its growing importance may be said to date from January 1929, when it was placed under the command of one of the Party zealots, the ex-poultry farmer Heinrich Himmler, who retained his position as *Reichsführer-SS* until his death in 1945. By 1934, when three armed battalions of the SS took part in the Roehm purge, a special uniform had evolved. This comprised a black tunic, single-breasted, with four pockets; black flared

breeches; black belt and shoulder-belt; and a high-fronted black peaked cap. A single epaulette was worn on the right shoulder, and a swastika brassard, distinguished by strips of black ribbon, was worn on the left arm. Insignia of rank and unit symbols were worn on braid-edged collar patches; silver was the predominant colour in all SS insignia, and the cap badges consisted of a silver death's-head on the band and a distinctively shaped silver eagle clutching a wreathed swastika on the crown. Officers' caps were fitted with two braided aluminium cords, in place of the leather chin-strap worn by other ranks. Cap piping, around the crown seam and the top and bottom of the band, was in white, and later in silver for commissioned ranks.

Fig. 142: Lance-corporal (left) *and* Feldwebel (right) *of German infantry, 1944. The soldier wears the original pattern tunic, with dark green collar, and standard insignia of service. The senior N.C.O. wears the simpler M1944 tunic with unpleated pockets, and his rank is indicated by shoulder-strap braid and pips and by the braid collar edging. He has been awarded the Iron Cross, 1st and 2nd Class, and the Infantry Assault Badge.*

The relationship between the Army and the SS was one of wary goodwill. Official Nazi policy was that the Army should remain the principal fighting force, but there was increasing pressure on the Army High Command to ensure the political indoctrination of the forces. The symbol of the Army's commitment to the New Germany came in 1934, when the swastika of the National Socialist Party appeared on the Army uniform. All ranks and all branches of the Army, Navy and Air Force were to wear on the right breast a badge depicting an eagle clutching a swastika in a wreath of oakleaves in its talons. The Army wore a straight-winged eagle, the longest wing feather at the top; for Army Officers and senior N.C.O.s this was woven in silver thread, and for other ranks in white or pale grey. Apart from this there were few major changes in the uniform worn by the German soldier since the First World War.

The steel helmet was almost identical to the First World War model, although smaller and lighter. To the right side was

applied a decal in the shape of a shield with diagonal bands of black, white and red, and to the left a black shield charged with a silver eagle with closed wings, holding an unwreathed swastika in its claws. A uniform cap or *mütze* was similar to the 1914–18 pattern, though with a higher front to the crown. All ranks wore this cap with a black peak, and officers and other ranks wore double aluminium braid cords and black chin-straps respectively. On the front of the crown was pinned the *Wehrmacht* eagle, and on the band appeared the national cockade surrounded by a wreath of oakleaves. Non-commisioned ranks wore these badges in pressed alloy; officers initially wore a metal eagle and a woven silver-thread main badge, but it was not uncommon for both to be woven, especially later in the war. It was not usual for ranks below sergeant to wear the peaked cap, although it was official parade dress.

Round the crown seam and the top and bottom of the dark green band appeared piping in a wide variety of colours, which indicated the branch of service; this *waffenfarbe* is believed to have originated as early as 1900, when a German contingent was sent to China with the international force which protected foreign embassies during the Boxer Rebellion. Some of the more important shades were white (infantry), golden yellow (cavalry, and thus reconnaissance troops), lemon yellow (signals), bright red (artillery), bright rose pink (armoured troops), light green (mountain troops, *Jäger* units), and black (pioneers).

Two other main types of headgear were issued. In 1938 a field service cap—a side-cap, known to the troops as a "boat" in obvious reference to its shape—was issued. This was of the same shade of slate grey as the uniform, and had cloth badges sewn to the front, in the form of the eagle and swastika surmounting the national cockade. The latter was often enclosed within an inverted V of *waffenfarbe* piping. Officers' caps of this pattern were distingu-

ished by silver braid round the crown seam and in the front arch of the "turn-up", and by badges in silver rather than grey thread. A second cap, of the shape generally referred to as a "ski-cap", with a cloth peak and an arched "turn-up", was issued to mountain troops and later to all branches of the forces, under the designation M1943. This was also worn with cloth eagle and cockade badges, and with silver crown piping for officers. Mountain and *Jäger* troops wore additional badges on the left side, in the form of an *edelweiss* and an oakleaf spray respectively. By 1944 it had largely replaced the side-cap, and was even worn in the field by generals.

The Army uniform was basically a slate grey, although in some batches the collar was of dark green cloth, particularly in the case of officers' uniforms. The quality of the cloth, and the fact that all commissioned ranks wore flared breeches with the "number one" uniform, were the only major distinctions between officers and men, apart from applied insignia. Collar badges, in the traditional German form of braided bars, were sewn to the tunic; these were in silver thread for officers, and grey for other ranks. Strips of *waffenfarbe* were applied to these, and the appropriate colour also appeared as the underlay and edging of the shoulder-straps. These carried the rank distinctions; other ranks wore plain straps with *waffenfarbe* edging, and senior N.C.O.s were distinguished by a system of silver braid inner borders and metal pips on the straps. Officers' straps were of silver cord on an underlay of cloth in the branch colour, the different ranks being distinguished by variations in the weave of the cord and by applied metal pips. Junior N.C.O.s wore rank patches on the left upper arm, in the form of a star on a circular patch for senior privates, and one or two chevrons on a triangular backing for lance-corporals and corporals. From sergeant up, the rank was indicated only by the shoulder-strap variations and by a

broad silver braid edge to the tunic collar. Generals wore special collar patches of most attractive design—stylised oakleaves embroidered in gold thread on a red background. Gold was also the colour used for the piping on generals' caps, and for shoulder-strap cord.

Specialists in various military trades— radio operators, farriers, mechanics, and so forth—wore trade symbols in yellow thread on circular green cloth background patches sewn to the lower left arm of the tunic. Mountain troops wore an *edelweiss* patch on the upper arm.

The armed units of the SS, or *Waffen-SS*, grew from small beginnings in 1939 into a force of thirty-eight divisions by the end of the war. Many of these were under-strength, and some were mere "paper" formations of untrustworthy Eastern European conscripts; but the eight or ten élite *Waffen-SS* divisions are judged to have been the most effective troops fielded by any army during the Second World War—never forgetting, of course, their savage reputation for atrocity.

They wore a grey uniform, initially of better cut than that of the Army, but this was replaced by Army uniform stocks as the needs of economy became pressing. The SS

colours of silver and black were preserved in the various insignia; to the collar were applied black cloth patches bearing, on the right side, the double lightning-flash SS runes, and on the left side a rank insignia. This was made up according to a system of silver braid bars and metal pips; from the rank of *Standartenführer* (full Colonel) upwards, woven silver oakleaves and pips were used on both sides of the collar. Officers' patches were edged with silver cord, and those of other ranks were plain, although senior N.C.O.s, in common with Army practice, had the broad silver edge applied to the tunic collar itself. Many thousands of foreign volunteers served in the *Waffen-SS*, and some of these foreign units wore special collar patches in place of the SS runes; many of these are still not positively identified, and they are much sought after by collectors—to the extent that a thriving industry supplies the market with faked items! Known variations include a silver "wolf's-tongue" rune, worn by Dutch SS units; a swastika of circular outline, worn by the Scandinavians of the *Nordland* SS Division; and a three-legged swastika, worn by the Flemish *Langemarck* Division. National flag arm patches were also worn.

Unique among German troops, the SS did not wear the eagle badge on the right breast. An eagle of special design, with the longest feather in the middle of the wings, was worn on the upper left arm; and the same design in metal and cloth was applied to the various headgear, in the same way as the Army eagle. Instead of the wreathed cockade, all SS troops wore the death's-head as the lower cap badge, again, in metal or thread depending on the type of cap. Peaked caps identical to the Army pattern were worn, with a black band replacing the dark green of the Army. The side-cap and "ski-cap" were also worn; as the skull badge occupied more space than the cockade, it was sometimes necessary to wear the eagle badge on the left side of the cap rather than on the front. SS shoulder-strap and *waffenfarbe* conventions followed those of the Army closely, although black appeared as the basic colour of the enlisted men's straps, and as an extra underlay on some officers' straps.

The German Air Force or *Luftwaffe*, which, unlike the Army, was formed from "scratch" by the Nazis, wore an entirely new uniform of slate blue, with an open collar showing the shirt and tie. It was conventional in cut, and all the basic types of headgear were issued. The peaked cap was piped in silver for all officers, and in *waffenfarbe* for N.C.O.s, the chin-strap distinctions following those of the other forces. The main cap badge was in the form of the cockade in a wreath of oakleaves supported by two stylised wings; the upper badge was an eagle and swastika of unique design. This was repeated on the breast of the tunic. Side-caps and "ski-caps" carried this *Luftwaffe* eagle surmounting a cockade, and were piped in silver for officers. Shoulder-straps paralleled those of the Army exactly, except that the base colour for enlisted men was, obviously, blue; the *Luftwaffe* also had its own system of *waffenfarbe*, the two most frequently encountered of the many shades being

yellow for flying personnel and paratroopers, and red for anti-aircraft artillery. Collar patches, edged in silver cord for officers, were of a different design from those of the Army. Basically patches of cloth in *waffenfarbe* colours, these indicated exact rank by a system of stylised wings and oakleaves (see Plate 22.)

The airborne forces were administered by the *Luftwaffe*, and wore the same uniform with special qualification badges on the left breast pocket. In action they were dressed in a thigh-length gaberdine smock, either in field grey or camouflage colours, and wore a special steel helmet; this had no peak or neck-guard and was secured by double chin-straps, to ensure a close fit and a reliable fastening. This, and the conventional helmets worn by ordinary *Luftwaffe* troops, bore a decal in the form of a *Luftwaffe* eagle, reversed, on the left side. On flying suits, and on airborne troops' smocks, a system of rank patches was worn on the upper arm indicating rank by stylised wings and bars in light-coloured cloth.

A most attractive uniform common to units of the Army, the *Waffen-SS* and even the *Luftwaffe* was the black tank outfit. This consisted of a short double-breasted jacket and baggy trousers tucked into ankle

boots, with black side-caps, and, later in the war, "ski-caps". The collar patches of Army *panzer* units were unique, being silver skulls set on black patches edged in pink. The pink-piped shoulder straps indi-cated rank in the normal way. The SS tank units wore the same basic uniform with the substitution of SS-pattern shoulder-straps and collar patches, arm eagles and cap badges. The *Luftwaffe* fielded several divis-ions of conventional troops during the war, including the *Hermann Göring Panzer Division* which fought with distinction in Italy; the tank crews of this unit wore Army *panzer* uniform with *Luftwaffe* breast and cap eagles.

The German forces had many different designs of metal badge, generally worn on and below the left breast pocket, which indicated qualification in certain specialist skills, participation in various grades and types of action, wounds on active service, and so forth. No brief study can mention a worth-while selection of these, so suffice it to say that they appeared in bronze, silver, and gold-coloured metal, that they were

usually oval in shape and based on the idea of an oak wreath containing a symbol—often almost self-explanatory—and that they more often than not included an eagle and swastika design.

One type of insignia peculiar to the German forces was the cuff-title. This was a strip of cloth embroidered with lettering and sewn around the forearm of the tunic. They had two main functions; to indicate service in a particular unit, or to indicate that the wearer had fought in some notable campaign. Unit titles were common in the *Luftwaffe*, whose cuff-titles were usually in the form of pale grey lettering on a dark blue band—e.g. "*Geschwader Boelcke*", "*Jagdgeschwader Richthofen*", etc. Divis-ional titles were often worn in the *Waffen-SS*, in the form of silver-grey lettering on black bands edged with silver—e.g. "*Adolf Hitler*", worn by past and present members of the 1st SS *Panzer* Division "*Leibstand-arte SS Adolf Hitler*"; "*Totenkopf*"; "*Das Reich*"; "*Wiking*"; "*Frundsberg*"; and many others. Both the Army and the *Luftwaffe* commemorated two campaigns of

Fig. 146: The Luftwaffe *paratrooper's helmet. Although the outline, bolts, decal and leather furniture are authentic, the sharp, unfolded rim suggests that this might be a post-war reproduction cut down from the conventional* stahlhelm—*an example of the caution which must be exercised by collectors in this popular field.* (Windrow Collection)

particular fame with cuff-titles; "*Afrika*" and "*Kreta*". These cuff-titles, popular with collectors, are also the subject of much spurious production.

Apart from submarine and coastal formations, the German Navy did not play a great part in major actions during the Second World War. Like the Army, the *Kriegsmarine* did not change its uniform greatly between the wars; and like all navies the world over, the officers and men wore various different types of uniform for various different duties. The normal headdress for ordinary seamen was a peakless cap, higher in the front of the crown than the back, with two ribbons hanging down the back, and a detachable band bearing the word "*Kriegsmarine*" in gold lettering. The metal or cloth rosette in the national colours appeared low on the crown, and a small yellow eagle in metal or thread above it. The officers' uniform caps differed with rank. No cap cords were worn; instead, braid was worn round the edge of the peak, in different designs according to rank. On the band a national cockade was surrounded by woven gold oakleaves, and a gold eagle, in metal or thread, was fiixed to the front of the crown. Senior petty officers wore a less elaborate peaked cap with a black raised edging to the peak, and the same badges pressed in yellow metal. Sidecaps were worn by all ranks for certain types of duty, those of officers being distinguished by the conventional line of braid piping round the "turn-up"; cloth eagle and cockade badges, the former in yellow thread, were sewn to the front. For full dress occasions officers wore cocked hats, decorated with gold braid for admirals and black mohair for lower ranks. As already mentioned, a gold or yellow thread eagle and swastika was worn on the right breast of the tunic or jumper. Trade and rank badges were worn on the arm; in the case of commissioned ranks, these latter were in the form of the conventional gold rings surmounted, for general duty officers, by a small star, and by various branch insignia in the case of specialist officers. Shoulderstraps were worn on certain types of uniform, and were far more frequent than in the Royal Navy or the United States Navy.

These, then, were the basic uniforms of the four main branches of the German armed forces. There were a myriad of specialist insignia, each worn according to some minutely-worded regulation, but it would occupy the whole of this volume if one were to attempt to describe them all.

So popular has this field become that, as already mentioned, the market for collectors has been flooded with spurious items which range in quality and accuracy from the excellent to the childish. It is thus a field into which the inexperienced should venture only warily.

Badges and Buttons

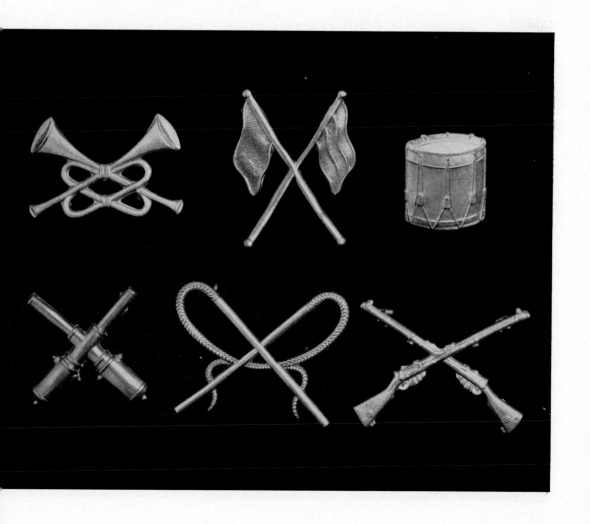

12

Badges and Buttons

Title page, *Fig. 147: Arm badges of the British Army.* Top, left to right: *Trumpeter (reversed here), Signaller, Drummer or Fifer—not worn in Foot Guards.* Bottom, *Artillery instructor, Driver, Marksman.*

Left, *Plate 23: Selection of British Army headdress badges. The large plates were worn on the 1879 pattern helmet. The grenade number 102* (left centre) *pre-dates 1881 since it still bears the regimental number. The acorn is that of the South Nottinghamshire Hussars Yeomanry. The grenade at lower right is a plume holder for a Royal Artillery busby of the mid-19th Century. "Britannia" is a cap badge of the Royal Norfolk Regiment, and the "(Death) or glory" badge is that of the famous 17th/21st Lancers.*

Right, *Fig. 148: General Service shako plate pressed in bronze, circa 1810; 5½ by 3⅜ inches. (Gyngell Collection)*

Both badges and uniforms have a common origin in heraldry, and for many centuries the two were indistinguishable. It seems that during the latter part of the 16th Century there may have been some slight development of separate badges, for there is at least one reference during Elizabeth's reign to the wearing of the "Queens' Badge". Whether this referred merely to the wearing of the Royal Arms or to some specific badge is not clear from the context. It is probably true to say that badges, as separate items, developed during the 17th Century. Mention has already been made of the use of field marks and scarves; both were fairly general all over Europe at the beginning of the 17th Century, being used during the Thirty Years War (1618–48) as well as during the English Civil Wars. Field marks were rather haphazard and chancy, and thoughtlessness could lead to fatal results. The Earl of Orrey, in his book *"Treatise of the Art of War"* published in 1677, tells the oft-quoted story of an unfortunate officer who, finding a dead enemy officer with a better quality hat than his own, took it and wore it, forgetting to remove the enemy field mark first. He was attacked by some of his own men and killed; and such unfortunate occurrences were repeated on several occasions.

One slightly unusual use of the field mark is recorded as being made by General Monck at the Siege of Dundee in 1651; he ordered his men, besieging the city, to wear "a white cloth or shirt behind". At first sight this may appear a little strange but, in fact, during a siege the attacking forces would see the backs of their own men and therefore the field mark was obviously situated in the best place. It also offered some extra encouragement to the attackers to face the enemy, for if at any time they turned their back they presented a better target to the defenders inside the wall! The use of field marks continued into the early part of the 18th Century, but by this time badges, in the broadest sense of the word, were becoming more commonplace.

The earliest badges were heraldic and usually comprised the reigning monarch's cypher, part of the Royal Arms, or the arms of the Colonel commanding the regiment. These badges were to be found on the uniform and on pieces of auxiliary equipment; many coats worn by troops had the Royal Cypher embroidered thereon, and holster cases, worn at the horse's neck, often bore the Royal Cypher on their covers. These embroidered badges were frequently quite elaborate, and thick silver or gold wire was used together with coloured threads.

Badges on headdress seem to have been limited in the 17th Century to the Grenadiers' caps, and the majority of the troops wore three-cornered hats devoid of all badges, although an odd button, piece of lace or plume was sometimes attached to the brim. Grenadiers' caps, with their stiffened front and folded flap, offered a useful embroidery area. Surviving examp-

les and contemporary illustrations indicate that the majority of them were covered with embroidered Royal Cyphers, grenades, or, occasionally, an associated national emblem. Tapestries depicting troops at Blenheim show Foot Guard Grenadiers with a large star on the cap, bearing at the centre the St. George's cross encircled by a large garter; this motif was repeated subsequently on many badges. In the Dublin Museum is a Grenadier's cap which is reputed to have belonged to an officer serving with the Royal Irish Regiment of Foot during Marlborough's campaigns; this is decorated with a crown, a harp, sprigs of shamrock and the word "Royal" on the front, whilst at the back, the lower brim bears a grenade and further sprigs of shamrock.

During the early part of the 18th Century this practice of embroidering the front of Grenadiers' caps became well established, and there are numerous surviving examples to indicate that it was general usage.

According to a book called "*Rudiments of War*" published in 1778, a Royal Clothing Warrant was issued in 1743 and another in 1749, but no trace of the original warrants has so far been found. The first warrant that is available for study is one dated 1751, and, in the preamble, it specifically states that no Colonel was henceforward allowed to place any parts of his arms, crest or livery on any appointments of the regiment or any part of the clothing." The "Regulations for the Colours, Clothing, etc. of the Marching Regiments of Foot and for the Uniform, Clothing of the Cavalry, their Standards, Guidons, Banners etc." is the full title, and this warrant contains the first specific use of the word "badge". The paragraph describing the Grenadier's cap goes into full details, stating that the front should be the same colour as the facings of the regiments, that the Royal Cypher should be embroidered on the large front, that the small flap was to be red with the white horse of Hanover and the motto embroidered on it, and that the back part of the cap was to be red with the number of the regiment "on the middle part behind". The Warrant then goes on to list "devices and badges of the Royal Regiments and of the six old Corps"; the distinctions are then listed for all the appropriate regiments. All the badges described in the 1751 Warrant, and there are many, were embroidered on to the cap, or painted on certain other accessories belonging to the regiment. Coloured worsted seems to have been most commonly used for this embroidery. There appears to have been no standardisation as far as the method of displaying the number was concerned, for surviving examples bear the regimental number in either Roman or Arabic numerals.

The Royal Cypher still figured on many pieces of equipment, including the cartridge pouch. One of the earliest use of tools or specialised items to indicate the occupation of certain soldiers appears in the "March of the Guards to Finchley" a famous painting by Hogarth. In this picture a pioneer, that is a soldier employed in construction, defence and siege work, is shown wearing a loose cap with a white tassel and a blue brim; on the upturned blue brim, embroidered in white, is a saw and mattock (a form of pickaxe). Around the middle of the 18th Century there is a fresh development, for it seems that certain of the cartridge pouches were now being fitted with the Cypher in brass instead of having it painted or embroidered as previously.

IN 1747 Highland Grenadiers were given permission to wear a fur cap (see Fig. 103) in place of the usual cloth caps. These fur caps are basically the same shape as the normal Grenadier's cap, but in place of the decorated cloth front there is a small crescent section which is decorated with a crown and "G.R." It is difficult to decide from an illustration made in 1751 whether this is a metal plate or a piece of cloth. It would also seem from some contemporary paintings that in the case of Hanoverian

Fig. 150: Similar badge of the 1st Volunteer Battalion, the King's (Liverpool) Regiment, retaining its red cloth backing patch. This regiment was unusual in having no less that seven Volunteer Battalions in 1900.

regiments the front of the Grenadier cap was decorated with cut-out metal plates, but this cannot be stated with certainty. However, the evidence is soon much firmer, for in 1768 another Clothing Warrant was issued and, after repeating the injunction that no Colonel was to put any part of his arms on any part of the regimental equipment, the paragraph dealing with Grenadier caps states that they will now be of black bearskin (the model introduced for the Highland Regiments in 1747) and goes on to say that on the front was to be the King's crest "of silver plated metal on a black ground with the motto Nec Aspera Terrent". This is definite evidence for the existence of the metal cap badge, and it is likely that they were already in use prior to this date. It is of interest to note that the use of badges seems still to have been limited to Grenadier's caps, for another paragraph in the Warrant, which details

Above, *Fig. 151: White metal plate of the 6th Tower Hamlets Rifle Volunteers—the area furnished Trained Bands as far back as 1643.* **Opposite,** *Fig. 152:* Left to right, top to bottom: *brass Connaught Rangers badge; embroidered crown worn above chevrons by Victorian sergeant; pre-1881 badge of 19th Foot; helmet badge of the Eton Rifle Volunteers.*

the hat, makes no mention of a badge at all.

In the 1760s the fusiliers were issued with a leather headdress rather in the style of a helmet, and these too were fitted with white metal plates at the front. Despite all these innovations and the increasing use of metal plates for badges, the cocked hat still seems to have been left unadorned, apart from a black cockade worn from early in the 18th Century. Towards the end of the 18th Century a cap was introduced for the light dragoons, fitted with a small metal plate which bore the name of the unit or some other designation.

The 1800s saw the emergence of the badge as an established feature of military dress, for in this year the tall shako, worn previously by certain units, was made a general issue to the infantry. The tubular shako was fitted at the front with a stamped brass plate embossed with the Royal Cypher, and those for regimental use were identified by the number. The shako did not entirely displace the other forms of headdress; new fur caps were authorised in 1802, and these too were fitted with brass plate at the front for other ranks and a gilt plate for officers.

In 1181 the light infantry were also ordered to fit a badge to their shako and, in keeping with the general practice for the light infantry, theirs took the form of a bugle horn with the number of the regiment below it. During the 1820s there was an abandoning of the old shape of cap plate and a more general adoption of a basic pattern consisting of an eight-pointed star with regimental insignia set at the centre; covering the topmost point of the star was the Royal Crown. This crown had downward-curving top bars and is usually known as the "Queen's Crown"; it continued in use until the death of Queen Victoria in 1901, when it was replaced by the so-called "King's crown" with upward-curving top bars (see Figs. 152, 154). The badge was attached to the headdress by means of two, sometimes three, loops which were pushed through the material and then held in place at the back by small wedge-shaped pieces of leather, or later by long brass split pins, pushed through the loops on the inside of the headdress. Although there had been changes in the badges during the 18th Century, by the 19th Century the regimental badges had become more or less standardised, although there were to be numerous variations in detail. Most of them carried the regiment's name and number as well as some device associated with the regiment.

The numbering of regiments, begun in 1751, continued until 1881. A committee was set up by Edward Cardwell in 1878 to consider the entire organisation of the British Army. This committee reported and, in effect, dispensed with the numbering of regiments; certain regiments were amalgamated, and all were placed on a far more provincial basis, being associated with a particular part of the country. The abandoning of the numbering of regiments meant, obviously, that badges had to be altered; and from 1881, although the Queen's crown was retained, the badge displayed only the name of the regiment. This loss of the regimental number applied only to the infantry; cavalry units retained the old system.

The distinction between Militia and Regulars, originally made by the use of different coloured lace on uniforms (gold for regular forces, silver for Militia) was extended to these badges, and those of the Militia were cast in white metal while the Regulars wore brass or gilt. One exception was in the Scottish regiments where, almost invariably, the badges were of white metal.

Naturally the size of the star varied according to the shako worn; the largest were on the bell-topped and Albert Shakos, and the size was progressively reduced as the height of the shako decreased. With the adoption in 1878/9 of the spiked home-pattern cork helmet, large style badges were introduced once again. These large shako and helmet plates were usually made from die-stamped brass for other ranks, but for officers' models the star and crown were pressed and the regimental insignia made separately and secured by loops and pins. In the case of the cavalry the basic star plate was also used, both for Yeomanry and Regulars; one distinctive plate was produced for the lancer cap, which was roughly semi-circular and curved to fit the *tschapka*.

In addition to the large star-type badge worn on the shako and blue cloth helmets, a smaller version, usually the centre device from the larger star, was worn on the small Scottish-type side-cap, known as the glengarry, which was introduced into the British Army in 1874—this was largely an undress hat. The older style of embroidered badge was used for the round forage cap worn by officers.

With the adoption of the Broderick and the Field Service cap a smaller badge was introduced, and it was at about this time that an alternative form of attachment was used on some cap badges. In place of the two loops at the back of the badge an L-shaped metal bar was fitted, and this slid into an appropriate recess on the Field Service cap or side-cap. Nearly all badges at this time were made of brass, and certainly until the commencement of World War I the majority of other ranks' cap badges were of solid brass. A number were of bi-metal construction, that is a white metal and brass; in the case of officers, the equivalent materials were gold and silver.

In addition to the regimental badge worn on the headdress, small badges known as collar dogs were worn on the lapels. These lapel badges were either miniature versions of the cap badges or comprised a part of the main regimental badge. As they were made in pairs the figures normally faced in opposite directions (see Fig. 154); again, these were usually fixed in place by the loop and split pin system. On the shoulder-straps of the tunic were fixed the titles of the regiments, although they were sometimes abbreviated to the point of obscurity—thus

Fig. 153: Top, *brass cap badge—with slider—of The Ayrshire Yeomanry (Earl of Carrick's Own), a unit dating originally from 1793.* Bottom left, *cap badge of the Carabiniers (6th Dragoon Guards): this unit amalgamated with the 3rd Dragoon Guards in 1922.* Bottom right, *brass cap badge of the Duke of Lancaster's Own Yeomanry—see Fig. 156.*

T.4.P.W.V. was used by the 4th Battalion The Prince of Wales' Volunteers (South Lancashire). Yet another style of badge worn by certain N.C.O.s was the arm badge, usually based on part of the regimental badge. Sometimes these were of metal but cloth ones were commonly worn—those of Victorian times were often beautifully embroidered.

During the First World War another form of badge made its appearance in the British Army; this was the Divisional Sign, fashioned from cloth and stitched to the sleeve. Originally the device was used to identify transport without disclosing the details of the Corps or Division owning it. The devices, initially simple patches of colour, were gradually adopted by the men who comprised the Division, and became a standard part of the uniform. Choice of design was fairly arbitrary and at the discretion of the commanding officer; thus the

sign for XIX Corps comprised three white question marks on a red background, suggesting "Whats?"—the formation was commanded by Lt. General Sir Hubert Watts, K.C.B., C.M.G.! The use of these cloth badges was continued by nearly all participants in the Second World War.

SEPARATE badges of rank appeared late on the military scene, and it would appear that during the 17th Century rank was distinguished only by the form of dress of the officers. A further distinction was made by the wearing of a bunch or knot of ribbons on the right shoulder. It also appears that officers were distinguished by having gold lace on their coats while the lower grade officers, subalterns, wore silver. Sergeants and Corporals were also distinguished in the same way by silver of different widths and edging to their hats. A further distinction for officers was the sash; in the 1740s it was laid down that sashes of infantry officers should be of crimson silk and worn over the right shoulder. Silver or gold aguillettes should be worn on the right shoulder as the distinguishing mark of an officer. These augillettes were plaited cords which passed around from the shoulder under the armpit and draped over on to the chest. Sergeants were to wear worsted sashes, which were usually red with a stripe in the colour of the facings, and Corporals wore a white worsted shoulder knot.

The Warrant of 1751 describes the distinctions for non-commissioned officers of the Dragoon Guards, and again these depended on the arrangement of gold and silver lace on lapels, sleeves and pockets. The Royal Warrant of 1768 specifies for the first time that the uniforms of the officers were to include epaulettes; officers of the Grenadiers were to have one on each shoulder while battalion officers wore one only, on the right shoulder, and the choice was to be either embroidery, lace, gold or silver. Sergeants wore sashes of crimson with a stripe of the regimental facing colour, whilst the Corporal's coat had a silk epaulette on the right shoulder. These epaulettes consisted of a narrow strip, sometimes parallel sided, sometimes swelling out at the end, from which hung a tassel or frill of gold or silver braid.

In the Continental Army of America during the Revolutionary War, General Officers wore a sash across the breast, over their waistcoat and beneath the coat, whilst other officers had cockades and N.C.O.s had epaulettes or strips of cloth on their shoulders. Field officers wore red or pink cockades on their hats, Captains yellow and Subalterns green. In the case of N.C.O.s the material was stitched to the right shoulder of the coat, and was red for Sergeants and green for Corporals. In 1780 the regulations were changed and officers thereafter wore a special uniform, their rank being indicated by the number of silver stars fixed on gold epaulettes and by the plume on their hats. A plume of black and white and two stars indicated a Major-General, a white plume and one star a Brigadier General; Colonels, Lieutenant-Colonels, and Majors wore two epaulettes, and Captains and Subalterns one epaulette,

Captains on the right, Subalterns on the left. Silver was used by the infantry and cavalry, and gold by the artillery. All officers wore a black cockade on their hat, a practice also followed by the British Army.

In 1786 officers of the British Army lost another distinguishing feature—the spontoon, a short pole arm with a single cross-bar. Sergeants still carried the long halberd as an indication of rank, but in 1791 an army order authorised the issuing of a short pike, or spear, in its place. It was carried until 1830 by infantry Sergeants although its use was apparently continued in the artillery until 1845. Also in 1791, Grenadier officers were ordered to add grenade insignia to their epaulettes, and officers of the Light Company to add the traditional bugle emblem. Field officers were given two epaulettes. By the beginning of the 19th Century officers' epaulettes became very elaborate, being made stiffer

Fig. 154: British Army collar dogs. Left to right, top: *The Argyll & Sutherland Highlanders, The Royal Scots Greys (2nd Dragoons), The King's Own Royal Regiment (Lancaster), and The Monmouthshire Regiment.* Bottom: *The 13th Hussars (1901–22), Army Veterinary Corps (1903–1918), Royal Tank Regiment (pair) and The Northamptonshire Regiment (Victorian).*

and fitted with quite fancy fringes. In the 1830s the Guards tunic was fitted with white-fringed epaulettes for other ranks and gold for Sergeants. The gorgeous epaulettes of the officers were finally discarded in the 1850s, but this raised another problem, for badges of rank had been displayed on these fittings. The alternative position chosen was the collar; field officers then had lace all around the collar, Colonels were given a crown and star, and so on down through the ranks to a single star for a Sub-Lieutenant; for ranks below

Major the lace was restricted to the front and top of the collar. With the removal of the epaulettes the crimson sash was no longer wrapped around the waist, as it had been for some time past, but was now turned into a shoulder sash, passing over the left shoulder where a thin crimson cord retained it in position.

In the 1880s the insignia of rank for officers was moved back to the shoulders, where they were fitted to twisted gold cords. Officers' rank badges largely stayed on the shoulder although there were variations which became quite complex with certain ranks being distinguished by insignia on the cuff. Certain grades of service were indicated by the wearing of gorget patches, that is red, blue or green strips of material with strips of braid down the centre, worn

Fig. 155: British Army shoulder titles, including 15th (King's) Hussars, pre-1922; Army Catering Corps; King's Dragoon Guards; 15th/19th The King's Royal Hussars (post-1922); 3rd Dragoon Guards (post-1922); 13th/18th Royal Hussars (Queen Mary's Own), post-1922; The 9th (Queen's Royal) Lancers, pre-1960.

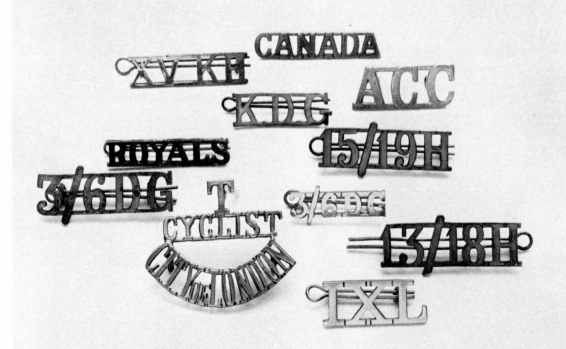

on the lapels. Distinction was also made by the colour of the brand around the peaked cap worn by officers.

In addition to badges of rank, further badges were worn on the arms at various times. The practice became particularly common during Victoria's reign, such badges being an indication of proficiency or specialised skills; crossed swords indicated the best swordsman in every twenty men, a spur was for the rough rider, axes for an infantry pioneer, and obvious motifs such as a brass drum indicated a bandsman. Early examples of these badges were embroidered but later metal, usually brass, was adopted.

Buttons were designed originally as mere ornaments, being mentioned as far back as the 14th Century, but they were adopted as a means of fastening in the 15th Century. They came to play a very important part in military uniforms, as did the loops to secure them, which were often one of the most decorative features of the uniform. By the 17th Century large numbers of buttons were being used on the uniform coat, sometimes in double or triple rows, some tunics carrying as many as fifty or sixty individual buttons. Buttons were also used to decorate the breeches, being arranged in rows down the side. Most of these buttons, particularly for the officers,

Fig. 156: Shoulder pieces. Gilt shoulder scale with silver rose, 7¼ by 5 inches, Duke of Lancaster's Yeomanry, mid-19th Century; silver shoulder cord of a Lieutenant-General, 5¾ by 3¼ inches, c.1910; shoulder chain worn by cavalry units and Royal Horse Artillery; chain of East Lancashire Yeomanry, 6½ by 3½ inches.

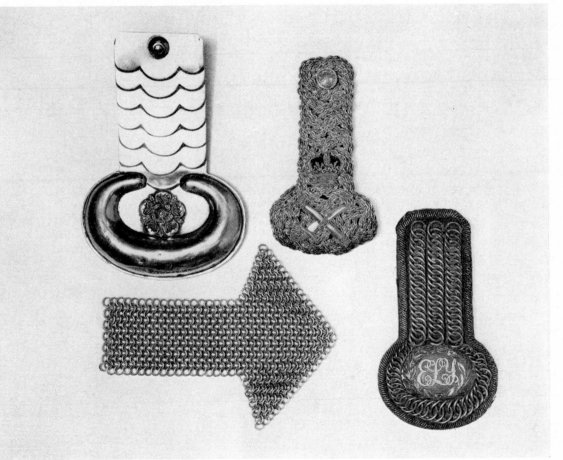

appear to have been gilt, that is covered with a thin layer of gold.

Large quantities of buttons were produced in Birmingham from the 17th Century onwards, and brass buttons are mentioned as a product of Birmingham in the latter part of the 18th Century. Every other kind of material has been used—ivory, horn, bone, mother-of-pearl, porcelain, glass and wood, even cut steel—although the expense of these latter precluded their use in general army dress. As early as the beginning of the 17th Century there is a mention of pewter buttons for other ranks. It was apparently not until 1767 that it was ordered that buttons should bear the regimental number, although the French had adopted this practice five years earlier. This detail is included in the warrant of 1768, which states that the number of the regiment should be worn on the buttons of both officers and men.

The same practice was followed in the colonies, and in July 1775 the Massachusetts Provincial Congress ordered that coats of the state regiments should have pewter buttons with the number stamped on the face, and this became general policy.

A number of buttons have been excavated from the sites of various forts in the U.S.A. and Canada, and since it is known in which years any particular regiment was serving in North America, it is possible to date the buttons accurately. Most of those for officers are made of two pieces, a back of wood or bone which is covered with a thin sheet of silver; those for the men were flat and made of pewter with the number embossed or occassionally engraved on the surface. The flat single-piece button was gradually changed in design and became slightly domed, and around the turn of the 18th Century the manufacturers of military buttons began to put their name on the back. It is interesting to note that the majority of those examples excavated in

Fig. 157: A selection of foreign badges. Top, *a Bulgarian officer's cap badge from pre-Communist days. Second row, Soviet Naval officer's cap badge, and a Netherlands cavalry badge. Third row, badges of the Netherlands Pontooneers and French (armoured) cavalry. Bottom row, pre-Communist Polish Air Force collar badge, Netherlands anti-aircraft artillery, and French artillery school badge on leather panel for suspension from breast pocket button.*

Above, *Fig. 158: German (Nazi) blockade runner's badge, of self-explanatory design; this is typical of German breast badges of the 1933–45 period. The miniature is for wear in the lapel.*

North America dating from 1800 onwards are made by the firms of Nutting and McGowan. The doming of buttons became more pronounced, and eventually a new type of two-piece button was produced in which the back, to which the shank was attached, was made separately from the high domed front piece. These continued in general use until about 1855 when a larger-sized button with a rim was introduced; at the same date pewter buttons were abolished for other ranks and brass ones substituted. In 1871 the regimental button bearing the number, title or both was abolished for most regiments and a single general service type which bore only the Royal Arms was issued to other ranks—although, in certain cases, N.C.O.s retained

Below, *Fig. 159: British Army Buttons. Top, left to right: Royal Engineer Department (Victorian); Control Department (Victorian); Army Pay Department (Victorian, 1878–1901); Army Ordnance Department (Victorian, c.1900). Bottom Medical Staff (Victorian, 1878–1898); The Royal Scots (1901); The Royal Scots (Victorian).*

Right, *Plate 24: Shoulder and arm badges of Europe and America. Top left is the shoulder strap of a British Admiral, and top right the shoulder cord of a British Lieutenant-General. The Russian shoulder-boards to the left of the bulldog patch are those of Captains of Pioneers— note crossed axes—and Infantry. The shoulder-boards marked 15 and 75 are Imperial German pieces, and the twisted shoulder-cords with red underlay were worn by the Connaught Rangers, pre-1881. Bottom left is the embroidered arm badge of a Sergeant in the army of Queen Victoria; and among the other pieces may be recognized the patch of the U.S. Army's Tank Destroyer battalions, an R.A.F. pilot's wings, a Polish cap badge, and the famous "Bloody One" shoulder-patch of the American 1st Infantry Division.*

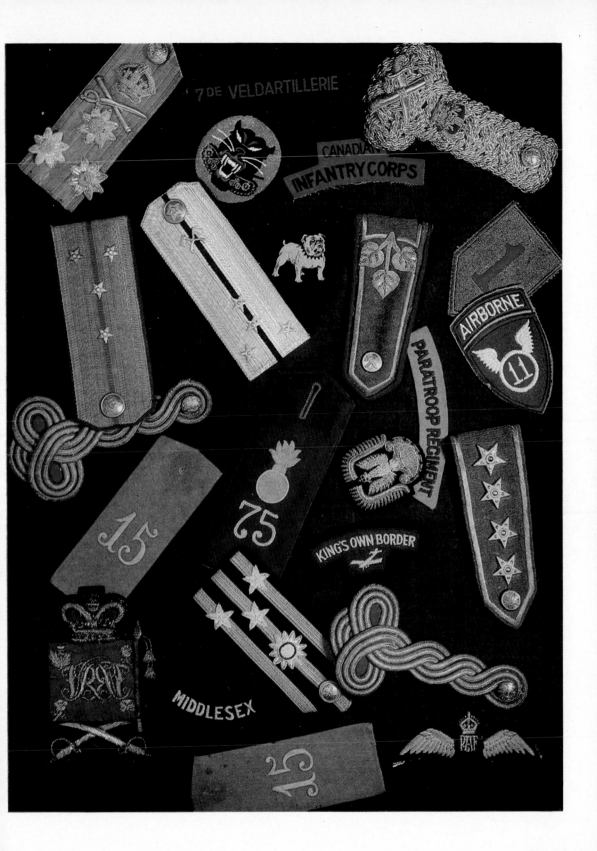

Fig. 160: White metal badge pinned to dark green patch and worn on the turban by the old 20th Madras Native Infantry. The patch measures 4¼ by 3¼ inches.

the older pattern. Other ranks regained their regimental buttons in 1928.

Most of the British Army buttons, during the period 1800 to the present day, were supplied by a small group of makers who had been in business for very long periods. Firmin, Gaunt, Pitt and Nutting are probably the best known of London makers, while Smith and Wright of Birmingham and London was another well-known supplier. Brass was the most common material used, although certain units such as the Rifle Regiment used dark composition materials for buttons, so that there should be no danger of reflection from shiny surfaces. Modern buttons and badges have utilised— or suffered from, as traditionalists would hold—modern technology, and since the Second World War various plastics have been used in their construction.

In general the development of badges has followed much the same path in most countries, although the method of display has varied. French badges, which in recent decades have included many very attractive designs of coloured enamel, are frequently suspended from the breast pocket button on leather panels. During this century Germany has followed the practice of displaying many types of metal badges and decorations on the breast of the tunic. The British Army has retained the general practice of wearing unit badges on the headgear, and in certain circumstances on the lapels, through several progressive redesigns of the service uniform; and the United States Army has proliferated the use of shoulder and arm badges. Most of the American Corps signs originated on an unofficial basis during and after the First World War, but during the Second World War the enormous increase in the size of the forces led to the official endorsement of many others. Unlike earlier examples these Divisional and Corps patches were precision-made by machines and were of colourful and standard designs, being worn at the shoulder at the top of the sleeve. These shoulder patches have been adopted by many other nations in the past twenty years, as being both attractive and practical for wear on the various types of combat clothing in which the modern soldier spends much of his life.

Belts, Buckles, and Accoutrements

13

Belts, Buckles, and Accoutrements

Title page, *Fig. 161: Waist belt and metal-lined cartridge box of The Queen's Westminster Rifle Volunteers, c. 1860. The belt is secured by a slot and tongue buckle.*

Left, *Plate 25: Shoulder belt plates of top left, 9th (The Earl of Norfolk's) Regiment of Foot, Other Ranks, c. 1820; top right, 17th (Leicestershire) Regiment of Foot, Other Ranks, c. 1790, brass; centre left, Loyal Chelmsford Volunteers, c. 1805, gilt; centre, helmet plate of 3rd Volunteer Bn., The Welsh Regiment (Cardiff), late 19th Century; centre right, St. Margaret's & St. John's Association, c. 1805; bottom left, 2nd West India Regiment, c. 1835–55; bottom right, 88th Regiment of Foot (Connaught Rangers).*

Right, *Fig. 162: Solid silver shoulder belt plate bearing hallmarks and date letter for 1791, of the 2nd (Queen's Royal) Regiment of Foot; 3 by 2¼ inches.*

APART from the most primitive warriors, soldiers of all periods have been festooned with equipment of one kind or another. One of the first accessories to appear was a sword belt and scabbard, and their design was regulated by the pattern of sword currently in use. The Roman legionary was fitted with a wide waist-belt of leather which was decorated with metal plates. During the 1st Century A.D. these plates were quite elaborate, being gilded, silvered or covered with applied niello work. By the end of the century they had been simplified and had cut-out patterns, so that when the plate was fitted over a coloured background the colour showed through the spaces. Not only did the belt support a dagger and scabbard but it also afforded some abdominal protection, for a number of weighted leather thongs, covered with small metal plates, hung from the front to cover the groin.

Dagger scabbards, secured on the left, were quite highly decorated, as was that of the sword. This short, broad-bladed weapon hung from a shoulder strap on the right, for its length allowed it to be drawn easily with the right hand. Nearly all the contemporary illustrations show the sword worn fairly high up under the arm, thus ensuring that it would not entangle the legionary's legs and trip him. The strap from which it hung was almost certainly of leather and, conceivably, was also fitted with small metal plates in the same fashion as the waist belt.

Not for nothing was the Roman legionary nicknamed "Marius mule", for in addition to his armour and weapons he was expected to carry (according to Josephus, writing during the period of the early Empire) rations, a wicker basket, a rope of leather, and a hook, as well as a dual-purpose tool known as a *dolabrum* which was a combined axe, pickaxe and adze. The sharp edge was protected by a bronze guard, and this too could be hung from the belt.

During the so-called Dark Ages informa-

tion about the details of swords and their decorations is less easy to come by, and there is doubt as to the best interpretation of the surviving evidence. It seems likely that warriors of the Franks and Almani decorated their swords with charms or amulets in the form of small balls fastened to the scabbard by leather thongs. The practice seems to have been common from the 5th Century, but the evidence is somewhat contradictory. In the 7th Century taste seems to have changed and in place of the balls, little metal pyramids were fashionable; they were of bronze, and hollow, with a bar at the base to which a cord could be fastened. The tops were often decorated with small, semi-precious stones.

It seems likely that there was some form of retaining cord fitted which, presumably, looped around the scabbard to hold the sword in place. The Anglo-Saxon sword was carried in a sheath of wood which was covered with leather; sometimes the inside was leather-lined, and one or two excavated examples have been found with strips of

Above left, *Fig. 163: Other Rank's shoulder belt plate of the 86th (Royal County Down) Regiment of Foot, c.1850. Pressed brass, 3½ by 2¾ inches.*

Above, *Fig. 164: Officer's shoulder belt plate of the 88th (Connaught Rangers) Regiment of Foot; the back plate and central device are of "frosted" gilt, and the star of white metal. On the back is engraved: "Prestd by J. Gore Esq. to Serj Major Hendley Depot 88 Reg." Circa 1835; 3¾ by 3 inches.*

Right, *Fig. 165: Types of fitting found of belt plates; left to right, top to bottom: 86th (Royal County Down) Regiment— see Fig. 163; 88th (Connaught Rangers) Regiment—see Fig. 164; 17th (Leicestershire) Regiment—see Plate 25; St. Margaret's & St. John's Association (Volunteers)—see Plate 25.*

lamb's fleece fastened on the inside. This wool served a double purpose; it gripped the blade securely but not too tightly, and the natural lanoline or grease in the wool helped to lubricate the blade and reduce rusting. On some scabbards an embossed effect was given to the leather by carving the wooden case and then shrinking the outer leather into place. The chape or metal tip to the scabbard was often quite elaborate, as was the mouth piece.

These swords were worn on the left, the scabbards being attached by rings. The short Roman *gladius* had given way to much longer weapons, which had to be worn on the left and drawn across the body with the right hand.

Contemporary illustrations indicate that both shoulder and waist belts were used to support the sword. Shoulder belts appear more frequently during the earlier period but by the 7th Century A.D. waist belts begin to predominate. The evidence of the Bayeux Tapestry suggests that by the 11th Century the waist belt was fairly general, since every armed figure is shown with a sword on such a belt. At one point Harold is shown holding his sword in its scabbard and from the top, just below the cross guard, the tapestry shows the ends of a straight belt hanging down, complete with buckles. Armoured knights in their mail have no visible belts, but some figures are shown with the sword hilt sticking out through the hauberk. If this represents the facts then it may be assumed that there was a slit at the

side of the hauberk and the sword was worn beneath it with the hilt arranged as to project through the slit. However, the evidence is too fragmentary to draw firm conclusions.

The waist belt seems to have been firmly established by the 13th Century, and much more is known about belts of this period, for they are illustrated on many of the incised brasses of the time. By and large, as swords became longer it became necessary to tilt the scabbard so that the tip did not touch the floor. Sword blades were now too long to hang down straight, and so the belt was designed to tilt the scabbard forward. Belts were made in two pieces; one fairly short and the other long enough to encircle the hips. The short section was secured to the scabbard just below the mouth, whilst

Below, *Fig. 166: Waist belt tongue and loop buckle of the East Surrey Regiment, in gilt and white metal; the central device is composed of the Arms of Guildford. 3¼ by 1⅞ inches.* **Right,** *Fig. 167: Brass belt pouch of the Italian Field Artillery, with spring catches to clip to the belt; 6 by 3¼ inches.*

the longer section was fixed to it some inches lower down. The two ends either buckled or tied together, and by tightening the belt the degree of tilt on the scabbard could be altered. By the mid-14th Century the belt was no longer laced to the scabbard, but fitted on to attached rings.

By the mid-14th Century a tight-fitting hip belt was popular, and for the richer members of the community it was common to decorate the belt with jewelled plaques. At first this belt appears to have been purely decorative, but later the sword and dagger were attached to it by securing cords or hooks. The weight of the two weapons could well have dragged this belt down over the hips so it may be assumed that it was held in place by some lacing or hooks. During the first part of the 15th Century this hip belt continued in use, and in some cases it was actually secured to the skirt of the armour, but during the same period there was a return to a belt which hung loosely from the waist and crossed the thighs diagonally. Small rings at the top of the scabbard were used to attach it to the belt. During the latter part of the 15th Century the belt was divided to form a Y-shape; and the top of the scabbard was

fastened to the waist belt while the other arm of the Y was attached lower down on the edge of the scabbard so tilting the sword forward slightly.

DURING the early part of the 16th Century this diagonally-shaped waist belt seems to have remained predominant and again the belt appears to have been split, but during the second part of the century the entire system of suspending the sword was altered. A narrow waist belt was worn and from this hung a triangular support terminated by as many as a dozen small straps. This hanger hooked on to a ring on the waist belt and the scabbard pushed through the small buckled straps at the base. To prevent the sword flapping a second strap extended from the front of the sling round the front of the waist. The sword hung fairly securely and was almost parallel with the ground since the blade was often of an excessive length. During the 17th Century there was a general drift back to the older shoulder belt, although waist belts were still worn by many. The shoulder belt terminated in a greatly simplified version of the sword hanger with its many small straps. The waist belt used basically the same pattern to secure the scabbard, which often had a straight hook-like arm to hold it in place in the hanger. Naturally enough, for the "other ranks" belts were far less elaborate. Those of the very late 17th and early 18th Century seem to have been of buff leather and very plain, and crossed the shoulder to terminate in a widened section which held the scabbard.

For the greater part of the 18th Century and indeed for the latter part of the 17th Century the most common form of sword belt was that worn around the waist. Illustrations by contemporary artists suggest that it was essentially a white leather belt probably of untreated leather, fitted with an oval or rectangular buckle, usually of brass. They had either a double strap which connected to the scabbard or a special fitting as shown in an illustration of

Dutch infantry *circa* 1680, in which the belt has the bayonet attached near the front buckle and an extension coming round to connect to the sword scabbard. A series of paintings which show a member of the Second Troop of Horse Guards performing manual exercises, dated around 1740, shows the same form of belt except that this one appears to have some form of decoration, probably lines of lace running along the centre and edges. A second wide belt with blue edging crossed the shoulder and supported a cartridge case. This cross belt was

Fig. 168: Pair of plain leather pistol holsters of the type carried at the horse's neck, dating from the mid-19th Century. Note that one has a bullet hole in the tip.

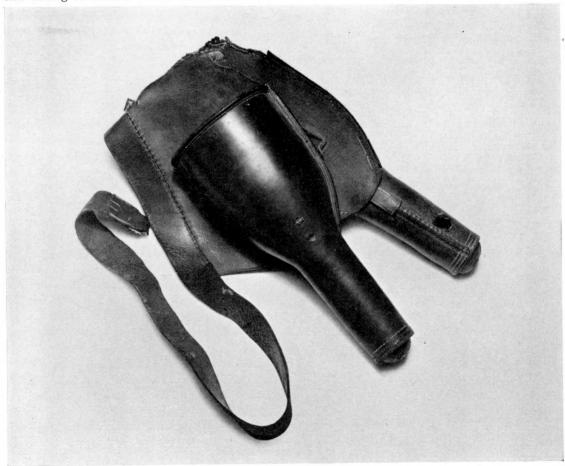

often secured on the left shoulder by a strap with a button, and is illustrated on the painting of David Morier in 1751. The buckle shown is again very large and rectangular, with a double prong fitting. Practice evidently varied, for this artist shows cavalry, for example the 2nd Queen's Dragoon Guards, wearing the waist sword-belt of buff leather, complete with suspension straps. A sword knot of the same material was fitted to the hilt of the sword. This same soldier wears across his shoulder a cartridge box belt, but a private of the 1st Horse is shown wearing two very wide cross belts, one of which holds the broadsword and the other the cartridge pouch. The cartridge pouch shown on the private of the 6th Inniskilling Dragoons is fairly large with a quite ornate flap, and it fits on the right hand side of the body. The artist Morier also painted a farrier of the 11th Dragoons, and the man's trade is shown clearly on his fur cap by a horse shoe and hammers on the metal plate. Paintings of infantry regiments show more or less the same arrangements as for cavalry, with the Grenadiers wearing a very wide cross belt to which was attached the pouch; they had a double-pronged rectangular buckle. The sword and bayonet were suspended from a waist belt with an oval buckle, worn over the waistcoat and under the coat. Even the method of wearing the belt varied, for Grenadiers of the 4th King's Own, 5th, and 6th Regiments of Foot wore the sword belt over the outside coat and passing over the shoulder belt. The 7th Royal Fusiliers follow the same system, but the 8th King's reverts to the belt worn under the coat.

There are variations too in the wearing of sword knots. In general, this series of paintings shows the Grenadiers with a sword knot, but many of the other regiments depicted have no such fitting. Originally they were simply leather loops which were passed around the wrist so that the sword might not be lost by accident or in combat. As with all things military they tended to become more ornate and decorative, and soon many regiments or units were distinguishing themselves by the design of their sword knot, and this tendency was to continue throughout the 19th Century. Around the middle of the 18th Century most appear to have been of natural, untreated leather but by the end of the century and the beginning of the 19th Century quite elaborately decorated gold and scarlet ones fitted with fringes, tassels and acorns were commonly used.

In another of this series of pictures by Morier a Grenadier of the 49th Regiment of Foot is depicted with a double cross belt; a very wide one suspending a pouch, and another coming quite high up under the shoulder which holds a sword and bayonet. To judge by Morier's paintings, and he covers quite a large number of troops, the arrangement of cross and waist belt seems to have been fairly general for English, Prussian and Hanoverian troops. When the British Infantry had their sword withdrawn in 1768 the belt was naturally simplified, since it no longer had to support both bayonet and sword.

By the early 19th Century the decorations on these belts had developed quite considerably and although the waist belt was still worn by many of the cavalry it no longer fitted tightly but draped across the thighs. In place of the large buckle some were secured by a serpent-type buckle in which a hook engaged with a loop.

At the beginning of the 19th Century, to judge from the illustrations available, there were many forms of belt in service. Some were fitted with oblong buckles, others obviously favoured the serpent type fitting, whilst one painting dated 1803 shows what appears to be the tongue and loop system being used by a volunteer. By this period cavalry officers had developed another form of belt decoration, for they had a shoulder pouch worn in the small of the back and fitted by means of spring clips to a shoulder belt. During the 1820s, at least in the Coldstream Guards, there was a reversion to the shoulder belt for suspending the sword; it is shown as a wide white one with a frog attachment to hold the sword secure, by means of a slot to receive the stud fitted to the scabbard.

DURING the latter part of the 18th Century it became quite common for a large securing plate to be fitted on the shoulder belt. So far no order authorising them has been traced. In general the earlier examples appear to have been oval and fairly large. For other ranks they were usually stamped out of brass but many, particularly those of officers, had separate numbers and crowns fitted by means of a wire attachment at the back or by means of pin and socket attachments (see Fig. 164). During the period of the Napoleonic Wars most of the volunteers wore these plates, and they seem to have retained the oval shape throughout their active lives. Although known by collectors as shoulder belt plates, the contemporary term was "breast plate", and this is the expression used in all references to uniforms of the period.

In the case of volunteers these shoulder belt plates were nearly always of gilt, as were most buttons and badges worn by officers. The trend was towards a larger, more rectangular form, at first with rounded corners, but from about the 1820s it became a basically rectangular shape with square corners. As with the helmet plates the star was incorporated into the design of the shoulder belt plates, and in the case of those fitted with various regimental insignia each item was often made separately and secured by a lug which passed through the star and the main plate of the shoulder belt plate, to be held in place by a retaining pin. These plates gradually became more and more elaborate until they were finally abolished in 1855, although they were retained by certain Scottish Regiments and were worn by officers. Many surviving examples are fitted with a thin sheet of leather on the back, presumably to prevent scratching on buttons and wear on tunics. Shoulder belt plates secured the two ends of the belt and, in the case of oval versions, most have two studs and a hook, but with the later 19th Century examples there are usually two studs and two hooks, although the design was by no means standard (see Fig. 165).

With the general adoption of the waist belt in the latter part of Victoria's reign there was a common use of a rectangular belt buckle with the Queen's cypher and various regimental badges applied. The design of the waist belt was subject to dress regulations, and details of the design of lace and badges on the belt were all set down. From the main waist belt hung two straps, one short and one long, and these were clipped on to the rings on the sword scabbard. For convenience the sword could be

Below, *Fig. 169: Stirrup of the Viking period, decorated with simple repetitive patterns. (British Museum)*

secured to a single hook fitted at the side of the belt. Towards the latter part of Victoria's reign there was a more general use of the D-shaped tongue type buckle, usually bearing a lion and crown. Another type which seems to have come into general use at the same period was a more complex model with a double oval on either side of a serpent clasp.

Attractive as these belts were they were not really suitable for hard usage, and in 1900 a far more practical and workmanlike belt, known as the Sam Browne, was officially adopted. The name was derived from the traditional inventor, General Sir Sam Browne, V.C.; it consisted of a wide, stout leather waist belt with shoulder supports. Two cross braces were available, although Dress Regulations (1900) state that the one passing over the left shoulder need not be worn unless required to support a revolver holster. To the waist belt could be secured a holster, ammunition pouch and scabbard supports. For officers required to wear their sword belt under their tunic a webbing belt was available.

The sword and holster were not the only items secured to the waist belt, and the cavalry and horse artillery had an extra fitting known as the sabretache. These flat cases were adopted in 1814 and were originally designed for the practical purpose of carrying messages; they were, in effect, a separate pocket attached to a uniform which generally speaking had none. The sabretache was usually secured by three straps to the waist belt, and bore on the front flap some regimental insignia or detail. Dress models were quite elaborate, with bullion embroidery, but undress ones were far simpler—red Russian leather for Colonels on the Staff, and black patent leather for other mounted officers, with approved regimental devices. Their original purpose was soon obscured by the embroidery and embellishments which were added

Below, *Fig. 170: Early 17th Century iron spur, with common five-point rowel and— unusually—a brass buckle. (Mungeam Collection)*

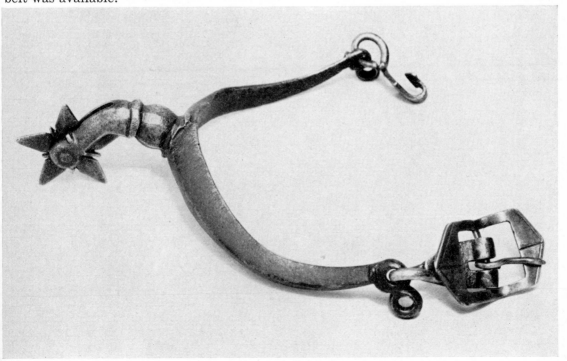

to these items. They were officially discontinued in 1901.

Until the adoption of the 1796 pattern Light Dragoon Sword it is true to say that all British scabbards were of leather with metal fittings. With the 1796 pattern a metal sheath made its appearance, although the issue of such did not become general practice. Metal scabbards were not really favoured by the experts, for it was felt that the withdrawing and replacing of the sword tended to dull the edge as it rubbed against the steel scabbard. In general terms the light cavalry favoured a curved slashing sword, and the heavy cavalry a rigid-bladed one primarily designed for thrusting; whilst the infantry officer favoured a cut and thrust sword which sought to combine the best features of both types.

Holsters for pistols were used from the 16th Century onwards, but since military

pistols tended to be rather large and heavy the holsters were usually secured at the horse's neck. In the case of infantry officers the pistol was secured either to the shoulder or waist belt by means of a belt hook, which was simply a metal arm secured to the side of the stock and pushed behind the belt. Some of the earliest examples of personal holsters designed to allow an officer to carry a pistol at his belt appear to have been made in France, and several Napoleonic troops, especially defenders of the standards, were shown wearing personal holsters. In Britain the personal

Below, *Fig. 171: Pair of standard British Army spurs dated 1918, complete with leather straps and guards.* **Opposite,** *Fig. 172: Gorget which belonged to Lt. Col. William Miller, 1st Foot Guards, who was killed at Quatre Bras during the Waterloo campaign of 1815. (National Army Museum)*

holster does not appear to have gained general acceptance until the 1840s or '50s when pepperbox pistols and percussion revolvers, capable of firing five or six shots after each loading, became popular. The holster was then transferred from the horse to the waist belt, and generally consisted of a leather body with a top flap which folded over to hold the pistol firmly in place. A later feature was the adoption of a lanyard passing round the neck or shoulder and tied to a loop fitted to the base of the butt of the revolver, again to prevent accidental loss.

CAVALRYMEN wore spurs, which had been in use since the earliest times. In the 11th Century they were basically a U-shaped arm fitting over the back of the heel, to the centre of which was fitted a short spike. By the 13th Century the prick spur was a little more elaborate, having a ball-shaped fitting on the back of the U-piece from which projected the spike. In the early 14th Century a new feature appeared; this was the rowel, a spiked plate, free to rotate, mounted at the end of the shank. The wearing of horse armour meant that the foot of the rider was held further away from the horse and for this reason the shank of the spurs tended to be very long. As armour was gradually abandoned the shape of the spur was modified and the shank made shorter. 17th Century British spurs are characterised by the sharp bend in the shank. By the early 18th Century the cavalryman's spur had acquired the shape which was to remain largely unchanged until the present. A rowel was mounted at the end of a short shank, and the U-shaped base fitted over the heel and was held in place by straps or chains, usually with a large square leather patch at the front. In the 19th Century many spurs were secured lower down on the foot and were fixed directly to the heel of the boot. Shanks were fairly short and straight, or acutely angled upwards. Like all other military finery the wearing of spurs became

systemised, and Dress Regulations detail the distinctions, such as box spurs with "dumb rowels" for review and Mess orders —these were secured to the boot by engaging an arm on the inside of the spur with a recess in the heel. To avoid the possibility of unfortunate entanglements the rowel was devoid of spikes.

The New Model Army of Cromwell had worn a helmet, an elbow gauntlet, and a breast and back plate—and, on occasion, a gorget. This had been a piece of armour designed to protect the upper chest and throat. From a functional piece of armour the gorget evolved into an embossed plate hung around the neck. Development continued and there was a simplification in design, until the gorget was merely a crescent-shaped piece of metal decorated with the Royal Arms in one form or another. Earlier examples appear to have been fairly large, with the Arms engraved on the surface. Occasionally the Arms were made separately, and fastened on to the base plate. During the latter part of the 18th Century the gorget became smaller, with a more pronounced curve, and the engraving too became simpler. General service models were decorated either with G.R. and

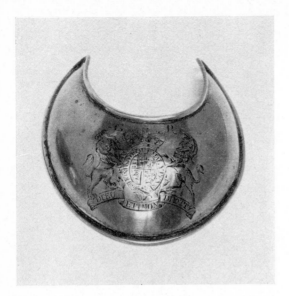

two branches of laurels, or with the Royal Coat of Arms. Many were identified by the engraved regimental number. These gilded gorgets were lined, like the shoulder belt plates, with thin chamois leather, and were secured around the neck by pieces of ribbon which passed through two holes punched in the two topmost points of the crescent. Blue ribbon appears to have been commonly used for this function. The gorget lingered on until 1830 when it was finally abandoned, although its presence was remembered by the so-called "gorget patches" of red which were worn by British infantry officers to indicate staff status. On the Continent gorgets were retained in service for a much longer period; they were revived under the Nazi regime, when large gorgets suspended from chains became part of the uniform of the standard bearer and the military police-man.

Although the infantry might have their gorgets and shakos, they were as nothing beside the splendour of the 19th Century cavalryman and his mount. As already pointed out the uniform of the mounted man was always a little more gorgeous than that of the infantry, probably because the foot soldier was subject to greater physical strain, having no mount to help him. In

Above left, *Fig. 173: British officer's gorget bearing the Royal Arms used from 1714 to 1801, although this specimen dates from the latter part of that period; 4¼ by 3¼ inches.* **Above,** *Fig. 174: Similar gilt gorget of the early 19th Century, though slightly wider than previous subject. It bears the Royal Cypher and laurel leaves.*

Top, *Plate 26: a waist belt of the Royal Medical Corps, 1910–1936.* **Centre** *is a waist belt of the late Victorian period, and* **bottom** *is an Army Veterinary Department waist belt of the Victorian period.*

addition to the man there was always the horse to be decorated, and naturally this was an opportunity not to be missed. The holsters mentioned above were often fitted with large, beautifully decorated flaps and covers during the 17th and 18th Centuries. More mundane ones of plain leather were general during the first half of the 19th Century.

Saddles had been decorated at various periods—many were actually fashioned

from ivory—but during the 18th Century it became common to fit decorative covers at the back of the saddle, "housings", which usually repeated the decoration on the holster covers. Early in the 19th Century a far more elaborate decoration was adopted, known as the shabraque (see Plate 27). This profusely decorated cloth covered the entire saddle, with a hole to accept the cantle. Some were fitted with sheepskins or leopard skins, and others were covered with heavy embroidery, bringing the weight up to seven pounds for this item alone. As with all military fittings various distinctions were introduced; heavy cavalry were supposed to have shabraques with square corners, lancers' were supposed to be rounded, while those of the Hussars were pointed.

Less decorative, but far more important, were the extra items such as carbine holsters and lance buckets. Carbines, a smaller version of the infantry rifle, had for long been carried suspended from a shoulder strap, but this was later replaced by a form of holster fitted on the right side of the saddle. To support the lance a narrow, tubular leather bucket was fitted to the left stirrup, into which was placed the ferrule of the lance.

Fig. 175: Gorget of a French Infantry officer of circa 1856; the plate is gilt and the eagle silver. The loops secured the gorget to the epaulette buttons.

Books

and

Prints

14

Books and Prints

Title page, *Fig. 176: Two from a very early set of 50 military cigarette cards issued by John Player Ltd. in 1900; on the back of each card was listed the battle honours of the regiment.* $1\frac{3}{8}$ by $2\frac{5}{8}$ inches.

Left, *Plate 27: Coloured print of an Officer of the 1st Regiment of Life Guards—No. 1 in a series of Officers of the British Army by L. Mansion and St. Eschauzier, published in 1831: 19 by 15 inches.*
Right, *Fig. 177: Made for an illustrated edition of Virgil, printed in Strasbourg in 1502, this print is typical of the period; all the characters are armed and armoured in contemporary fashion.*

It is perhaps a sad commentary that so much of man's earliest pictorial art should have been devoted to recording deeds of violence. The carvings and paintings of Egypt and Assyria abound with illustrations of victories in war, and the inscriptions boast of the slaughter and destruction. Assyrian sculptures show the attack and capture of towns, and Egyptian carvings and paintings show Pharaoh triumphant, with prisoners and booty pouring into his royal palace. Some of the earliest writings, too, are devoted to the reporting of wars; Polybus, Xenophon, Cæsar, Josephus and Tacitus are just a few of the classical immortals whose writings abound with references to the glories, adventures, misery and excitement of war.

During the Middle Ages, with the emphasis on chivalry and feudalism, it is not surprising that many of the best known books should be devoted to the knightly arts and to glorifying battle; and with the advent of printing in Europe in the late 15th Century the number of books devoted to war, its management, study and usage, multiplied enormously. As far as Britain is

concerned probably the most fruitful period was the early part of the 17th Century. Learned books on the management and conduct of war begin to appear in catalogues of printed books from the latter part of the 16th Century. Sir Edward Hoby's *The Theorique And Practise Of Warre*, published in 1597, is typical of the period, containing learned discussions on which form of weapon was preferable and how best the weapons might be used. During this period and the 17th Century there was, of course, considerable discussion amongst military thinkers as to the best form of weapon. Each school of thought had its advocate; some were all in favour of the new firearms, others preferred the traditional long bow and pike, and many were the suggestions, arguments and reasons advanced by the experts for the retention of one or the other.

Sir John Smythe, in *Certen Instructions, Observaconns And Orders Militarie Requisite For All Cheeftaines, Captaines And Higher And Lower Men Charge*, published in 1594, bitterly opposed the new weapon and praised the virtues of the long bow. William Neade, in *The Double-Armed Man*

By The New Invention, published in 1625, put forward the theory that a soldier armed with a long pike and a bow would give far better service than a musketeer, and included in the book some woodcuts showing how this might be done. Judging by the illustrations the entire process would have been extremely unwieldy. It is interesting to note that this idea was not completely abandoned, and as late as 1798 Richard Mason produced a book called *Pro Aris Et Focis* in which he seriously advanced the idea that a form of folding pike, coupled with the use of the long bow, would be an extremely effective way of repelling the anticipated invasion from France.

One of the best known of all military books of this period is that illustrated by Jacob de Gheyn, *The Exercise Of Armes For Calivers, Muskettes And Pikes*, printed in various editions although originally appearing in 1607. This, although it varied according to the edition, contained 117 plates showing the various movements for the musketeer to load and handle his matchlock, how the caliver—a smaller form of matchlock—was used, and also how the pikeman should cope with his cumbersome 16 or 20-foot long weapon. The plates are beautifully done and the series was copied innumerable times over the next two centuries. Although originally in black and

Below, *Fig. 178: Engraving from* Introduction à la Fortification, *1693—No. 95 of a series of 118. The volume consists of an introduction to the science of fortification, and includes plans of a large number of towns and fortresses. 10¾ by 8¼ inches.* **Opposite**, *Fig. 179: This title page is typical of 18th Century books; this particular volume, dated 1798, contains an essay on the history and use of cavalry and some 25 rather inept but not atypical plates.*

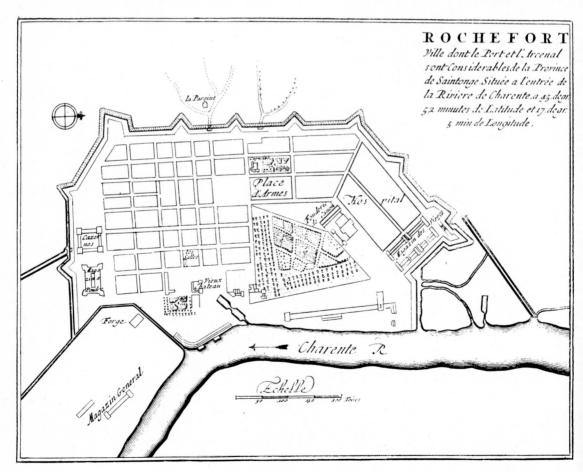

white, many will be found with the figures coloured in, but this is invariably a later addition.

During the 18th Century the flood of books by no means abated and some, such as the *Duke of Marlborough's New Exercise Of Firelocks And Bayonets*, circa 1710, were in effect, up to date versions of De Gheyn showing the correct management and use of the flintlock musket of the period. Others were more general, and some remained best sellers for many years; for example *A Treatise Of Military Discipline* by Colonel Humphrey Bland ran through many editions, nine at the very least, and became a sort of standard reference book for military orders and discipline during the greater part of the 18th Century. There were also a number of translations made available at this period, such as the *Regulations For The Prussian Infantry* which was translated by Sir William Fawcett and published in 1754.

With the outbreak of the American War of Independence, and later the Napoleonic Wars and the growth of the Volunteer movement, the number of military instruction books multiplied even more; large numbers offered advice on how to train troops to use the various weapons or carry out complicated manoeuvres of the period, whilst others advocated the pet fancies of the author. Exactly the same phenomena were apparent when the second outburst of volunteer enthusiasm took place around the middle of the 19th Century, and there was a flood of books dealing with the rifle and how to use it, how to form a volunteer unit, the duties involved, designs of uniform, methods of practice and, in fact, everything that the "do-it-yourself" soldier could possibly want to know.

The majority of the books so far discussed were, so to speak, privately published ventures; but there were, in addition, a number of official publications which were issued by Horse Guards—in modern parlance, the War Office—and these were basically vol-

REMARKS

ON

CAVALRY;

BY THE PRUSSIAN MAJOR GENERAL OF HUSSARS,

WARNERY.

TRANSLATED FROM THE ORIGINAL.

umes which set down the regulations current at that particular period. As with the privately published volumes the number of these greatly increased during the latter part of the 18th Century and the early 19th Century. Many of them included not only the regulations but also sample forms for the information of adjutants, etc., who would be required to fill in such returns. Some, but not all, were illustrated, and one of the best known of the illustrated official publications was *The Rules And Regulations For The Sword Exercise Of The Cavalry*. It contained 29 engraved plates showing the various positions of the sword and the correct procedure for the use thereof. It was originally published in 1796, and remained a standard work for some years.

Other immensely valuable books from the student's point of view, which first appeared during the 19th Century, were the official dress regulations. These were intended only to cover the dress of officers, since other ranks' uniforms were supplied by the government. As officers purchased their own it was very easy for them to deviate from the approved pattern, and these dress regulations were intended to give them guidance as to the official uniform. The first appeared in 1811, with a subsequent one in 1816, but these were in fact fairly brief and were largely devoted to the details of staff uniforms. The first really comprehensive set of dress regulations gave details of the whole of the military forces and was issued in 1822. Various amendments and alterations were made over the years, and a number of new editions were published—indeed, the latest was issued this year (1970). The earlier ones contained no illustrations but from 1900 they were illustrated with photographs showing such things as headdresses, lace, buttons, badges and accoutrements.

Another immensely valuable source of information for the military historian are the Army Lists. These vary in content; some merely list officers in the Army and Royal Marines whilst others include militia, and sometimes separate volumes cover only the Volunteers. In general the make-up is the same, with the regiments arranged numerically, and brief details of any special

honours as well as a list of all officers serving with that regiment. Earlier issues usually have blank pages interspersed so that alterations could be entered to keep the list up to date. Similar lists were issued for the Navy and both sets are, of course, invaluable for the purpose of tracing specific officers during the period of their service.

In order to run such a complicated machine as the British Army general orders and regulations obviously had to be issued from time to time; these were often produced in bound editions and many such volumes will be found inscribed with various attributions such as "*For the use of the Brigade Major of the 1st Brigade in the 5th Division of Infantry*"—this appears on the fly leaf of a set of general orders for Spain and Portugal. These regulations are full of fascinating but largely useless information; for example, on 28th February 1811, from the Adjutant General's Office in Cartaxo comes a list of the officially approved contractors for the sale of snuff to the seven Divisions together with the contract prices, including "fourteen reas per pound for Segars". These orders also cast

Left, *Fig. 180: Plate No. 12 from* Remarks on Cavalry—*showing a Tartar horseman, and demonstrating the relatively poor quality of these pictures.*

Opposite, *Fig. 181: Rare example of ephemera; a Safe Conduct issued to a member of the French Republican Army dated "29 Prairial au Cinq de la République française." Instituted in 1793, this system of dating was one of the wilder excesses of the revolution; in conventional terms the pass is dated 14th June 1797.*

interesting sidelights on life in the army at that time, giving details of charges, court martials and the opinion and sentence. For example, on 3rd March 1811 the opinion and sentence of the court was that "Private John Cordlar of the Chasseurs Brittanniques . . . is guilty of the charge preferred against him, being breach of the articles of war and do, by virtue thereof sentence him . . . to be shot to death at such time and place as His Excellency, Commander of the Forces may deem fit. Which sentence has been confirmed by the Commander of the Forces". The execution was planned to be carried out on 5th March, and on 4th March it is interesting to read that during the past two years the Brigade of Guards, which had been under the command of the Commander of the Forces, had had no soldier "brought for trial before a general courts martial, no one confined in a public guard"; therefore this group were excused attendance, which was normally compulsory at all such executions.

Another series of official publications are those devoted to various mechanical and technical aspects of army life. A large number of these were normally issued in a small size, approximately four by five inches, presumably to enable them to be carried in a pocket. They covered tremendously diverse subjects, and include handbooks on Guns, Hostilities Without Declaration of War from 1700–1870, and Musketry Regulations, as well as an Urdu Primer for the use of the Colonial Artillery, 1899.

If one turns to consider the books dealing with the histories of the various regiments, corps and other groups comprising the British armies, the field is enormous. One series which must be accorded a special mention are the *Historical Records of the British Army*, by R. Cannon. These were published over a number of years around the middle of the 19th Century. Most volumes contain at least two colour plates showing the colours and uniform of the regi-

ment, and some have additional plates illustrating events relevant to the regiment. Cannon's series of books take the history of the various regiments up to the mid-19th Century, and since then dozens of other regimental histories have been published to bring the story up to date. Some of the histories are very dull reading but others are enjoyable and instructive, and contain photographs which are valuable sources of information on uniform and equipment. There is fortunately a very good bibliography—*A Bibliography of Regimental Histories of the British Army*, compiled by A. S. White and published 1965—which lists the main histories of each regiment. Many regiments have also published magazines, some for many decades, and these are valuable sources of incidental information. For the general history of the British army, the standard work, with its minor inaccuracies, is still Sir J. W. Fortescue's *History of the British Army* (London 1899–1930), which comprises thirteen volumes.

In addition to the myriad of volumes, official and semi-official, devoted to army

Fig. 182: Coloured print of an Officer of the 1st (King's) Dragoon Guards—one of a series of 70 prepared by Mansion and Eschauzier for Spooner's Military and Naval Uniforms *1833/40.*

There were other similar series published over the century, and one of the most useful for the student is *The Navy and Army Illustrated*, which was edited by Commander C. N. Robinson R. N.; first appearing in 1895, it ran into many volumes and included articles on almost every aspect of military life of the period, both in the British forces and overseas. One of the most valuable features of this series is the selection of photographs, which give so much information about the minutiae of military life at the turn of the century. Others were more specific in their content, and of these possibly one of the best known is *The Cavalry Journal*, which contained numerous articles on the history, use and equipment of the cavalry; they even set some tactical exercises to assist in the training of officers.

Over the last few decades a number of societies devoted to the serious study of military history have developed, and many issue magazines which have established a well-deserved reputation for scholarship and accuracy. The Society for Army Historical Research and the newer, but very active, Military Historical Society, both publish articles which cover many facets of military history. The National Army Museum, soon to move to its new building in Chelsea, London, has already issued a number of pamphlets devoted to specialised items, such as sabretaches, and plans are in hand to extend the range.

There has been one development over the last few years which clearly indicates the growth of interest in things military, and this is the number of reprints and facsimiles of previously out-of-print volumes issued by various publishers. The general standard has been very high and it has meant that

life, there are numerous autobiographical accounts of campaigns and life in the army. They range from Xenophon's account of the march to India to the latest memoirs of 20th Century generals. Fortunately many of the accounts devoted to famous campaigns like Waterloo, the Crimea and others, are full of incidental information, and give a vivid picture of life in the army. In addition to these full-length memoirs there were a number of periodicals which collected together anecdotes and snippets of information for the general reader. A number flourished early in the 19th Century, and one such was *The Soldiers Companion or Martial Recorded*—Volume 1, published in 1824. This is a glorious hotchpotch of anecdotes and scraps of information, and poems such as the immortal—

students have been able to acquire reference books previously beyond the range of most collectors. Dress Regulations for 1900 (reprint by Arms and Armour Press, 1970) is of great value, since it was the first of the illustrated regulations, whilst for general information on the British Army up to 1900 the fine reprint of *Records and Badges of the British Army* by Chichester and Burges Short (reprint by Frederick Muller Ltd., 1970) is of tremendous use, including as it does a number of colour plates of uniforms. The number of such reprints continues to grow and many others are planned.

In addition to books there is a vast amount of associated printed matter which is of interest to the military enthusiast. Much is best described as ephemera, intended to be used and then to be disposed of, and consequently it is usually scarce and difficult to find. Within this category come such things as recruiting posters, leaflets, official returns, souvenir programmes and similar items.

M ANY of the early military books were illustrated with woodcuts the quality of which varied considerably, ranging from the crude to the delightful. In the very early examples the illustrator used material with which he was familiar and clothed his combatants in contemporary armour. It was not unusual for Greek heroes to be shown in armour of the 16th Century and fighting with halberds—but even so they provide many valuable incidental details. Some books like De Gheyn's *Exercise Of Armes* have illustrations which are outstanding examples of draughtsmanship and accuracy. During the 17th Century a number of military books were published which gave accounts of various campaigns, and many of these are illustrated with marvellously detailed panoramic views of attacks on towns, or pitched battles. With so much compressed into a comparatively small space fine detail is lost, but for general impressions of tactics and marching they are invaluable. Some delight in the horrors of war, showing the multitude of unpleasant ways in which one might dispose of a defeated enemy.

Many of the handbooks of war were illustrated with woodcuts showing details of machines and stratagems, and one such is *Animadversions Of War* by Robert Ward, published in 1639, which contains a large number of small illustrations of infernal machines and various devices. It also gives details of the various movements in arms drill, as well as advice on how to fight an enemy. Many books of this period also illustrate the fortifications of various strongpoints and towns throughout Europe;

Fig. 183: Page of sketches of military headdresses over the years, from A History of the Dress of the British Soldier *by Lt. Col. John Luard, 1852.*

A.D. 1625–1824.

again, the draughtsmanship is usually of a high standard.

During the early part of the 18th Century the standard of line illustration was not very high, with a general crudeness and lack of fine detail, but in the field of painting there were outstanding exceptions. Portraits of leaders and paintings of battles were popular, and when Hogarth painted his famous "March of the Guards to Finchley in 1745" the soldiers were depicted with great care. In the collection of Her Majesty Queen Elizabeth at Windsor there are a series of paintings by David Morier (1705–1770) which depict the troops commanded by the Duke of Cumberland during his campaigns in the Low Countries from 1747–9. The 120 canvasses are detailed, if somewhat static, but have proved of immense worth in the study of the history of uniforms. Morier also did some paintings of battle scenes and, again, although the general style is stiff the paintings are valuable records of warfare of the period.

During the latter part of the 18th Century the number of military illustrators increased and numerous coloured plates were produced in folio or bound in volumes. Colour printing did not become a commercial proposition until the middle of the 19th Century, so that most of the plates were hand-coloured. The artist painted the picture which was then engraved and printed off in quantity, and water colour added as in the original painting.

A number of artists followed the armies

Figs. 184, 185: The Duke of Wellington was awarded a magnificent funeral by a grateful nation in September 1852. A coloured panorama was published, more than 60 feet long; this section shows a contingent of the Royal Horse Artillery in the procession, and (right) is a drawing of the funeral car with the Duke's coffin, decorated overall with captured French trophies. The monstrous vehicle was so heavy that it sank into the paved roadway.

into the field and John Clark, originally noted for his landscapes, gained the nickname of "Waterloo Clark" from the series of scenes of the battlefield which he produced. Thomas Heaphy, a water colourist of repute, went through the Peninsular Campaign and painted many portraits of serving officers.

British military feats from the taking of Seringapatam to the Battle of Waterloo were commemorated in *The Martial Achievements of Great Britain and her Allies from 1799–1815*, published by James Jenkins in 1815. The pictures were designed by a well-known illustrator of the period—William Heath—and the plates were engraved by a craftsman whose name occurs frequently on 18th Century prints, T. Sutherland. Shortly after this, in 1818, there appeared *Historic Military and Naval Anecdotes of Personal Valour, Bravery and Particular Incidents which Occurred to the Armies of Great Britain and her Allies*. This was published by Edward Orme, and contained forty aquatints dealing with incidents in the Napoleonic Wars; these were done by M. Dubourg and D. Dighton—again names seen on many period prints.

THE FUNERAL CAR DRAWN BY 12 HORSES.   10 BANNEROLS BORNE BY OFFICERS.

For the volunteers of the Napoleonic period there were printers and painters anxious to instruct and please, and they produced handbooks illustrated with a series of colour plates. One of the most attractive and highly desirable volumes was that entitled *The Loyal Volunteers of London and Environs*, published in 1799 by Ackermann, with eighty-seven coloured plates by the famous artist Thomas Rowlandson. Each plate depicted a movement of arms drill being performed by a member of one of the volunteer units. Opposite each plate was printed a brief history of the unit as well as details of the uniforms and officers. Rowlandson also illustrated an instruction volume entitled *The Hungarian and Highland Broadsword*, with twenty-four coloured plates showing the various positions of the sword and a text by Henry Angelo, a noted swordsman of the period. In many ways it was a civilian version of the official publication *Rules for the Exercise of the Sword* mentioned above.

From this period on the military illustrator flourished, and the quantity of portraits, uniform plates, cartoons and battle scenes increased beyond count. With such an enormous output the quality was naturally variable, but most were surprisingly good. In the period 1833–40 two artists—L. Mansion and L. Eschauzier—executed seventy plates which were coloured by two fine painters, Martin and Bowen. These large plates (see Plate 27) depicted regiments of the British Army, and are extremely attractive examples of meticulous workmanship. Similar plates were issued in the 1850s, engraved by J. Harris and designed by H. Masters. Another prolific military artist of the period was the appropriately named Michael Angelo Hayes. Many of the better class prints and paintings were copied and modified, and a multitude of versions will be encountered.

The large output of martial illustrations was not limited to Britain; France and Prussia, or later Germany, were well served by their painters and engravers. There seems to have been less interest in the United States, for the amount of material appears to be much smaller and the majority are of comparatively recent production. In 1893 A. Tholey painted a series entitled *Military Types of U.S. Militia and National Guard Past and Present* which was pub-

THIRTEENTH,
PRINCE ALBERT'S REGIMENT OF
LIGHT INFANTRY.

Left, *Fig. 186: Typical coloured plate from one of Richard Canon's series of regimental histories,* Historical Record of the Thirteenth, First Somerset, Regiment *(1848). 8¾ by 5½ inches.*

Below, *Fig. 187:* Top left, *coloured postcard by H. Montagu Love prepared for Raphael Tuck and sons in 1905; the incident depicted occurred on 2nd January 1858. 5½ by 3½ inches.* Top right, *card published by Gale and Polden Ltd., one of a series giving badges and other details of the various British regiments.* Bottom, *Christmas card showing the Cameron Highlanders, painted by R. Simkin, c. 1890. 5 11/16 by 4½ inches.*

Left, *Fig. 188: Ticket which entitled a ratepayer to enter the grounds of the National Rifle Association shooting area on Wimbledon Common. The range was important to the Volunteer movement and was graced by Queen Victoria, who fired a shot there to mark the opening of the Volunteer shooting competition in July 1860. 3 by 1⅕ inches, with red diagonal stripes.*

Right, *Plate 28: Original water colour of an Officer and man of The Black Watch, by the well-known artist Orlando Norrie.*

lished by L. Prang & Co., and another fine series showing the changes in uniform from the War of Independence up to the late 19th Century was prepared by H. G. Ogden.

For the print enthusiast two books must be regarded as essential; these are *British Military Prints* by Ralph Nevill (London, 1909) and *Prints of British Military Operations* by Lt. Colonel C. de W. Crookshank (Lonond, 1921). Both these volumes omit two names that will soon become familiar to all interested in prints, namely Richard Simkin (1850–1926) and Captain H. Oakes-Jones, for these two artists produced a vast output of good quality material. Their paintings will be found in many books dealing with the British Army.

With the outbreak of the South African War there was a burst of military enthusiasm in Britain, followed by another surge of patriotism in 1914, so that this period is marked by the amount of military publishing that went on. Many of the books were illustrated with numerous colour plates, some of indifferent quality. *Her Majesty's Army* by Walter Richards, in three volumes (London, undated, *circa* 1900)

contained numerous competent but uninspired coloured plates by G. D. Giles and Frank Feller. A later companion set of four volumes—*His Majesty's Territorial Army* (London, undated, *circa* 1910)— was illustrated by a famous painter of battle scenes, R. Caton Woodville, and plates from all these volumes are frequently found loose.

At the same time there were a large number of postcards, monochrome and coloured, issued by various firms. Raphael Tuck & Sons issued a series on the Chelsea Hospital, and *Types of the British Army*, while Max. Efflinger & Co. Ltd. of London and New York did a coloured series *Life In Our Army*. Wrench Postcards Ltd. issued a most attractive set of coloured cards by A. Montague Love. Raphael Tuck & Sons also issued a series under the title of *How He Won The Victoria Cross*, which were fine examples of the bravura style of boys' adventure illustrations—these were also painted by Love. Gale and Polden Ltd., a long established military printer, issued a series of postcards which showed the badge of each regiment together with collar badge or shoulder belt plate or similar accessories, and these too

SOUVENIR IN COMMEMORATION

OF THE

FEED THE GUNS

Campaign in Trafalgar Square

OCTOBER 1918.

LONDON'S WAR SAVING "BIG PUSH"

Trafalgar Square will be transformed into a 'life-like' reproduction of a ruined village on a section of the Western battle front.

The fountains and statues will be covered with shell-shattered buildings. Where the Gordon statue is a ruined church will stand. The prosaic lamp-posts will be shell-torn and withered trees. A battered windmill will conceal the west fountains. The east fountain will be hidden by a half demolished farmhouse.

Three will be trenches along which visitors will pass to the guns. The breech of each of these will be fitted with a special stamping machine, so that visitors feeding the guns with Bonds and Certificates will be able to have them stamped with a special souvenir stamp.

Famous TANK and GUNS as Prizes.

The famous tank Egbert will be given as a prize to the city or town which raises the largest amount per head of population in National War Bonds and War Saving Certificates during the period from October 1, 1918, to June 30, 1919.

To the five towns in the category of those with over 50,000 inhabitants next in merit to the winner of "Egbert" heavy guns will be awarded.

The second prize will be a 9.2 Howitzer; the third prize an 8in. Howitzer; the fourth prize a 60-pounder, and the fifth a 6inch Howitzer. There will be prizes for the places under the 50,000 mark, which will take the form of engraved shells.

Buyers of War Bonds and War Saving Certificates at the St. Pancras Feed the Guns campaign on Tuesday will participate in a scheme offering a hundred gifts including a £100 War Bond.

Burgess, Printer, York Place, Strand, W.C.2.

Fig. 189: Printed on tissue paper, this souvenir programme commemorates what must have been one of the last fundraising efforts of the First World War.

have become collectors' pieces. Simkin also did some illustrations for postcards, but one of the best known names to collectors of military postcards is that of Harry Paine, so popular that facsimiles of some of his cards have recently been published.

Cigarette manufacturers were not to be left out of the military rush; many firms issued sets of picture cards of uniforms or military exploits and later, in the 1920s and 1930s, issued some quite elaborate silk reproductions of regimental colours. There were a number of series of cigarette cards devoted to military matters such as famous regiments, battles and cavalry units of the world, published during the period 1900–1939. Reference to the appropriate catalogues will supply the details, and many are now highly prized by collectors.

During both World Wars there were a number of specially produced items aimed at increasing savings or creating support for the war effort. Recruiting posters were often striking, and reproductions of many of these are now available. Wartime post-cards were also produced with appropriate patriotic sentiments expressed in words and picture. One scarce form of ephemera is that shown in Fig. 189; these souvenirs were printed on near-tissue paper and their chances of survival were extremely small.

Propaganda leaflets were a feature of the Second World War, but it must be admitted that the majority of them were distinctly uninspired and have little value beyond that of curiosity.

Photographs may not strictly be counted as prints in the collectors' sense, but they are obvious sources of immense value. From the mid-19th Century onwards there was an increasing use of the camera, and from the Crimea onwards the photographic coverage of war and the military scene has become increasingly complete. Many of these pictures dating from the latter part of the 19th Century and the early part of the 20th Century are full of interest, showing items of equipment and uniform that in many cases, according to official sources, either did not exist or were never used!

Colours and Campaigns 15

Plate 29: Infantry regimental standard of the Prince of Wales' Own Fencible Infantry, a unit raised in June 1798 and disbanded in May 1802. Measuring 76½ by 71 inches, the standard is of silk and bears the pre-1801 Union Flag. (By courtesy Sotheby & Co.)

Colours and Campaigns

Title page, *Fig. 190: Colours of 1st Royal Sussex Regiment—on the right the Queen's Colour, on the left the Regimental Colour, bearing the battle honours. Tradition and mystique demanded that the flags continue in use despite considerable battle damage. The soldiers wear the Colonial pattern helmet; the picture dates from the turn of the century.*

Below, *Fig. 191: From* Historical Record of the Thirty First, The Huntingdonshire, Regiment of Foot *by R. Canon, 1850; these are typical of the majority of infantry colours. The top bears the regimental number in gold, while the Regimental colour is of buff, as were the facings, with a red circle and the battle honours in blue.*

M ENTION has already been made of the use of banners and flags as rallying points and means of identification, and the concept may be traced back to the Classical world. One of the best-known examples was, of course, the Roman standard, the eagle, which played such an important part in the assembly and structure of the Roman Legions. Standards are shown on many monuments and carvings, although surviving examples are practically non-existent. The origin of the Roman standard is a matter of conjecture but it seems not unreasonable to assume that there was some totemic significance, for many featured various animals at one time or the other. Early references speak of such creatures as the minotaur, but under Marius (155–86 B.C.) the eagle was promoted to the prime position, probably because it was closely associated with the senior deity Zeus. The eagle standard (*aquilla*) was depicted as having its wings outstretched and grasping in its claws a flash of lightning signifying a thunderbolt.

In addition to the eagle most legions had their own more personal standard, with figures based on the signs of the Zodiac appropriate to the unit's birthday or to

Fig. 192: Waterloo medal, bearing the Prince Regent's head and a figure of Victory; this example retains the fitting for suspension from a ribbon—crimson with dark blue edges. (Wallis and Wallis)

rest of the troops. A large horn-like trumpet, known as a *cornus*, was blown on the command of the officer, and this sound directed the attention of all troops to the standard, movements of which then indicated the next manoeuvre to be carried out by the legion.

Standards were not the only emblems carried by the legion and one form, which was to be used for many centuries, was the dragon. This particular type seems to have originated with the Sarmatian horsemen, who are shown on Trajan's column carrying a representation of a dragon. It was made of cloth in a tubular shape, so that as the wind blew through it the "wind-sock" effect made it twist and flutter in a lifelike fashion. "Dragons" appeared during the 2nd Century A.D. but their use appears to have caught on, and by the 4th Century most of the legions seem to have had this type of banner. A second form of cloth standard was the *vexillum*, resembling the mediaeval banner; this was a square piece of material —a surviving example found in Egypt measures approximately twenty inches square, and consists of linen, dyed scarlet and bearing a golden image of victory. The *vexillum* was attached to a crossbar mounted at the end of a short pole and it seems to have been more commonly carried by cavalry. The hoisting of a red flag, probably symbolic of blood, appears to have been the signal to mark the commencement of battle.

The standard or *vexillum* apparently fell into disuse after the decline of the Roman Empire, although there are some references during the Saxon and Viking times to "the banner of Odin" and "the Raven banner".

Firm evidence for the use of banners is afforded once again by the unavoidable Bayeux tapestry. Many of the lances depicted thereon have fitted just below the head a small flag with a number of tails. These *gonfanons* seem to have been primarily badges of rank, for they appear to be carried only by those in authority, although

some notable associated with that particular legion. Another type of standard, the *imago*, bore a portrait of the Emperor. These chief standards were, according to Vegitius, placed in the care of the First Cohort, but other, smaller sub-sections of the legion appear to have had their own standards.

The physical construction of the standard was a long pole at the very tip of which was bolted either the eagle, in the case of the *aquilla*, or an outstretched hand. Beneath this figure was arranged a series of wreaths and circular discs the purpose of which is not at all clear, although it has been suggested that the wreaths were marks of meritorious service; also fitted just below the hand was a crossbar, a device repeated further down and, judging by the reliefs, from this were hung wreaths and streamers. In battle the standard served as a rallying point and a means of indicating movements to the they would also have served much the same function as the Roman standard. Most of those shown have three tails, and the section nearest the staff is embroidered in a different colour from the rest; some bear a cross or other simple pattern.

Two special banners are featured in the tapestry, and one is roughly semi-circular with nine pointed projections around the edge and includes a peculiar symbol; the suggestion has been very tentatively put forward that this might represent a chalice and this could, therefore, be the sacred banner which was blessed by the Pope. It was given to William as an indication of Papal approval, since William had promised to reform the church in England.

The second interesting variant occurs in the sequence illustrating the actual Battle of Hastings, when the Saxons are shown clustered around a staff from which flies a dragon standard very similar to that carried by the Roman auxiliaries. That this fashion persisted is shown by the fact that in 1244 Henry III is known to have ordered a dragon to be made from red silk bedecked with gold, "the tongue to resemble fire".

During the Middle Ages banners began to acquire more general characteristics; there were three main types known as the pennant, the standard and the banner. Of these the pennant most closely resembled the *gonfanon* and was essentially a personal flag bearing some device identifying the owner. The banner was larger, either square or rectangular, but this, too, bore a personal device. The standard was much larger and came to be the prerogative of the ruler; as its name suggests it was essentially an indication of position, both physical and statutory. Today the Royal standard would be the closest equivalent to this flag.

These, then, were the origins of the colours of the modern army; however, most of the later flags of the various regiments featured somewhere in their design the national flag. When James I united the crowns of Scotland and England it was ordered that the national flag should bear the red St. George's cross and the white cross of St. Andrew joined together "according to a form devised by the Heralds". The resulting flag was the Great Union Flag—strictly it was only a "jack" when flown from the flag-staff of a ship at war. During the Commonwealth (1649–1653), when the union with Scotland was officially broken, the flag carried the cross of St. George only, but when Cromwell became Lord Protector in 1653 the union flag was brought back into service with an Irish Harp added at the centre. In 1660 Charles II had the harp removed again, leaving the original union flag.

Fig 193: Naval General Service Medal. (1793–1840) with four bars on a white ribbon with dark blue edges. The top bar, for Boat Service 14th December 1814, recalls an action off New Orleans. (Wallis and Wallis)

Fig. 194: Army Gold Cross bearing names of battles in which the recipient fought— Pyrenees, Nivelle, Albuhera, Orthes (1811–14). These were attached to the buttonhole by a wide crimson ribbon with dark blue edges. (National Army Museum)

During the English Civil Wars the number of flags which saw service was enormous, for each unit carried their own distinguishing flag. Each troop of horse had its own standard, and since these were designed by the Commanding Office or some other notable, the variety of decorations to be found on them was considerable. Many were almost political cartoons or at least political comments on the times, and consequently were quite elaborately fashioned. As the war progressed the designs became somewhat less flamboyant and there was a greater use of devices or portions from the coat of arms of the commanding officer. In general, standards carried by the infantry seem to have been far less fanciful and more mundane than those of the cavalry. The Trained Bands were equipped with a more

or less standard flag, but each company had a minor distinguishing feature to pick it out from the rest, and it seems likely that the same idea was in use amongst the regular soldiers. The custom of using some form of flag to distinguish officers was continued; the colonel of the regiment had a white or red flag, whilst the Lieutenant-Colonel had a flag bearing a small St. George's cross in the upper left hand corner. Other officers had their flags distinguished by one, two, three or more devices according to rank.

IN 1661 a Royal Warrant was issued by the Earl of Sandwich, Master of the Great Wardrobe, ordering "twelve colours or ensigns for our Regiment of Foot Guards of white and red taffeta, of the usual largeness, with stands, heads and tassels, each of which to have such distinctions of some of our royal badges, painted in oil, as our trusty and well beloved servant Sir Edward Walker, Knight, Garter Principal King-at Arms shall direct". Most of the Restoration colours seem to have featured the King's Royal Cypher, and from a review of 1684 there survives a list of units taking part together with a description of their standard. The King's Own Troop of Horse Guards, a troop of Grenadiers, had a crimson standard with the Royal Cypher and crown, as did the Queen's Troops. The Duke's Troops of His Majesty's Horse Guards, troops of Grenadiers, had a yellow damask standard with his Royal Highness' cypher and coronet.

During the 18th Century standards began to take on a more or less common form; one carried in 1747 at the Battle of Dettingen is described as being of crimson silk brocade, about two foot square and edged with a gold and silver fringe, in one corner the "small union" three inches square, on the other side of the crest and motto of the Colonel. The reverse gave his full coat of arms, and trophies of stands of muskets and weapons worked in gold embroidery. Again, from the above description it will be seen that there is an emphasis on the arms of the colonel commanding the regiment. This practice was stopped in 1743 by a Royal Warrant which stated clearly that the Union colour was the first colour in all regiments except the Foot Guards, in which isolated case the King's standard was to be the first; but, even more important, no colonel was henceforward to put his "arms, crest, device or livery . . . in any part of the appointments of his regiment". The flag which from thence forward led every marching regiment of foot was to be the Great Union; following this was to be the "colour", in the facing of the regiment with the union flag in the upper corner, and in the centre was to be painted, in Roman figures of gold, the number and rank of the regiment within a wreath of roses and thistles. Exceptions were allowed in the case of long-established badges. The simplification of regimental design must have been beneficial as far as the troops were concerned, for in place of a quite complicated armorial bearing all that needed to be recognised was the number of the regiment.

The next addition to the standards and colours were the battle honours. The first appears to have been bestowed on the 15th Light Dragoons in 1768, when they were given the battle honour "Emsdorf" for a battle fought in Germany on 16th July 1760. When the regiment returned to England it presented to the King 16 colours captured from the enemy—an event commemorated by crossed flags on their shabraques. The next honour to be granted was that of "Gibraltar", and this was awarded to four regiments—the 12th, 39th, 56th and 58th—who took an active part in the defence of Gibraltar when the French and Spaniards laid siege to the rock for four years, 1779–1783; despite many hardships the British defenders held firm. It was directed that the battle honour might be worn on their grenadier and light infantry caps, their accoutrements, drums and on the second colour of each of the regiments, just below

their respective numbers, but it was not to be placed on the King's standard and this general rule—there are exceptions—applies to the present.

With the Act of Union in 1801 theoretically joining Ireland to England and Scotland, all current colours became obsolete, and the Great Union obviously had to be modified. In many cases entirely new colours were provided, but in others the cross of St. Andrew was modified with red stripes to incorporate St. Patrick's cross, and shamrock leaves were added to the wreath of leaves around the regimental badge.

Fig. 195: Small medal awarded by 2nd London Rifles to those who did well in recruiting new members—red ribbon with green edges and centre strip. $\frac{9}{10}$ by $\frac{9}{10}$ inches.

Fig. 196: Silver medal awarded to Corporal Charles Collard of Bridgwater Troop, West Somerset Yeomanry in May 1859, as Best Swordsman. (Webb Collection)

With the addition of new flags, battle honours and shamrocks the opportunities for evasion of the official regulations were obviously greatly increased; many of the colonels and commanding officers were no longer conforming and the position became more and more involved until, in 1806, an official Inspector of Regimental Colours was appointed, the York Herald, one of the members of the College of Arms. The Inspector sent a leaflet to every commanding officer which set out the official policy on the King's and Regimental Colours and included a representation of each, stating that this was to be the standard pattern. If the commanding officer had any special devices or modifications in mind, he had to indicate these on the sample and return it to the inspector.

Following the end of the Napoleonic wars there were a number of changes, the most

obvious being the abandoning of the heart-shaped shield usually placed at the centre of the colour. In many cases the regimental number was no longer given in Roman figures but in the more conventional Arabic, although this process was reversed later on. Again in this period there were many deviations from the standardised practice, and in 1844 a new order emphasising previous instructions was sent out, the most important being that, with the exception of the Foot Guards, no regiment was to place battle honours on the King's or Queen's colours, which henceforward would bear no extra devices other than the regimental number.

Many of the cavalry units carried conventional square standards but others retained the guidon which was, in many ways, a direct descendant of the bifurcated gonfanon of the Bayeux Tapestry. There were numerous distinctions made; whilst the Household Cavalry and Dragoon Guards possessed standards, the Dragoons had guidons. Hussars and Lancers had no flag at all and their devices and battle honours were embroidered on wide strips of heavily decorated material hung around the drums of the regiment. Again, in the Yeomanry only the Dragoons carried flags; these were normally guidons made of crimson material edged with gold and red fringes, and the pole was surmounted by the royal lion and crown. The only battle honour accorded to any Yeomanry regiment was that of South Africa.

In the case of infantry colours it is almost impossible to generalise; a minimum of two colours were carried by every regiment—the King's colour, which bore the union flag with the regimental number or badge and the Imperial crown in the centre, and the regimental colour, which was so various as to defy classification. In general all carried a central device bearing a badge and the regimental number; around this was a ring bearing the name of the regiment, above the badge was the Imperial crown, and encircling this was the union wreath incorporating shamrocks, thistles and roses springing from a single stalk. Battle honours could be arranged in any one of a number of fashions depending on the number awarded to the regiment. In addition there might be other devices, such as a small flag, in the corner. The colour of the flag was determined by the facings of the regiment. Blue facings meant that the flag was blue and yellow, buff or green facings were all matched in the colour of the flag. If the facings were scarlet or white the flag was white with the red cross of St. George, and in the case of black facings the flag was black with a red cross on top. One exception in the infantry was that rifle regiments did not possess colours, probably in keeping with the tradition that these were light, fast-moving and unencumbered troops.

THE British Army was not alone in its reverence for its colours, and similar practices were adopted by the young American Republic. The Continental army made use of three colours—the National colour, which was flown largely as an identifying mark on ships and Government installations, a regimental standard, and Grand Division colours. In May 1775 the regimental standards were given to each regiment; first yellow, second blue, third scarlet, fourth crimson, fifth white and sixth azure—but as blue cloth was extremely scarce the second regiment had its colour changed to green. In July 1775 two more regiments were added; the seventh was awarded a blue flag and the eighth was given orange. In January 1776, under the reorganisation of the army, General Washington stated that the regiments were to have two flags, a regimental standard and a Grand Division colour. He ordered that both flags were to be small and display some connection with the uniform of the regiment. On June 14th 1777 the Continental Congress agreed that the flag of the United States should take on its basic form with

Fig. 197: Reverse of Collard's medal, showing additions scratched on by the owner—"Sargt 1860, Rsine July 1871." (Webb Collection)

alternate red and white stripes and stars on a blue field. In 1782 the position was to be standardised, and it was planned that there would be a hundred silk standards each needing $4\frac{1}{2}$ yards of silk and bearing the name of the State and the regimental number in gold leaf. Each was to have two silk tassels whilst the tip of the carrying staff would be mounted in brass.

The Emperor Napoleon I was well aware of the dramatic and sentimental value of flags, and in December 1804 he awarded new standards to all his regiments. At the top of the pole on which the flag was carried was an eagle with wings half outstretched, strongly reminiscent of that of the Romans. From henceforward the colours were known as "the eagles". By an Imperial decree of February 1808 infantry of the line and light infantry were somewhat reorganised and the post of Le Port-Aigle—eagle-carrier or

standard bearer—was created. Each eagle was to be carried by an ensign who had had at least ten years service and had fought at Ulm, Iena, Friedland and Austerlitz. Two other old soldiers were to be created second and third standard bearers, and these three soldiers were to be approved by the Emperor himself. The second and third standard bearers or *port-aigles* were to be armed with halberds and two pistols carried in holsters slung across the chest, one of the earliest uses of personal holsters. The flag itself was supported in a bucket fitted to a cross belt passing over the chest of the *port-aigle*. The design of the standard varied somewhat; many were basically the French tricolour with the name of the regiment embroidered across the flag. Many of the standards were of other patterns, although most incorporated three colours, and on them were embroidered the various battle honours granted by the Emperor. The capture of an eagle was, of course, either a great honour or a disgrace depending upon which side carried out the operation, and such an event was usually honoured in some fashion. The 2nd Dragoons (Royal Scots Greys) gained one of their nicknames—

"Bird Catchers"—because a Sergeant Ewart captured one of the French eagles at the battle of Waterloo. One of the last occasions on which the British lost their colours was at Isandhlwana on 22nd January 1879 when the Zulus annihilated an invading British force and, despite gallant efforts, the colours of the 1st and 2nd Battalions of the 24th Regiment were lost.

During the American Civil War (1861–65) the Regiments took their colours into battle with them and each regiment had a colour guard of four men, two as carriers and the other two as guards. Each Union regiment had two silk colours: the national colour, that is the stars and stripes with the number and name of the regiment embroidered on the centre stripe, and the regimental colour. This was blue with the arms of the United States embroidered in silk at the centre and the name of the regiment placed beneath the eagle. The standards were roughly six feet square and were carried on a ten-foot pole with a finial in some fanciful style. In the case of volunteers and militia units the coat of arms was normally that of the state. The Confederate battle flag bore the "stars and bars"—a starred red St. Patrick's cross on a

Fig. 199: Left, *Indian General Service Medal (1854–95), ribbon crimson with dark blue stripes; the bar* Chin Hills 1892/93 *commemorates one of the numerous punitive campaigns of Victoria's reign.* Right, *Indian Mutiny Medal (1857–58); white ribbon with scarlet stripes.* (*Wallis and Wallis*)

blue field—and was smaller in size than that of the Union.

Like so much of the historic glamour of warfare, the carrying of colours in battle was gradually abandoned, and during the First and the Second World Wars the greatest use of flags, apart from marking government buildings, was in the form of small pennants. Few, apart from these pennants, saw "active service". The Third Reich, however, was not blind to the emotional value of flags, and produced a plethora of variations. Many, such as the *Handelsflagge* and the *Reichsdienstflagge* (Reich service flag), the flag of the Commander in Chief of the Army, and others, incorporated both the Swastika and the old German Teutonic Cross. In addition there were numerous smaller flags for the various levels of field command, as well as the regional flags of the Nazi Party itself.

IN the case of whole regiments due honour could be afforded them for their part in any action by permission to bear the appropriate title on the colour. Sometimes an associated device served to remind future generations of some past glory; a well-

known example is provided by the Gloucestershire Regiment, which was granted the right to wear a small badge on the back of the headdress as a result of an action at Alexandria in Egypt in 1801. When attacked by cavalry and unable to form a square, the rear rank about-faced, and the two lines fought back to back until they had repulsed the enemy attack. However, for the recognition of bravery by individuals the battle honour was insufficient, and there arose the practice—in the British Army a very late practice—of awarding medals. The granting of medals was both a public and private affair, for long before the Government adopted the policy of issuing medals to all who took part in certain actions, it was not uncommon for officers, at their own expense, to issue some form of regimental medal. Such medals were not necessarily issued for bravery, they might be awarded for any action or service which merited some recognition. When in 1830 a Long Service Medal was officially introduced, this practice was largely abandoned. The material for the construction of such medals was obviously limited by the expense that the officers were prepared to undertake,

and pewter, gold, copper, silver and bronze were all used. This practice of issuing private medals was particularly prevalent inside the Volunteer and Yeomanry movements, and large numbers have survived; they were awarded for such distinctions as best marksman, best swordsman and so on. The design was obviously a matter for personal preference and many variations are recorded, although the majority are circular or oval in outline.

Bravery by serving soldiers has always been recognised in some form or other. Polybus, writing in the 2nd Century B.C., tells how the Roman soldier was rewarded with cups and spears, and cavalrymen were probably given specially decorated trappings for their horses. During the Middle Ages knighthoods could be conferred on the battlefield, but for the majority of soldiers the only rewards were likely to be monetary, in the form of loot. The awarding of medals in the modern sense of the word seems to date back to Elizabeth I, who had struck a number of medals for the officers commanding the ships which fought against the Spanish Armada in 1588; these were not general issue medals, but were probably intended only for the commanding officers. These so-called "Armada medals" were oval and were designed to be worn suspended around the neck. The English Civil Wars saw similar issues of medals, and a warrant issued by

Charles I in 1643 authorised badges of silver intended for those who took part in the "Forlorn Hope"—the group which led the attack and so were in particular danger. Regulations were laid down which prohibited the sale or wearing of these medals except by those authorised.

The first general issue of medals to both officers and men who served in a campaign was that for the battle of Dunbar in 1650, when the House of Commons voted in gratitude that all who were engaged should be issued with a medal. A number of other Civil War medals were issued mostly for Naval engagements.

Individual or small groups of medals continued to be awarded to officers or select crews for various naval engagements over the years. The Honourable East India Company awarded a number of campaign medals, but it was not until the great battle of Waterloo in 1815 that a general issue was made to all those who took part. In April 1816 the London Gazette reported that the Prince Regent had authorised a medal which should "be conferred on every officer, non-commissioned officer and soldier present on that memorable occasion". The medal was struck in silver and was originally suspended from a ribbon around the neck. It bore the Prince Regent's representation and the words *Wellington, Victory* and *Waterloo*. The ribbon was dark crimson with blue edging. The name of the recipient was struck into the edge in block capitals, and on many of them the suspension ring for the ribbon around the neck was replaced by a straight slot bar, as on later medals.

Long after the issue of the Waterloo medal, in fact some thirty years later, it was somewhat belatedly decided that a medal should be issued to all those who served in the wars between 1793 and 1814. The Duke of Wellington, with his strong sense of the fitness or otherwise of such gestures, disapproved and opposed this

general issue. He was gently but firmly overruled by Queen Victoria, and the medal was duly issued in 1848, 34 years after the last campaign to qualify for the medal. Obviously large numbers of potential recipients never received it; illiteracy prevented many from even knowing of its existence, and in 34 years many of those qualified had long since died, but a large number were issued. In fact the actions recognised as entitling a person to receive the medal were not extended as far back as 1793, and the earliest to be recognised was the Egyptian campaign in 1801. With these general issue medals such as the Army General Service Medal recognition of participation in several battles was marked by the issue of bars, that is strips of silver or some other metal which bore the name of the action. For the Army General Service some twenty-nine battles or campaigns were recognised although, as far as is known, no recipients qualified for more than fifteen. A similar medal was the Naval General Service Medal which was issued for campaigns, actions and battles fought

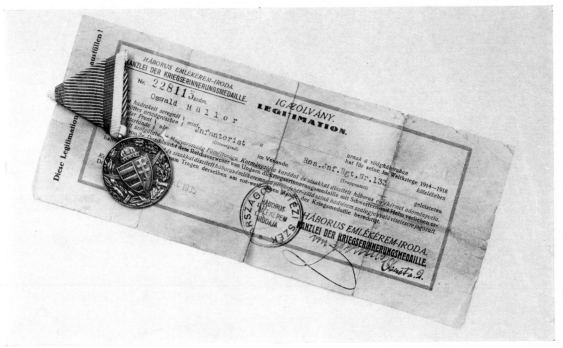

between 1793 and 1840. Some 223 different actions were recognised, and the maximum number awarded to a single individual appears to have been seven. A similar retrospective award was made with the India Medal, which covered actions between 1799 and 1826; this was known as The Army of India Medal and was issued in 1851 with a possible total of twenty-one bars of which seven seems to have been the highest number awarded to a single individual. From then onwards awards began to multiply and the numbers issued increased enormously; notable was the Crimean War Medal, of which something like 275,000 were awarded. There were five bars although only one person seems to have re-

ceived four. The Sultan of Turkey also awarded medals to English, French and Sardinian troops who took part in the Crimean campaigns.

The issue of campaign medals became standard practice, and almost every action of any size from the mid-19th Century to the present has been suitably commemorated; and there has been a consequent and inevitable depreciation in esteem of such medals.

This has not been the case with gallantry awards and decorations, and in certain cases the reverse has been the case. The Victoria Cross, the supreme British award for gallantry, was given far more liberally in the years following its inception in 1856 than has been the case during the 20th Century. On the other hand medals such as the Iron Cross were given fairly freely, although there are different classes of the award with the higher grades being far less frequently granted. This is an old-established order, instituted in 1813.

As with all things military the appearance of so many medals and awards soon necessitated rules as to precedence and the sequence of wearing ribbons, which should come first, or whether one may be worn with another, and etiquette on this matter is strict—dare one say pedantic?

Care and
Collecting

16

Care and Collecting

Opposite *Plate 31: White Imperial German Navy flag with black and gold eagle motif, and red Naval flag of the Third Reich, both 18 by 135 cm. Metal Royal Engineers epaulette of* circa *1860* (left) *and Hospital Staff epaulette. Sabretache and shoulder-belt pouch of the Royal Artillery, Victorian period. Duty gorget, with luminous lettering, of the German army* Feldgendarmerie—military police—*of the 1940s. Confederate style slouch hat. South African Medal awarded to 5747 Private T. Skipp, Yorkshire Regiment, with bars for Belfast, Diamond Hill, Johannesburg, Driefontein, Paardeberg and Relief of Kimberley.* (Jeffcoat Collection)

Title page, *Fig. 204: Forage cap with japanned travelling case and brass padlock (stamped V.R.) for an officer of The Prince of Wales's Own (West Yorkshire) Regt. These caps varied in details such as the embroidery round the sides; this pattern was adopted in 1896.* **Above, Fig. 205:** *16th Century Italian tilting helmet, lipped at the base to lock on to gorget. The skull, fashioned from a single piece of metal, is strengthened by a reinforcing plate on the brow. Weight, 8 lbs.* (Gyngell Collection)

COLLECTING antiques has become one of the major industries and interests of many people over the last two decades. This growth of interest has had an effect rather like the dropping of a stone into a pond, for there have been fashions and phases in antique collection which have inflated demand for certain classes of object. This has obviously meant a corresponding increase in prices, and higher prices tend to elevate the articles socially. What was perhaps, only a few years ago, collected by the undiscerning amateur gradually climbs into the category of items sought-after by intelligent amateurs, then by the professionals and finally only by the wealthy, who may be any or all of these things. This social climbing effect has been particularly noticeable in the field of arms, armour and militaria.

At the end of the 19th Century interest in such items was restricted to a very limited number of wealthy amateurs, and although prices paid for good quality pieces were often quite considerable, the market was more than adequate to deal with all demands. Then came the First World War, and the Depression in Britain and America precluded any widespread collecting of antiques. With the Second World War came the peaceful invasion of England by many Americans, and there was a greater demand for all antiques; and as there was more money about, the prices began to rise. One of the areas of peculiar interest to the American collector was that of arms and armour, especially firearms. This encouraged dealers to look out for specimens and gradually the spiralling effect of heavy demand and rising prices began to operate. During the early 1950s the effect was slight but nonetheless noticeable, and there was a gradual upward trend; but it was in the mid-1960s that prices really began to rocket. Associated with this growth of interest was the publication of numerous books devoted to this field of collecting, so that gradually increasing knowledge began to stimulate further demands. As each new book came on to the market its particular subject began to increase in value; a good example was the case with the publication of H. Blackmore's *British Military Firearms* in 1961. This effect was particularly noticeable in the field of fine firearms, which began to realise prices placing them beyond the reach of the

small collector. This drove large numbers of enthusiasts to widen their interest, to cover less popular and less expensive items, and some of the interest was funnelled off into the field of armour and swords. An increasing interest here produced exactly the same effect, and gradually prices began to rise. Driven now further and further from his original interest in firearms the smaller collector looked around and found that, as yet, militaria had been neglected.

Militaria, a loose generic term, has come to include almost anything remotely associated with the military forces. Within this volume it has only been possible to give a very cursory glance at some of the fields associated with this topic. In general the collector of militaria tends to specialise, and the old story of demand forcing up prices has already made its impact. To take but one example, some six or seven years ago blue cloth helmets, in good condition, were fetching somewhere within the region of £7 or £8; today the same model, in only reasonable condition, would normally fetch

at least three times that figure. A few years ago military cap badges could be purchased for a few coppers, but today the cheapest is likely to be five shillings and for the earlier examples the figure runs into pounds. Military prints have always been in demand, not only by the militaria enthusiast but by art collectors and by those who simply like something a little different with which to decorate the walls, so that they have always been a somewhat special case, but prices have risen. The same is true of some of the earlier books which were often collected for their antiquarian value quite apart from their military association.

Uniforms have always presented something of a problem for the collector since to display them well a fair amount of space is needed, and consequently demand for such items has never been as high as in other fields. Prices, therefore, have not risen on a comparable scale with other items of militaria. Items of equipment are of interest but again often present a display problem and therefore these are rather variable as far as price and demand are concerned, and it is difficult to generalise on the state of this market.

What advice, then, can be offered to the collector? Undoubtedly people come into this field knowing full well what their main interests are, and consequently specialise, but there is a lot to be said for the "magpie" collector who buys anything relating to militaria. This sweeping together of "unconsidered trifles" has been the foundation of many a good collection, simply because the collector had bought cheaply and when prices rose was able to dispose of some items at a reasonable profit. With the increased return he was able to acquire better quality pieces to enhance his collection. Whatever the style of collecting, whether it be general or specialist, there are certain guide lines that are worth bearing in mind. Obviously the degree of commitment must depend on many external factors such as the amount of space available for display and, of supreme importance, the amount of cash available. Undoubtedly one of the best policies is to buy only the best that funds will allow.

This can be a policy of perfection, and there are many enthusiasts who are content with a second-best item rather than none at all. In the case of medals, for example, many of the experts would be most definite and categoric in their advice that on no account should an altered medal be purchased, but although this is sound advice the collector must decide for himself whether he is happier to have a renamed example of a scarce medal rather than none at all. The answer to this dilemma must be a matter for personal choice, but in general it may often be better to have a slightly poorer example of a particular item rather than a gap in the collection. With items such as British military cap badges, where a

sequence of line regiments, yeomanry or indeed any particular group is being collected and a particular example is not readily available, then a specimen which is perhaps battered or has the lugs or slide missing is desirable to ensure that the sequence should be completed.

MILITARIA is such an enormously wide subject that it has the advantage of offering the collector an almost unlimited choice. Most established collectors would probably agree that the pattern of their

Opposite, *Fig. 206: Sallets are extremely rare and invariably expensive, but this example, with throat defences, is in mint condition. This piece is complete with interior padding and securing straps; it is, in fact, a superb model made by H. Russell Robinson, and measures only 6⅞ inches long.* (*Blackmore Collection*) **Below,** *Fig. 207: Mitten gauntlet in fine condition; note "fingernail" detail on top lame. Such pieces—this is a German example dating from c. 1525— are in great demand by collectors.* (*Blackmore Collection*)

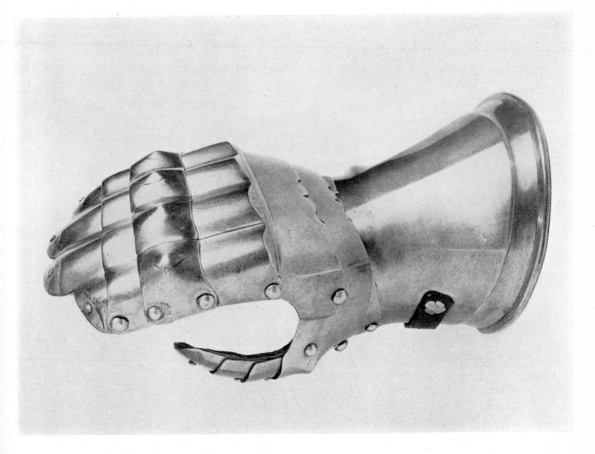

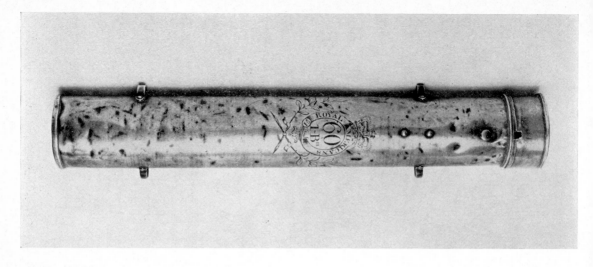

collecting was basically the same. Most started with a general magpie attitude, acquiring anything and everything that is even remotely concerned with the subject. The usual pattern that follows is that one particular theme will begin to assume a position of supreme importance. Specialisation may occur for any one of a number of reasons, but once that specialisation has developed all the interest and energy of the collector will be devoted to this one theme. One of the most popular and, in broad terms, one of the cheapest, is undoubtedly that of cap badges, mostly of the British Army, for they offer one of the widest ranges in the whole field. The approaches to the collecting of cap badges are manifold; some seek to acquire examples from each of the regiments serving at some particular period, say the 1914–18 War, or the Boer War. Other collectors will be more interested in concentrating on cavalry units, and some will go for Yeomanry; others may just aim to acquire as many variations as possible, perhaps connected with one particular regiment. The collector of military cap badges is in a fairly fortunate position for it is true to say that hardly any fakes are being produced in this field and the majority of those that are being produced are fairly easily detectable.

As far as the collector is concerned this ability to distinguish between the genuine and the false is obviously of great importance. In many cases there is little or no problem, for close examination will soon indicate which is the genuine piece, but in some fields, alas, this is far from true. One of the greatest phenomena in the collecting of antiques has been the enormous growth, over the last twenty years, of interest in the men, material and history of the German Third Reich. To those who lived through the period 1933–45 there is still something rather distasteful about this, but for younger collectors no such repugnance is felt and they regard it in exactly the same way as the older generation would look at something Victorian. Following the collapse of the German Reich in 1945 the amount of available material was absolutely enormous, but so much of it was destroyed in the de-Nazification programme that the demand has now outstripped the supply. A very large number of the German badges and insignia were cast with pins attached to the back and this has meant that it was a comparatively simple matter to reproduce them. Given a single genuine example and a reasonably careful caster the item may be duplicated *ad infinitum* and at a fairly small cost. This is exactly what happened, until today it has become extremely difficult, if not impossible, to detect with certainty the genuine article from the reproduction. There are few, if any, firm guide lines that may be accepted with complete confidence. Certainly most of the cruder examples are easily detectable because of the poor quality casting and lack of fine detail, but probably the majority are sufficiently good to confound any but the absolute expert. One guide, and it is by no means a totally reliable one, is to examine the pin attachment and compare it with a known, genuine article. Many of the cheaper castings have a comparatively crude fitting which does not approach the original in quality. However, it must be once again emphasised that this is by no means an infallible test. Not only have the badges been duplicated but the glut of films and television programmes devoted to the Second World War have meant that German uniforms and equipment have been almost mass produced to equip these film armies. Much of this material found its way on to the antique market and again it is often very difficult to distinguish reproduction from the genuine article, so much so that one or two auction houses now state quite clearly that whilst they offer items as being genuine to the best of their knowledge they cannot guarantee them. Arm bands, embroidered badges and all similar items have also been duplicated, and this is especially true in some of the rarer fields. It is ironic that the group probably guilty of the greatest excesses, the *SS*, should be the formation whose equipment is most highly prized by a modern collector.

Badges and insignia offer one great advantage to the small collector in that their size allows him to obtain, identify and display large numbers of pieces in a comparatively small space. Modern, man-made materials have come to the aid of the badge collector, offering help in the number of ways in which he can use them to display the collection. Expanded polystyrene, either tiles or large sheets, makes an ideal base on which to lay out the various badges; the lugs and slides can be very easily pressed into the material with no risk of damage. This material offers a tremendous advantage in that badges or buttons may be arranged or re-arranged with minimum difficulty. Even simpler and cheaper to use are pieces of card on which the badges can be placed and small holes made to accept the lugs or slides, which are then simply pushed into place and, more often than not, held there by friction fit. Coloured card, preferably dark, enhances the appearance of badges quite considerably. Similar forms of display can be used for medals although many collectors prefer, as with badges, to

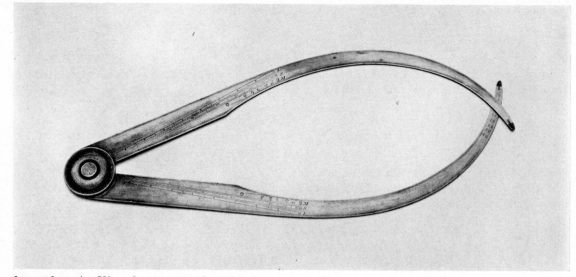

keep them in filing drawers so that they are kept under cover and out of danger and dirt of everyday life. It is still very easy to examine the collection simply by pulling out the drawer.

Campaign medals offer serious hazards for the inexperienced collector. Most, but by no means all British campaign medals bear, around the rim of the medal, the name of the recipient, sometimes engraved in light script or, more commonly, indented in block capitals as with the South African Medal; most also carry an indication of the holder's unit or ship. The rarity value of any medal usually depends upon the fact that whereas one regiment may have taken part in an action and the whole unit been awarded the medal, a small detachment from another regiment also took part. Since there were far fewer of this group it follows that a medal bearing the name of that unit will be far less common and consequently more valuable. This fact has encouraged a number of less scrupulous persons to remove the name and regiment of the original recipient by shaving off a thin layer of metal from the rim and replacing it with that of the smaller group. Most of the purists in medal-collecting would say that a renamed medal is useless and valueless, but for the majority of the smaller collectors a

Above, Fig. 210: Large pair of gunner's callipers made by G. Adams of London sometime between 1730 and 1795. They were used to give details of size and weight of shot and the various bores of cannon barrels. The arms are steel-tipped, to reduce wear and ensure acuracy. Length, 25 inches. (Durrant Collection)
Opposite, *Fig. 211: Brass shako plate of a French infantry officer of c. 1850; Louis Napoleon based the design of most of his military accessories on those of the First Empire. Length, 4½ inches.*

"renamed" is better than none at all, and with the scarcer and more expensive items such as the Military General Service, the Waterloo Medal and others, the collector may well be happy to acquire a slightly inferior example rather than nothing.

THE cleaning of badges and medals have some common features and, in general, the best advice is to use the minimum force possible. It must be appreciated that every time the medal or badge is rubbed a small amount of metal, microscopic though it may be, is removed from the surface. Too frequent rubbing and polishing will wear away the surface, especially if it is one of the softer metals such as silver. Care should therefore be taken to see that medals and badges are cleaned as infrequently as is compatible with the generally desired standard of display. When cleaning is to be carried out then the mildest cleanser available should be used; many of the badges and medals respond very well to a dip of one of the patent silver renovators. Used in moderation these are extremely good, but it must be remembered again that the surface is being attacked by the liquid and therefore the item should not be left immersed for too long a period. Once the item has been gently cleaned then it is possible either to coat it with lacquer or cover it as far as possible with some material to exclude the air and so reduce the tarnishing effect of the impurities of the atmosphere.

Owing to certain inherent problems one of the cheapest fields of collecting is that of uniforms. Most collectors are not terribly interested in uniforms for the reasons stated above—namely that they are difficult to display. For anyone able to overcome this problem it is still possible to acquire examples of uniforms well over a hundred years old and yet in good condition, for a comparatively small amount. Accepting the limitations of space and so on, uniforms are an attractive item of militaria and many collectors regret their inability to build up numbers of these attractive items.

One of the other more popular fields is that of military headdresses and here, of course, each piece has a unity and uniqueness of its own; for while a tunic represents only part of a uniform, the helmet or shako is a complete piece in its own right. The demand for earlier examples is, of course, quite considerable; and pieces such as the early patterns of Dragoon helmets will realise prices of several hundred pounds. Similarly high prices will be easily achieved by Imperial German *Garde du Corps* helmets. At the other end of the scale the simple blue cloth helmet, the universal pattern introduced in 1878 is, if not common, certainly not rare, and it is quite possible to acquire good examples of this British army headdress for £20 or so. Shakos worn by the British Army are be-

coming increasingly scarce, and an Albert-type shako (1844–55) will fetch within the region of £100, but the last type of shako issued will probably make little more than the blue cloth helmet.

All things being equal, metal helmets will usually cost more than a soft headdress, and they have become quite expensive in recent years. It is, of course, important to ensure as far as is possible that the correctly coloured plume or crest is mounted on the headdress. For the very early examples of helmets prices do rise quite considerably. The demand for helmets of the 16th and 17th Centuries has risen sharply over the past few years and pieces which were quite common a few years ago, such as the 17th Century cavalry helmet with the three or single bar faceguard, have acquired a considerable rarity value and now realise something within the region of £50. For close helmets and the much scarcer armets, then the figure immediately rises to hundreds of pounds.

Display of headdresses does present certain problems, but they may be quite attractively mounted on some of the new style polystyrene heads commonly used as wig stands, which can be modified and adapted to this purpose.

Armour presents even greater problems of display than uniforms, but as a complete suit, or harness, will cost many hundreds of pounds the number of collectors owning a large number is quite limited. Single pieces of armour such as a knee piece or arm are still in demand and fetch reasonable prices. Gauntlets, complete in themselves, are more popular with collectors and fetch higher prices. The collectors' biggest problem with armour is, of course, the same as the original wearer's—rust! It is imperative that this should be removed as soon as possible. Again, it is always best to use the minimum amount of rubbing, and fine emery or wire wool and oil are probably the best means of cleaning the surface. Once clear of rust the metal can be polished with a good wax or furniture polish, which will help keep the danger at bay.

During the Victorian period there was a strong demand for armour to decorate the "baronial hall"—despite its having been built within the last six months! A number of reproduction armours, helmets, gauntlets and so on were produced in the theatrical workshops of the country, but in most cases there is little or no problem in distinguishing genuine from false. The genuine article almost invariably has a different feel about it, being thicker and heavier than the Victorian pressed steel pieces. Even more important, the inside surface of the genuine articles was usually left rough from the armourer's hammer while the armour made from Victorian plate has an inside surface almost as smooth, if not as highly polished as the outside of the genuine article.

Frequently the Victorian armourer lacked understanding of the technological problems involved in the production of armour, and produced helmets, arm pieces or complete suits that would be virtually impossible to move in. Anybody who has visited museums and looked at a genuine piece of armour, and studied the way that the pieces articulate and their general appearance, is unlikely to be misled by these "tin-plate" Victorian constructions.

Books and prints are a rather specialised field of collecting, but fortunately a certain amount of research and collation of information has been done on this subject. It is therefore possible to identify and locate most of those prints which are likely to turn up in the ordinary everyday market. For the collector of early books the field is likely to prove a fairly expensive one, especially if the books are illustrated; for it is sad but true that the print dealer can often obtain a bigger return by breaking up an illustrated book and disposing of the prints individually than he can by selling the book as a complete unit. Since a single De Gheyn print is likely to fetch within the region of £8 to £10, and there are over a hundred plates in his book, obviously the book is likely to be extremely expensive! With the standard military print the majority of those available have usually been removed from a book and on occasions it may be difficult to identify the source of the print. This is not such a problem with British prints, but in the case of Continental plates identification can sometimes be quite difficult.

The condition of the prints can vary enormously, but obviously it is desirable to collect only those which have not suffered unduly from staining, folding or tearing. A print which has been lightly stained or has become dirt-marked can often be cleaned quite simply by soaking in lukewarm water and occasionally, very gently, agitating the print; leaving it for a while; then removing it and laying it down to dry naturally, preferably on some smooth surface such as glass. The transformation can often be quite remarkable. It is sometimes recommended that a few drops of hydrogen peroxide be added to the water in order to whiten the paper, but this is a policy to be treated with caution, for too liberal a use of this bleach can damage the paper. Ob-

Opposite, *Fig. 212: Selection of military buttons: top left to right, 9th Lancers (Victorian) by Jennens of London; 49th Regiment of Foot (or the Princess Charlotte's Regiment of Wales, or Hertfordshire) by Sherlock & Co. of London, 1816–1855; 80th Regiment of Foot (Staffordshire Volunteers), in pewter, by Nutting of London, pre-1850; bottom left to right, 71st (Highland Light Infantry) by Kemp & Wright, Birmingham; 50th (or Queen's Own) Regiment of Foot, by Tait of London, c. 1850.* **Above,** *Fig. 213: Brass plate for Other Rank's lancer cap of the 12th (The Prince of Wales's Royal) Lancers. These were die-stamped, but officers' models were more elaborate with applied decoration in silver.*

viously the soaking method is not recommended for colour prints, for many of the early prints were done with water colours and therefore immersion will naturally remove the colouring.

Books are an essential tool of the collector of militaria, for source material is important if items are to be identified correctly. Generally speaking the value of 17th Century books is likely to be extremely high, and those of the 18th Century somewhat less; and the 19th and 20th Century values will depend very much on the book itself. Values will often be determined very much by the number of illustrations therein, even if they are not large enough to justify the dealers removing them to be sold as separate items. The worth of many of the regimental histories is a matter for debate; some which were seriously researched and carefully written realise reasonable prices, others are of little value. It is a strange but nevertheless apparent fact that some regiments, particularly those of the cavalry, are highly regarded by the collector, whereas some of

the lesser known and later formed regiments seem to arouse little enthusiasm, consequently books devoted to these latter regiments are little in demand.

Early 18th Century army lists are comparatively scarce and are therefore likely to prove an expensive buy for the collector, but those of the period following the Napoleonic Wars will not realise anything approaching similar prices. With all military books, particularly those of the 17th and 18th Centuries, it is always worthwhile to examine carefully the fly leaves and

blank pages since many were part of the property of commanding officers or adjutants of the regiments and may consequently bear their signature, rank and regiment. Since these can be fairly easily traced in the Army Lists the inclusion of such a signature in a book can add considerably to its value. Many of the early books, including Army Lists, are of course leather bound, and although this material is extremely durable and hard wearing, it can become very dry and dusty. Wherever possible it is recommended that the original bindings be retained, even if this involves a certain amount of repair. The covers can be treated with a number of proprietary compounds which will strengthen and revitalise the leather.

Obviously it is of tremendous importance that anybody concerned with the collection, care, research, preservation or indeed any

Left, Fig. 214: Designed to hold a lancer cap, this square tin case has a brass name plaque inscribed Major Fowle 21st Lancers. *John Fowle was born in May 1862 and was a Major from April 1898 to September 1902, serving in India, the Sudan, Egypt and South Africa.* **Below,** *Fig. 215: Odd items of interest, such as this brass plate, may still be found. These plates were hung by the bed in barracks—this one belonged to a soldier in The Worcestershire Regiment—and many are stamped to indicate whether the soldier was on duty. 4½ by 3½ inches.*

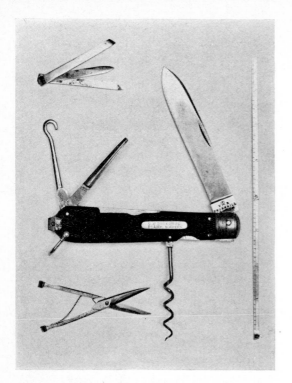

contact with militaria, should be in a position to differentiate between the genuine and the false, between the original and the copy. This is unfortunately much easier said than done for, as pointed out already, although the term uniform is always used to describe military dress, in fact this is the last thing that most of it ever was. In the case of the Prussian German armies documentation has been fairly continuous and extensive over the last two or three centuries, and changes in equipment, uniform, badges and organisation have been fairly well covered and extensively reported. In the case of the British Army this has not been the case, and there are numerous gaps in the knowledge and understanding of much of Britain's military history; it is terribly easy to dismiss, for example, a badge as being a copy or made up when, in fact, it was a variant carried by some particular unit. During the second half of the 19th Century when so many of the Rifle Volunteers were raised, the amalgamations, combinations and deletions of some of these units were very extensive and it is not an easy matter for the enthusiast to discover the lineage of some of these units; they simply disappear, leaving only a few odd badges or references. Again, as many of the volunteers had considerable control over their own uniforms and badges, a number of variations on them were produced.

There are scattered about in most countries a number of military museums devoted to particular units, and many of these collections are well displayed and well documented. However some of them were, in the past, in the hands of enthusiastic amateurs whose knowledge was not always as great as their enthusiasm, and it is sad to report that in many cases items are incorrectly described. However, visits to these museums, examination of contemporary prints wherever possible, reading of the regimental histories and newspaper reports, and study of any source likely to offer guidance is to be encouraged.

In the case of uniforms the amount of work involved in the production of good

quality copies of the Victorian and 18th Century uniforms, with their often elaborate decoration, makes it uneconomic to reproduce them accurately; and since, as pointed out above, the demand is fairly limited, fake uniforms are not common except in the Imperial German and Nazi fields. However, problems do arise, for during the latter part of the 19th Century and the early part of this century, military displays were very popular public spectacles and quite considerable sums of money were expended on equipping participants for these shows as accurately as possible, and consequently a certain amount of material was made with no consideration of expense. These pieces can present a problem to the collector and it is often not easy to decide on the authenticity of a particular piece. Some guidance can be obtained from the method of stitching; machine stitching did not appear until the middle of the 19th Century and therefore all earlier uniforms were hand-stitched and consequently far less even in the number of stitches, the length of stitch and, of course, the line of stitch.

For the collector of militaria the field is both exciting and rewarding, and it is a field which still affords the amateur opportunities for research and discovery.

Fig. 217: Items of Second World War vintage have already acquired a certain "collectability", largely because of their relatively low cost. This is the gas mask carried by German troops in the field, with its grey metal canister, inside the top of which are stored anti-dim patches to prevent misting of eyepieces.

INDEX

Numerals in ordinary type refer to page numbers; *italic* numerals refer to monotone illustrations, and numerals in **bold** type to colour plates. Certain general terms are indexed under their first mention.